"Tremper Longman is a highly respected name in Old Testament studies. I myself am a grateful beneficiary of his scholarly work and have appreciated his friendship and collegiality over the years. So when he writes about Old Testament controversies, we readers should take notice and ponder his well-considered perspectives, however challenging they may be. Longman's high view of biblical authority, his deep pastoral concern, and his commitment to the power of the gospel have shaped this insightful guide to help inform our conversation about difficult and hotly debated Old Testament topics."

Paul Copan, Pledger Family Chair of Philosophy and Ethics, Palm Beach Atlantic University; coeditor of the *Dictionary of Christianity and Science*

"Longman walks where mere mortals fear to tread, and he does so with erudition, honor, and grace. His scholarship is vast, and he takes those who hold different views seriously in a manner that is not only commendable but should be the standard for critique. I doubt there are many who will agree with him across the board on these challenging issues, yet the depth of reflection he offers is enough to help you return to the Scriptures to address your own presuppositions and aid you in articulating your current understanding of these controversies. I am profoundly grateful for Tremper for countless reasons, and this labor simply adds one more reason I consider him our generation's foremost Old Testament scholar."

Dan B. Allender, professor of counseling psychology and founding president, The Seattle School of Theology and Psychology

"Fools rush in where wise men fear to tread, but Tremper Longman is no fool. This book covers ground on which people can make fools of themselves, but he has been thinking for decades about the questions he discusses here. He has stayed abreast of changing

views among evangelicals and knows how to keep reflecting on issues without giving up ground when he knows one needs to stand firm. If you want not-too-conservative and not-too-liberal answers to the questions he raises, you will find them here."

John Goldingay, David Allan Hubbard Professor Emeritus of Old Testament, Fuller Theological Seminary

"What a wonderful opportunity to journey with the expertise of Tremper Longman and consider the Bible regarding some of the most difficult subjects facing Christians today! This is a valuable book and worthy of study and consideration."

Richard Hess, distinguished professor of Old Testament, Denver Seminary

"The Old Testament is full of difficult and controversial passages. These are often read without consideration of their original, ancient cultural contexts. Dr. Tremper Longman has tackled four of the most controversial topics: evolution, history, violence, and sexuality. Rather than settling for simplistic explanations that will not hold up under genuine scrutiny, Longman has brought many years of study and scholarship to bear on these problems. In a truly marvelous way, he explains these very complex issues with a clarity that will enhance readers' comprehension. Far from being a mere Christian apology, this book wrestles with the real issues and sheds light that brings about a full engagement. It is a pleasure to recommend this very significant volume."

K. Lawson Younger Jr., professor of Old Testament, Semitic languages, and ancient Near Eastern history, Trinity Evangelical Divinity School

"Many books on issues of faith and practice—and what the Bible has to say about both—gladly take on the author's ideological opponents. Tremper Longman's book is unique in taking on his friends, both literal and theological. He specifically addresses the arguments of scholars who could be characterized broadly as 'evangelical' (though some are fleeing the term) but who are embracing and advocating understandings of the Bible that have been more characteristic of liberal scholars. He defends the Bible's integrity and truthfulness authoritatively but with a wonderfully irenic spirit and accessible style that should be a model for such exchanges of ideas between people of good will."

Daniel Taylor, author of *The Skeptical Believer*
and *Death Comes for the Deconstructionist*

"Tremper Longman addresses the most controversial questions raised by the text of the Old Testament with courage and aplomb. Here we have a clear-eyed, common-sense treatment of the biblical text offering readers answers that many will find helpful. Indeed, the church will benefit greatly from this work."

Bill T. Arnold, Paul S. Amos Professor of Old Testament
Interpretation, Asbury Theological Seminary

"Tremper Longman is a rare scholar, and this book is a unique gift to the believing and doubting public. In a world divided over contentious issues, *Confronting Old Testament Controversies* somehow learns from all sides and then plots a path of balance, clarity, and grace. This will now be my number-one recommendation to all who ask about the so-called problems of the Old Testament."

John Dickson, honorary research associate, Department
of Hebrew, Biblical and Jewish Studies, University of Sydney;
founding director, Centre for Public Christianity

"With typical clarity, good sense, and balance, Tremper Longman tackles the most challenging questions related to the Old Testament. This is a volume I will be referring students and skeptics to for years to come."

Mark L. Strauss, University Professor of New Testament,
Bethel Seminary

"In this book Tremper Longman III is courageous, clear, charitable, and confessional. He is courageous in tackling subjects that arouse intense controversy as well as baffled distress. Any time I teach the Old Testament, someone will raise one or another of these issues. Longman writes with pleasurable clarity, making his deep scholarship available with lightness and warmth. His disagreements with other scholars, including evangelical friends, are expressed with respect and without vitriol. Above all he writes out of clear evangelical conviction on the inspiration, trustworthiness, and moral authority of the canon of Scripture. This book will be a blessing and resource for those wrestling with these contentious issues in honesty and faith."

Christopher J. H. Wright, Langham Partnership;
author of *Old Testament Ethics for the People of God*
and *The God I Don't Understand*

CONFRONTING
OLD TESTAMENT
CONTROVERSIES

CONFRONTING OLD TESTAMENT CONTROVERSIES

Pressing Questions about
EVOLUTION, SEXUALITY,
HISTORY, and VIOLENCE

TREMPER LONGMAN III

BakerBooks
a division of Baker Publishing Group
Grand Rapids, Michigan

Published by Baker Books
a division of Baker Publishing Group
P.O. Box 6287, Grand Rapids, MI 49516-6287
www.bakerbooks.com

Printed in the United States of America

Library of Congress Cataloging-in-Publication Data
Names: Longman, Tremper, author.
Title: Confronting Old Testament controversies : pressing questions about evolution, sexuality, history, and violence / Tremper Longman III.
Description: Grand Rapids, MI : Baker Books, a division of Baker Publishing Group, [2019]
Identifiers: LCCN 2018026904 | ISBN 9780801019111 (pbk.)
Subjects: LCSH: Bible. Old Testament—Socio-rhetorical criticism.
Classification: LCC BS1182.5 .L66 2019 | DDC 221.6—dc23
LC record available at https://lccn.loc.gov/2018026904

19 20 21 22 23 24 25   7 6 5 4 3 2 1

Contents

Contents

Acknowledgments

I entered the field of Old Testament studies about forty years ago for a number of reasons, but two stand out to me at this moment. First, I was deeply intrigued by these books that were written so long ago by a people who were chronologically and culturally foreign to us. I had a sense that there were theological riches to be discovered in these pages, and I was right. Second, I knew that most Christians—like myself up to that point—did not know what to do with the Old Testament. I wanted to dedicate myself to the study of this part of God's Word for my own spiritual growth and also to help others see that they could hear the voice of God in the Old Testament.

Now, toward the end of my career, I know that many Christians continue to struggle with the Old Testament. Part of the reason for this is that some of its teaching seems at odds with our thinking and even our values. Thus, I decided to write a book on what I perceive to be the four most controversial topics that face Christians today as they read the Old Testament: evolution, history, violence, and sexuality.

I want to thank in particular Jack Kuhatschek, formerly of Baker Books, for encouraging me to tackle these topics. I also want to thank Brian Vos and James Korsmo of Baker, as well as copyeditor Ryan Davis, for helping me express my ideas as clearly as possible. Of course, I remain responsible for any errors or infelicities in the final product.

I have many others to thank as well, particularly my friends whom I asked to read the manuscript and offer feedback. Let me be clear, though, especially since this is a book about controversial topics. Few of them read the whole book, and none of them agree with me totally. I did not always accept their advice. These friends include Reed Jolley, Timothy Keller, John Ortberg, Peter James, Paul Copan, Bruce Fisk, and Dan Allender. I in particular want to thank Peter Enns for reading this, since, as the reader will soon see, I am critical of some of his recent ideas. He remains a good friend whom I deeply respect and whose ideas I always find stimulating and sometimes even persuasive.

I also want to express my gratitude for two anonymous donors who provided me significant funds to work on this project. I am greatly encouraged by their support for my work—for past projects, this book, and two future projects.

I also want to thank my students at Regent College in Vancouver whom I taught on the topics of this book in the summer of 2017 and at Knox Seminary in Fort Lauderdale whom I taught in January 2018. Our interchange deepened my understanding and gave me new ideas.

Finally, and most importantly, I want to thank my wife, Alice. From our meeting in 1970 and our marriage in 1973 up to the present day, she has encouraged my work and my spiritual life. I dedicate this book to her.

Introduction

I became a Christian during the "Jesus Revolution" of the late 1960s and early '70s. Those of us who were teenagers or young adults at the time remember the period as turbulent, occasionally frightening, but also exciting. God used the social unrest of the moment to attract many of us to the message of the gospel.

I had grown up in a rather liberal church that was interested in the social gospel but not so much in encouraging members to cultivate a personal relationship with God through Jesus. The Bible was read during services, but there was no real encouragement to study it or to treat it as the Word of God. Thus, with my newfound faith came a new deep interest in the Bible.

In my sophomore year in college I decided to be a religion major, thinking that studying the Bible and theology in college would deepen my faith. And it did, but perhaps not in the way that I had imagined. My religion professors did their best to undermine my fledgling faith as well as that of my friends. They thought we were naive, and in many ways we certainly were. But they were more interested in questioning our faith than helping us build a more mature faith.

Readers today have their choices in Bibles (the New International Version, the New Living Translation, *The Message*, the English Standard Version, and on and on) and a plethora of books written by committed Christian scholars. But younger readers may not realize that this wealth of resources is a recent phenomenon. Back in the early 1970s we had only the Revised Standard Version (a high-style translation that for various reasons, good and bad, was not acceptable to the evangelical church), the King James Version (a seventeenth-century translation), or the Living Bible (a paraphrase).

In terms of evangelical scholarly material on the Bible and theology, there wasn't much. Our college fellowship did not have any real support from local churches either. They were either not evangelical and, like our professors, frowned on our passionate yet to-them-naive faith. Or they were conservative and did not support us because we were hippies. Looking back, it is hard to believe today, but when our college fellowship approached one pastor about our going to his church, he refused to let us in. He said that if we showed up with our long hair, he would be fired the next day!

Though support was hard to find, we did have help from a new college ministry in the area called the Coalition for Christian Outreach, a ministry that is still going strong in western Pennsylvania and Ohio. About once a month we got a visit from a young theologian named R. C. Sproul, who came from his home base in Ligonier, Pennsylvania.

Don't get me wrong. Some other resources were available to us from authors like Francis Schaeffer, Watchman Nee, and a young theologian named J. I. Packer, who was just starting to write. And there were others writing for a more scholarly audience, but I would not be exposed to them until I got to seminary.

I mention all this only to indicate why I decided to pursue an academic and writing career. I wanted to help provide the resources that would benefit people like me who wanted to learn more about the Bible. At this point I wasn't sure what field I would go into, and

I needed to start with a general master of divinity degree anyway, so I decided to make the decision about what specialty I would pursue while I was in seminary.

Early in my seminary career I took classes on the Old Testament with a young professor of the Old Testament named Ray Dillard, and I was hooked. Ray had the ability to open up the biblical text in ways that not only illuminated the ancient meaning but also demonstrated the ancient text's continuing relevance for Christian life today. Through his influence, I decided to get a doctorate in ancient Near Eastern languages and literature and pursue a teaching and writing career in Old Testament.

Ray not only inspired me; he also hired me even before I finished my degree. We worked together at Westminster Theological Seminary from 1980 until his untimely death from a heart attack in 1993. I continued to teach at the seminary until 1998, when I accepted the Gundry Chair at Westmont College, from which I retired in 2017. As Distinguished Scholar and Professor Emeritus of Biblical Studies, I continue to write and lecture.

I share this brief and selective life story with you to tell you how much I love the Old Testament and value its continuing significance for my life today. One of the reasons I went into the field was that I knew that Christians struggled with the Old Testament both in interpretation and in application. Our attention is naturally drawn to the New Testament because of its explicit focus on Jesus. Some Christians wrongly believe that that renders the Old Testament secondary, but the truth is that it is an integral part of the canon of Scripture (the standard of our faith and practice). Truth be told, we can't understand the New Testament without the Old Testament.

The present book, the first written after my retirement from full-time teaching, intends to help Christians appreciate the continuing relevance of the Old Testament in the light of current controversies over its teaching. All of these controversies have been around for a long time. The reason I am writing now is that they have a new dimension: some within the evangelical scholarly community are arguing for nontraditional interpretations of the text, and these new interpretations need evaluation.

Let me begin by saying that this book is written for the church and not the broader culture. I say this because at least some of these controversies have been taken up by some outside the church, notably the so-called New Atheists, in order to discredit the biblical text. This book does not "take them on" but rather addresses these issues among those who take the Bible as the Word of God. There is a place and there are resources for countering the attacks of people like Richard Dawkins, perhaps the best-known New Atheist,[1] but this book has a different purpose. It evaluates attempts from within the evangelical church to reinterpret texts in a way that is more culturally acceptable. We will look at what I consider to be the four most controversial issues in the Old Testament.

Creation and Evolution. Darwin published his theory of evolution in the mid-nineteenth century, so the issue of the relationship between the biblical teaching on creation and the scientific theory of evolution has been around a long time. That acknowledged, the past twenty years have brought powerful new evidence in favor of evolution, primarily in the field of genetics. Thus, many evangelical scholars, including myself, have suggested recently that the Bible is not in conflict with science, not even with the growing evidence that human beings go back to an original population of some thousands of individuals, not an original couple named Adam and Eve. I will make this case in the first chapter of the book.

Historicity. Non-evangelical scholars have questioned the historical veracity of the patriarchal narratives, the exodus, and the conquest since the early nineteenth century. In the past three decades, a group known collectively as "the minimalists" have argued

---

1. Though I don't agree with everything Paul Copan says, as will become clear later, one of the best resources for interacting with the ideas of Dawkins and others is his book *Is God a Moral Monster?* I also recommend the incisive comments found in Strawn, *Old Testament Is Dying*, 83–102.

that the entire history of the Old Testament from start to finish is largely fictional. What is new in the past decade is that some evangelical scholars have taken a position very similar to minimalism. Is it important that events like the exodus and conquest are historical? Or is the message of the story sufficient to establish its theological significance? In this section, I will argue that when the Bible intends the reader to understand an event as historical, the event's theological contribution depends on its being so.

Divine Violence. Divine violence in the Bible became a widespread matter of controversy after 9/11. When Islamic terrorists supported their violence with language that seemed to echo Old Testament warfare theology, people not surprisingly began to question the trustworthiness, relevance, and even the morality of the Old Testament. Some evangelical scholars have recently revisited the Old Testament texts to see if they can mitigate or even do away with the idea that God brings physical harm against his enemies. Here, I will make the case that such attempts are wrong-minded even if well intentioned.

Sexuality. Perhaps the most controversial issue of all has to do with sexuality, in particular homosexuality. Until the past few decades, the Bible was pretty much universally understood to prohibit homosexual activity, and even today the vast majority of the global church holds that view. However, some evangelical scholars in the Western church have reconsidered their opinion. Civil society recognizes same-sex marriages, and many churches, typically non-evangelical churches, welcome openly gay people into membership and even the clergy. What is new and what is addressed in this book are recent evangelical arguments that go along with the non-evangelical viewpoint and support affirmation of this new cultural trend. I will defend the long-standing and widely held traditional view. But I won't stop there; instead, I will go on to ask how we might show our love toward same-sex-attracted men and women.

At this point, let me say that there is absolutely nothing wrong with reconsidering traditional interpretations in the light of new cultural questions. As I will explain in more detail in chapter 1, while the Bible is faithful and true (inerrant, if you prefer), our interpretations are not as certain.

Indeed, when it comes to traditional interpretations of creation, I am in large agreement with the view that creation and evolution can be compatible. But I will differ from those who want to do away with any sense of historical background to Genesis 1–3, particularly those who deny a historical fall and deny that there is anything like what we call "original sin." That said, I will explain and critically engage attempts to reinterpret the biblical text in a way that denies the historicity of events presented as historical, divine violence, and traditional understandings of sexuality.

I desire and intend to be irenic in my critique of those with whom I disagree. There is way too much bombast in these inter-Christian debates. Labels like "heretic" or "fundamentalist" are used to stifle honest questions and discussion. Sometimes our theological discussions sound like the worst of political rhetoric these days, trying to ridicule and belittle opponents rather than grappling with their ideas and presenting our own.

I may be able to be irenic more than many because I personally know most of the people I critique. Indeed, Peter Enns, one of the people I critique in these pages, is one of my closest friends. He's a former student and colleague and a frequent drinking companion (maybe that is another controversial issue—no, the Bible is clear about that!). I know his heart and his love for Jesus and the gospel. I don't see people and scholars like Peter on a mission to undermine truth. Like me, they are trying to discover the truth in the Scriptures.[2] I hope that attitude comes through in my writing.

2. For those of you who do not know Pete personally, I recommend you read his book *The Sin of Certainty* to appreciate along with me how he shares his story

But still, as well intentioned and godly as these dialogue partners are, their ideas require a thoughtful response. This book is written for a broad audience and in a rather familiar style. The footnotes go a bit further in engaging the scholarly issues, and I hope they give the sense that I have reflected long and hard on these subjects.

Finally, at the heart of these controversies is the nature of the Bible and, related to this, the interpretive approach we adopt to read the Bible. I will address these issues throughout the book, but I will do so particularly in the first chapter as we consider the topic of creation and evolution.

---

to build up the faith of others. The charge made by some of his critics that he is trying to undermine the faith is ridiculous unless we are talking about an overly confident faith that needs maturing.

1

Creation and Evolution

Are the Bible and Science in Conflict?

After teaching all day at a church retreat in the fall of 2009, I was tired. Don't get me wrong. I was enjoying my weekend assignment to open up the grand narrative of the Bible to a group of bright young professionals from the San Francisco area, and the setting at a resort on Lake Tahoe was amazing. But still, I was hoping to get away that evening and fallow my mind by watching some football.

In a moment of weakness, however, I agreed to allow one of the attendees, a professional filmmaker, to ask me questions on film. I didn't know what he would ask or what he was doing with the film. But once we started, I enjoyed the time. He asked a number of questions about the Old Testament, and then came the one that ended up affecting my research and thinking agenda for the next decade. "Is it necessary that Adam be a historical individual for the early chapters of Genesis to be theologically important and true?"

I'll be honest. At this stage I didn't know that evolutionary biology provided overwhelming evidence that humanity did not emerge from its primate past through a single couple but rather

1

through a population of some thousands of individuals. I didn't even know that in some circles the question of the historical Adam was already a raging controversy. I was just thinking of the nature of Genesis 1–11 when I replied that, because of the highly figurative nature of the description of actual events in this first portion of Genesis, it was not necessary that Adam be a historical individual.

I didn't think much about this filming, and I went off and watched some football. About five days later, I got a call from an administrator of a seminary where I was going to teach a course in two weeks. While the following is not a verbatim recounting of our conversation, it is my best remembrance.

The administrator, a friend, said, "Tremper, our school has become aware of the clip that you did on Adam on YouTube."[1]

"What's YouTube?" (Remember it was 2009, and I am technologically challenged.)

"Do you really believe what you said about Adam on that video clip?"

"Of course, or I wouldn't have said it."

"If that is what you believe," he said, "you can't teach at our school. We have an unwritten policy, based on our understanding of the Westminster Confession of Faith, that people who hold that opinion can't teach for us."

"Really? I did not know that. Well, then, I'll teach this class and we'll part ways."

"No, you can't even teach that class."

"I have twenty-five students in that class who are expecting me to teach them!"

"Sorry, my hands are tied."

"Well, you are going to have to fire me, because I don't want you walking into class to tell them I resigned."

1. Tremper Longman III, "Is There a Historical Adam - Part 12," YouTube video, 1:37, September 16, 2009, https://www.youtube.com/watch?v=I8Pk1vXL1WE.

"Sorry, Tremper. It's not my decision. But because of the position of our seminary, I have to fire you."

I had violated an unwritten policy. Though my class had nothing to do with Adam, creation, or the book of Genesis, I was out.

I'm not looking for pity here. Though I enjoyed the job, I was being fired from a part-time adjunct teaching position. My day job (as the Robert H. Gundry Professor of Biblical Studies at Westmont College) was quite secure, and I had a lot more adjunct opportunities as well. Indeed, as word got out, I got even more speaking opportunities. Also, I want to be clear that I maintain my friendship with the administrator and also appreciate the school that fired me (though they have a blind spot here). I am telling this story to highlight how I discovered just how controversial the issue we are about to discuss is. Passions flare on all sides.

Let's dive in. The issue of creation and evolution has to do with the nature of the biblical witness, the relationship between science and faith, the theological impact of certain contemporary scientific theories, and much, much more. As I said, this issue evokes a lot of passion. Particularly in the present political atmosphere, there is a tendency on the part of both sides to demonize others. "What a fundamentalist!" or "Are you even a Christian?" are not arguments but rather attempts to silence what is an important discussion.

Recent surveys show that an alarming number of young people are abandoning the faith because they feel that they must make a decision between what they learn in their science class and what they hear in church.[2] Others decide not to go into the science field

2. A 2011 Barna survey on American Christianity discovered the six primary reasons why young adults leave church. Reason number three is that "churches come across as antagonistic to science," counting 23 percent of young adults polled as saying that they had been put off by the creation and evolution debate. And 29 percent of the Christian youth polled complained that "churches are out of step with the scientific world we live in." See "Six Reasons Young Adults Leave Church," Barna Group, September 27, 2011, https://www.barna.com/research/six-reasons-young-christians-leave-church/.

even though they find it intriguing. I believe that we must learn from science but that it is more important that we maintain our fidelity to God and Scripture than to what scientists may be telling us at any given time. But does the Bible actually teach that God created two humans from a nonorganic past?

How Do We Interpret the Bible?

Before we talk directly about creation/evolution, historicity, divine violence, and sexuality, we need to begin with a subject that will be important throughout all four topics: how we interpret the Bible. Everyone has a strategy for reading the Bible, even if it is just to pick it up and read it as if it were written yesterday, looking for what is relevant to one's life. God can use that type of reading in our lives, to be sure, but our desire should be to adopt the best possible interpretive approach to hear God's voice speaking to us from his Word rather than imposing our own meaning on the text.

This attention is particularly important as we discuss controversial issues, as I do in this book. With these issues especially, it is essential that we pay attention not only to what the Bible says but also to how we are arriving at our understanding of it. In each of the four areas we are investigating here, people who hold to the authority of the Bible and agree about what the Bible says still have widely divergent views about what the Bible means, so it is important to look clearly at how we interpret the Bible.

Hermeneutics is the technical term for the science of interpretation, which sounds a little sterile. But everyone who reads the Bible has a hermeneutic, even if they don't know it. Perhaps it will be clearer if we simply think of hermeneutics as principles of interpretation that lead to a strategy for reading the Bible.[3]

---

3. Of course, the topic of hermeneutics is relevant for reading anything written (or even listening to something oral), but we here focus on the interpretation of the Bible.

This book is not the place to do a full hermeneutics,[4] but I will focus on those issues that are particularly important to the questions of cosmic and human origins, historicity, divine violence, and sexuality. In this chapter I will look at the nature of the Word of God (canonicity, inerrancy, and clarity), the nature and goal of interpretation (how we find meaning in texts), and the role that genre plays in how we read—issues that are important for all four of the topics in this book. I will then look at the relationship of science and the interpretation of Scripture, an issue that has special bearing on the question of creation and evolution. In each subsequent chapter I will likewise bring in additional principles of hermeneutics that are relevant.

The Nature of the Word of God

As we begin our strategy for reading the Bible, we start by asking, Why do we, as Christians, care what the Bible says about these subjects? We care because the Bible is the Word of God, and that means we, the church, treat it as canon and believe that it tells us the truth.

CANONICITY

The church has recognized the Old and New Testaments as its standard of faith and practice from the very earliest times. But we must be careful not to confuse the church's long-standing recognition of the canonicity of the books of the Old and New Testaments with the *reason* they are canonical (the ground of canonicity).[5] The church does not define the canon; the canon defines the church. God reveals himself through the Scriptures; the Holy Spirit speaks to the church through these books; and the Spirit that dwells in the church hears and recognizes that authoritative voice.

4. For a fuller overview of my approach to the subject, see Longman, *Reading the Bible*.
5. For this distinction, see Ridderbos, *Redemptive History*.

In short, by saying that the Old and New Testaments are canonical, we mean that the church looks to the Scriptures as the source of authoritative teaching about God (doctrine) as well as for guidance for how we should live our lives (praxis). Though people can point to the occasional question about whether this or that book should have been included or excluded, the church's recognition of a stable canon through the centuries is remarkable. (One notable exception to this is Marcion, who questioned the canonical status of the Old Testament, and eventually much of the New Testament as well. Since his objections were specifically tied to the issue of divine violence, we will take up this example in more detail in chap. 3.)

Two important comments need to be made concerning the Old Testament canon. First, we acknowledge the difference that exists between the three great Christian traditions on the extent of the canon. Protestants affirm a narrow canon that does not include the apocryphal books recognized as canonical by Catholic and (with differences) Orthodox communities. But what is remarkable is that these three communities all recognize the same core books (those included in the narrower, Protestant canon). In addition, we should realize that recognition of the so-called apocryphal books does not result in significant doctrinal differences—and, most important for our purposes, no difference on the subjects on hand (creation/evolution, historicity, divine violence, and sexuality). Doctrinal differences, of course, do exist between these communities, but they are not the result of the differences of the scope of the canon.

Second, as a Protestant I recognize only the narrow canon as authoritative and, in keeping with Protestant beliefs, treat the apocryphal books as edifying, helpful books, though not canonical. We inherit our Old Testament from the Jewish community, in particular from the Pharisees. As Roger Beckwith thoroughly documents, Jesus disagrees with the Pharisees about a lot of things, but not about the extent of the canon.[6] But let me emphasize again the fact that, particularly as concerns the four topics we are covering in this book, even if one accepts the Apocrypha as canonical, it will not change the perspectives advocated here.

INERRANCY

By saying the Scriptures are the Word of God and therefore canonical, we are also making a statement about their reliability and veracity. After all, if we hear the voice of God in Scripture, then we can be assured that these words will not mislead us but, on the contrary, will be truthful, despite the fact that God used human beings to speak and write his words on his behalf. On this basis, evangelical Protestant scholars have generally used the term *inerrancy* to refer to the idea that Scripture is "without error." Here is a classic definition of inerrancy taken from the often-cited Chicago Statement on Biblical Inerrancy: "We affirm that Scripture, having been given by divine inspiration, is infallible, so that, far from misleading us, it is true and reliable in all the matters it addresses."

The term *inerrancy*, however, has been much abused in recent years, both by people who want to make it claim more than it does and by those who believe it claims too much or does so crudely. Those who want to make it claim too much confuse hermeneutics and inerrancy. In other words, they assert not only that Scripture is true but also that their interpretation of Scripture is true. Thus, if someone disagrees with their interpretation of Scripture, then that person must be denying the truth of Scripture. This difference

---

6. Beckwith, *Old Testament Canon*. It is true that the early Christians (and most Jews at the time) were using the Septuagint (the Greek version of the Old Testament), and it is also true that the earliest full manuscripts of the Septuagint that have survived to the present day contain the Apocrypha, but these are from the fourth century AD and do not directly bear on the contents of the Septuagint that would have been used by Jewish or Christian readers in the first century AD.

between inerrancy of Scripture and inerrancy of interpretation is extremely important for our study of controversial issues, which by nature will involve interpretive decisions. Thus, discussion of inerrancy also necessitates discussion of the clarity of Scripture, which we will take up below.

While some claim too much with inerrancy, others object to the word and even the very concept of inerrancy. This perspective has been growing in recent years, and I will be interacting with evangelical Protestant scholars who adopt this criticism of inerrancy in a way that affects their treatment of the issues of creation/evolution, historicity, divine violence, and human sexuality.

Let's first of all admit that *inerrancy* is not a perfect term. It has its liabilities. It is a term that focuses in on propositions: Is a proposition true or false? But the Bible is not all about propositions.

Take the Song of Songs, an anthology of love poems. How is a love poem true or false? Certainly not by way of propositions. We could perhaps think that these love poems rightly express the emotions and desires for physical intimacy that reflect God's intention for human flourishing. More could be said, but my point is that the term *inerrancy* has its awkwardness, though if it is understood as saying that the Scriptures as the Word of God are true in all that they intend to teach or affirm, then the word still has utility.

But there are those who think that more than the simple word *inerrancy* is misleading. We will observe this in the writings of Gregory Boyd, Peter Enns, and Eric Seibert, for instance, who argue that the God depicted in parts of the Bible is not the actual God (and thus there are parts of the Bible that are wrong, even on so central a thing as what God is like). We will note this particularly in the chapter on divine violence and interact with their ideas in a more detailed fashion there, but for now let me just say that such a view raises important theological issues, most significantly how we can tell the actual God from the depicted God.

CLARITY

Even as we recognize that God's Word is inerrant, we must also recognize that not everything in Scripture is clear. This admission does not infringe on the so-called doctrine of the clarity (or perspicuity) of Scripture. The Protestant church has always taught that the information and ideas that are essential for our salvation are clearly taught in the Bible but that this clarity does not extend to disputed issues such as the nature of the days of Genesis 1. We should pay attention to what the Westminster Confession of Faith, an influential Reformed creed from the seventeenth century, says on the matter: "All things in Scripture are not alike plain in themselves, nor alike clear unto all: yet those things which are necessary to be known, believed, and observed for salvation, are so clearly propounded, and opened in some place of Scripture or other, that not only the learned, but the unlearned, in a due use of the ordinary means, may attain unto a sufficient understanding of them."

The bottom line is that when it comes to the important main message of the Bible ("those things which are necessary to be known, believed, and observed for salvation"), there is clarity. OK, the Hebrew and Greek (and a smattering of Aramaic) still have to be translated, but as the confession says, these things "are so clearly propounded, and opened in some place of Scripture or other" that it would take a really bad translator to mess it up. All the translations typically used by evangelicals (NIV, NLT, NKJV, KJV, ESV, Message, CEB, NRSV) do a more than adequate job communicating the central message that is clearly taught by the Bible.

But what is necessary to know for salvation? Well, that would be "I am a sinner and I need help. Jesus died and was raised to save me from sin and death, and I must put my faith in him." Yes, that's pretty basic, and it is so clearly taught in Scripture that one must work really, really hard to miss the point.

This is the gospel, and it fits in with the big story of the Bible, which I think is also clear:

creation—fall (into sin)—redemption—consummation

This is the basic plot of the Bible from Genesis to Revelation. In Genesis 1–2, God creates all things, including human beings, whom he creates morally innocent. In Genesis 3, humans choose to rebel against God, thus explaining the presence of sin and death. In the bulk of the Bible, Genesis 4 through Revelation 20, God then pursues reconciliation by redeeming his human creatures from their sin. Finally, in Revelation 21–22, the biblical account ends with a description of the future consummation.

This big picture presented by the Bible is clear. But notice also how the statement in the Westminster Confession begins: "All things in Scripture are not alike plain in themselves, nor alike clear unto all." Not all things are clear in Scripture. We need to remember this when we interact with people with different opinions than ours on subjects that are not essential for our salvation.

When someone says that "the gospel is at stake" if one does not take the days of Genesis 1 as literal twenty-four-hour days, or believe that there was a global flood, or take a complementarian view of the relationship between the genders, or hold a particular position on any other matter that is not central to the big story of salvation, they misunderstand the nature of Scripture (or they are simply trying to win their point by dramatic overstatement).

I am emphasizing this point at the beginning of this book for a reason. The controversial topics that we will discuss are really, really important, but they are not "necessary for salvation." There is room for discussion among believers, and discussion only happens when we refrain from demonization. And that is true on both sides. I can't tell you how many times I have been told I am not a Christian or called a mindless fundamentalist for holding a particular view—and sometimes on the same issue (by different people of course). So we should enter the following discussion with the attitude that these are important issues but not issues that decide whether or not you are a Christian or whether or not you believe the Bible is God's Word.

In summary, as I approach the questions of creation/evolution, historicity, divine violence, and sexuality, I do so on the basis of my affirmation that the Bible is our standard of faith and practice (canonical) and that it is true in everything that it intends to teach (inerrant). I believe that the Scriptures are clear on the matters important for our salvation (perspicuous) but open to debate on many other topics.

Written for *Us but Not* to *Us: The Goal of Interpretation*

WHERE IS THE MESSAGE FOUND?

Interpretation seeks to discover the message of the biblical text that we are reading. But where is that message located? A written text—any text, including the biblical text—is composed by an author to readers. Stated this way, the goal of interpretation is clear. Readers want to know the intended message of the author.

This seems simple enough until we realize that, particularly with ancient texts like the books of the Bible, we have no independent access to the authors. We cannot interview Moses, David, Jeremiah, or Paul to ask, "What did you mean by that?" And truth be told, even if we did, it might not solve our problem. Authors don't always remember years later what they meant (and we have no reason to think God gave Paul infallible memory), or perhaps they themselves don't understand the full import of their words (especially for the Bible; see below concerning divine intention). But we don't even have the possibility of talking to the human authors of biblical texts, since they are all long dead. Thus, while the author's intended meaning may be our goal, our only recourse to discover that meaning is through a close study of the text itself.

The implication of this is that when we say the interpretation of a certain biblical text is such and such, we are making a hypothesis based on our reading of the text.[7] To read the text well, I will argue below, we have to be aware of the literary conventions that the author used to communicate their message, including most notably the genre of the text we are studying. Thus, to reach our goal of proper interpretation of a biblical text, we will need to become familiar with the writing practices of ancient authors.

In summary, the goal of interpretation is to discover the intended meaning of the author. We can only do this by doing a close reading of the text itself, since we have no independent access to the author. Thus, we need to be knowledgeable of the conventions of writing through which authors send signals to readers about "how to take" their words.

It's More Complicated Than That

So far we have given a rather straightforward and simple account of the model of literary communication: an author writes a text to communicate with readers, and the reader interprets the text in order to reach the intended message of the author.

We have already acknowledged some complications with this process. My view is that interpretation (discovering the author's intended message) is not untroubled or even perfectly achievable, but that recognition does not and should not paralyze us. While interpretation is not perfect, it can lead us to an adequate understanding of the message of the text, one that does indeed represent the intended communication. Literary communication is possible.[8] My confidence in getting at the message of the Bible is not diminished even as I recognize that, particularly when it comes to the Bible, the process of communication is more complicated, especially for those of us who affirm that God is the ultimate author of Scripture.

---

7. Strickland, *Structuralism or Criticism?*
8. The view that I take has been called "critical realism."

Let's start with the author, the one whose intention in writing we seek to discover. There are two complications here. The first is that—now restricting our comments to the Old Testament—the books typically have a history of composition. That is, the biblical books as we have them were not written by one person in one sitting. Rather, they were written over a period of time by more than one composer. A good introduction to the Old Testament will give the full story of composition, and there are differences among scholars regarding how certain biblical texts were written.[9] But most scholars agree that the Old Testament books came to their final form over a period of time. It is that final form that is considered canonical for the church.[10]

Sometimes the book itself reveals that it was written over time. The book of Jeremiah provides such a case, though all the details are far from clear. Here's what we can say with a considerable level of confidence. God called Jeremiah to preach his message of judgment starting in 626 BC (Jer. 1:1–10). A little over twenty years later, God told Jeremiah to write down these prophecies and read them in the temple precincts (Jer. 36:1, the fourth year of Jehoiakim, 605/604 BC). Jeremiah dictates his sermons to Baruch, who reads them in the temple precinct. Some of the king's men take the scroll to the king, and he doesn't like what he reads, so he cuts up the scroll and throws it page by page into the fire.

What is interesting for our present topic is that the narrator tells us that "Jeremiah took another scroll and gave it to the scribe Baruch son of Neriah, and as Jeremiah dictated, Baruch wrote on it all the words of the scroll that Jehoiakim king of Judah had burned in the fire. And many similar words were added to them"

---

9. For beginning students, see Longman, *Introducing the Old Testament*, and for more advanced students, Longman and Dillard, *Introduction to the Old Testament*.

10. Of course, debates will continue over the exact shape of the final form of many Old Testament books, but these debates do not prevent us from having an adequate understanding of the different biblical books.

(Jer. 36:32). The result? A second, longer version of the book of Jeremiah is written. And that was just the beginning, since we know that there are materials in Jeremiah that belong to at least the early exilic period, which begins in 586 BC. In addition, most scholars believe that there are materials added by disciples of Jeremiah, including Baruch, about Jeremiah. Indeed, we cannot be absolutely certain about when the final form of the book came into being.

Even though the case of the book of Jeremiah is complicated, the book gives us some concrete dates to go on. Often we cannot tell precisely when a book was written. Take the book of Daniel. Even granting (as I do)[11] the traditional view that the book contains reliable portraits of a historical Daniel living in the Babylonian and Persian courts (chaps. 1–6) and apocalyptic visions that came to him at that time, the book itself does not tell us when it was written or by whom. The stories are about Daniel, and a narrator reports the visions. Is the narrator Daniel himself? We have no reason to think so.

We need to acknowledge the fact that, often, we simply cannot precisely date the moment when the final form of a biblical book took shape, nor can we name all the people involved in the book's production. Yet our goal to discover the "author's intended meaning" remains intact, even though we can now see that the author is often an anonymous final shaper of a book. After all, we are not looking to interview the author. We are closely reading the text itself to discover the author's message.

But there is a second complication to our understanding of the author of a biblical book. This one is unique to those of us who believe the Bible is the Word of God. And that complication emerges from the fact that ultimately the author of the Bible is God.

Perhaps one of the best-known passages in the New Testament refers to the divine origin of the Old Testament, here referred to as

11. Longman, *Daniel*.

"Scripture": "All Scripture is God-breathed and is useful for teaching, rebuking, correcting and training in righteousness, so that the servant of God may be thoroughly equipped for every good work" (2 Tim. 3:16–17). This passage and others (Gal. 1:12; 2 Pet. 1:20–21) remind us that the ultimate author of biblical books is God himself, raising the question of whether passages in the Bible have a "deeper meaning" (*sensus plenior*) than the human authors would have been aware of. I believe the answer is clearly yes. And though he is not a biblical author, John the Baptist provides a good example of how a prophet speaks words whose meaning surpasses his or her understanding of their import.

In the wilderness, John baptized those who accepted his message of repentance. He announced the coming of one who was more powerful than he was. This one would cut down the rotten wood and throw it into a fire and would separate the chaff from the wheat and burn the chaff with "unquenchable fire" (Matt. 3:10–12). When Jesus appeared at the Jordan River, John recognized him as the expected one and baptized him. After the baptism, Jesus began his ministry, and John was later put in prison. In prison John received what he took as disturbing reports. Rather than burning the rotten wood and the chaff, Jesus healed the sick, raised the dead, and proclaimed the good news to the poor (Matt. 11:4–6). John sent two disciples to ask him, "Are you the one who is to come, or should we expect someone else?" (Matt. 11:3). Jesus was not acting in accordance with John's prophetic expectation.

But John, our example of a human author of a divine word, did not have full understanding of what he was saying. In this case, he did not realize that Jesus was coming not just once but twice. The book of Revelation, as well as other apocalyptic portions of the New Testament, makes it clear that Jesus will return to render judgment against those who resist him.

John provides a good example of an instance where the human spokesperson does not fully understand the importance of the words spoken (or written) on behalf of God. In spite of rather tortuous attempts to say otherwise,[12] the unexpected ways New Testament authors often use Old Testament passages (in ways that their original authors could never have anticipated) also illustrate our point.

Thus, in the Bible we have human authors speaking the divine message, and this complicates the picture of discerning a biblical author's intended meaning. That said, we must admit we can see beyond the human author's intention (and thereby presume that there is a meaning that transcends that intention) only if later Scripture itself brings out the deeper meaning. In other words, *sensus plenior* is not an excuse for assigning a meaning to a text that cannot otherwise be gained through normal interpretive method (the "ordinary means" of the Westminster Confession of Faith).

In terms of the text, we already mentioned above that no, or almost no, biblical books were written at one moment by one author. But we resolve this complexity by simply putting our focus on the final form of the text.

And that leaves the reader. The complication involved in the receiving end of the process of literary communication is quite simply that while the Bible was written *for* us, it was not written *to* us. In other words, it is absolutely imperative that we remember that the biblical books were written to a specific ancient audience and not to those of us who are reading them in the twenty-first century. Thus, it is critical that we recover what my friend John Walton calls the "cognitive environment" of any passage that we read.[13]

In this regard, I like to tell my students that they don't call the book of Romans "Romans" for nothing (yes, I occasionally use New Testament examples). Paul wrote this letter to a specific

12. For example, Beale and his "cognitive peripheral vision" (see Beale, "Cognitive Peripheral Vision").
13. Longman and Walton, *Lost World of the Flood*, 6–10.

church to address their particular issues. Reading a Pauline letter can be like listening to half a conversation—we occasionally wonder what issue or controversy he is explicitly addressing.

An Old Testament example is the history of Israel provided by the books of Kings and Chronicles. I like to use this example because these books recount comparable history but give us quite different takes on it. In a word, Chronicles gives a much more upbeat portrait of the history compared to Kings' emphasis on the sin of Israel and its leaders. To ask which is true misunderstands the purpose of these histories and does not recognize the importance of the first readers.

While neither Kings nor Chronicles explicitly mentions its original audience, we can identify their audiences by noting the last event narrated in each of their accounts. In Kings, the last event is the release of King Jehoiachin from house arrest in Babylon during the reign of King Evil-Merodach (known in Babylon as Amel-Marduk, the son of Nebuchadnezzar; 2 Kings 25:27–30). Amel-Marduk ruled a brief time (562–560 BC), but what is significant for us is that this event took place in the middle of the exile (586–539 BC). In other words, we can surmise that the author of Kings chose to point out the sin of Israel and Judah in order to explain to his exilic audience why they are in exile.

Chronicles, on the other hand, ends with the mention of the so-called Cyrus decree, which allowed the Jewish people to return to Judah. That means Chronicles comes from the postexilic period (after 539 BC). The Chronicler's audience is not interested in why they were in exile (because they aren't any longer) but rather in questions like What is our connection with the past? (thus so many genealogies!) and Now what do we do? (among other things, rebuild the temple, which explains why there is such an emphasis on the first temple).

Every biblical book had an original audience. In short, the biblical books are not addressed to us, and we need to remember that.

We are later readers living in a vastly different cultural context. To read the biblical books correctly, we must first of all read them as if we were living at the time of the original audience. Otherwise, we run the risk of imposing our meaning on the text.

And one more comment on readers. To read well, we have to remember that our reading is shaped by who we are as individuals. We are not blank slates who approach the text from a neutral perspective. Our reading is affected by who we are. I will take myself as an example. I am a male, getting up there in years (middle-aged would be too kind; I have four beautiful granddaughters after all). I am financially well-off (particularly if you buy my books). I am well educated (did I mention my Yale PhD?). I live in the twenty-first-century West (the United States, to be exact). And I could go on, but I have made my point. Who I am both helps me and limits me in my understanding of the text. But there is an easy solution to my limited perspective, though one not taken by many readers of the Bible: reading in community. I need to listen to a variety of voices (female and male, non-Western and Western, lay and clergy, poor and rich, young and old), especially of those who are different from me, as I interpret the text. These other voices can encourage or challenge my reading. They may correct my misapprehension, or I may conclude that they misunderstand the text.

Where do we hear these voices? They are readily available in commentaries, other writings, Bible study groups, sermons, and elsewhere. What keeps us from listening? Our pride. We need to be willing to listen to others (even those with whom we will eventually disagree) and question our own understanding if we are to grow in our interpretation. The Bible is inerrant, but our own interpretation is not. We need to be constantly open to changing our opinion.

Genre Triggers Reading Strategy

Let's remember that our ultimate goal is to hear the author's message in a literary text. Similarly, an author's goal is to be understood by readers. Thus, authors write in ways that are familiar to their readers, sending signals to the reader as to "how to take" their words.

A genre of literature is a group of writings that share features in terms of content, style, or form. The recognition of a genre raises expectations on the part of the reader, who then adopts an appropriate reading strategy. Let's consider a well-known type of text that occurs outside the Bible. If a text begins with "once upon a time," readers hear the author telling them that the text is a fairy tale. Fairy tale is a genre. If we recognize a text as a fairy tale, then we will not be surprised to encounter dwarves, dragons, witches, and elves and will "suspend our disbelief," because we know that it is not the purpose of the author to recount actual events but rather to entertain us or perhaps to impart a moral lesson.

Let's examine an example from the Bible to demonstrate how readers' identification of the genre of a text shapes their interpretation.

> While the king is on his couch
>   my nard gives off its scent.
> My lover is to me a sachet of myrrh
>   lodging between my breasts. (Song 1:12–13)[14]

Here, near the opening of the Song of Songs, the woman describes the object of her affection as sitting on his couch. She then expresses her affection and desire for intimacy by depicting him as a sachet (a small bag of perfumed powder) between her breasts.

How has this passage been interpreted and why?

Most readers today (scholarly and lay) would see this as the expression of a woman's desire for physical intimacy with a man, because we identify the genre of the Song of Songs as love poetry. After agreeing on the broad recognition of the Song of Songs as love poetry, there may be differences over a narrower genre identification that also triggers a certain reading strategy. Is the Song an

---

14. Translations from the Song of Songs come from Longman, *Song of Songs.*

anthology of love poems, which encourages the reader to unpack the metaphors and explore the emotional intensity of the speeches?[15] If so, then in Song of Songs 1:12–13 the woman expresses her desire to be as physically intimate with him as a sachet of myrrh between her breasts. The sweet smell of myrrh and her lover's touch are deeply pleasing to her. Or is the Song a narrative about the ups and downs of a couple's relationship or even the story of the conflicts that emerge from a love triangle?[16] If one believes the Song is a narrative rather than a collection of love poems, that shifts the goal of interpretation to focus on the discovery of a plot. Perhaps in this scenario Song of Songs 1:12–13 would be part of the courtship phase of the relationship between the man who might be identified as Solomon and the woman, perhaps the Shulammite. Here we have an example of how differences in genre identification trigger reading strategies that lead to somewhat different interpretations.

But compare the even more radical difference presented by readings common in the early church era and the Middle Ages. Cyril of Alexandria (ca. 376–444) presents a quite different understanding of the simile in Song of Songs 1:13. He says that the sachet of myrrh is Christ and the breasts represent the Old and New Testaments. The verse thus proclaims that Jesus Christ spans both the Old and the New Testaments.

You might say that that makes absolutely no sense. I would agree, but we have to ask how Cyril came to such an incorrect interpretation and why. Put simply, he (and virtually all interpreters during the early church era and the Middle Ages) misidentified the genre of the Song. He saw it as an allegory of the relationship between Jesus and the church (just as contemporary Jewish interpreters saw it as an allegory of the relationship between God and Israel). Thus, rather than expressing human desire for physical intimacy, the woman (the church) expresses desire to be intimate

15. See, for instance, Longman, *Song of Songs*, and Exum, *Song of Songs*.
16. See Provan, *Ecclesiastes and Song of Songs*.

in her relationship with Jesus. Once the reader identifies the Song as an allegory, there is logic to Cyril's interpretation of verse 13.

That said, we can be certain that Cyril and similar commentators got it wrong. First, there is absolutely nothing in the Song that would give the impression that the author expected the reader to take the text as an allegory (that is, there are no genre signals that point to allegory). Second, analogous love poems from ancient Egypt and the modern Middle East lead us to conclude that the Song of Songs is a love poem, not an allegory. The sensuous and intimate language between the man and the woman are clear signs of the former. And then finally we can see the motivation that early interpreters had for avoiding a sexual interpretation. The church at this time was heavily influenced by Neoplatonic philosophy, which held that the spiritual life was at odds with the physical life, so that things that had to do with the body (particularly sex) had to be subdued for the spirit to grow. Thus, a book that excites sexual passions just has to say something different than what it seems to say on the surface.

No matter what your views on the interpretation of the Song may be, however, there is no doubt from this example that one's genre identification triggers interpretation. Get the genre wrong and you get the interpretation wrong. We will see that genre plays an important, even pivotal role, in our treatment of the controversial issues in this book.

Science and Faith: The Two Books

We now turn to the relationship between science and faith, a topic that bears on creation and evolution. Many Christians and non-Christians alike buy into the "conflict model" of the relationship between science and faith. On the science side, some believe that science disproves the existence of God. On the faith side, some argue that the Bible trumps and undermines the conclusions of science.

Historically, though, the church has offered what may be called a "two books" understanding of the relationship between the Bible

21

and nature (the object of study of science).[17] Listen, for example, to the Belgic Confession, article 2:

> We know Him by two means: First, by the creation, preservation, and government of the universe; which is before our eyes as a most elegant book, wherein all creatures, great and small, are as so many characters leading us to see clearly the invisible things of God, even His everlasting power and divinity, as the apostle Paul says in Romans 1:20. All which things are sufficient to convince men and leave them without excuse. Second, He makes Himself more clearly and fully known to us by His holy and divine Word, that is to say, as far as is necessary for us to know in this life, to His glory and our salvation.

God reveals himself in Scripture and through nature. Both are "books" that involve interpretation. Hermeneutics provides interpretive principles that are applied to Scripture in order to exegete (bring the meaning out of) the biblical text. The philosophy of science yields the scientific method that provides the methodological principle to explore nature in order to support theories from nature.

God is the ultimate author of both Scripture and nature. When both are correctly interpreted, they will not conflict. Since God is the ultimate author of both Scripture and nature, both are true, though our interpretations of either may not be. To be open to a different interpretation than the one we hold is not to betray Scripture but to honor it. The same, of course, is true of our interpretation of nature.

Scripture does not trump nature, at least not in the way some people think.[18] Some people are so certain of their interpretation of Scripture that when they hear a scientific theory that doesn't fit with their interpretation, even a theory like evolution that is

---

17. For the question of the relationship between science and faith and different perspectives on the topic, see W. Dembski, "Science and Theology (Dialogue View)," and J. Stump, "Science and Theology (Reconciliation View)." My own view is closer to that of Stump.

18. It is correct to say that Scripture gives a fuller revelation than nature, but the point that the two will not conflict when properly interpreted still stands.

overwhelmingly supported by not only the fossil record but also genetics and numerous other fields of research, they don't even blink an eye as they reject it as "anti-Bible."

We should learn a lesson from the "Galileo episode." I am referring, of course, to the seventeenth-century reaction to Galileo's arguments in support of a heliocentric solar system earlier presented by Copernicus. Legends have grown up around this story, including the misunderstanding that Galileo was tortured. Indeed, as Kerry Magruder has pointed out, Galileo had powerful supporters within the church (like evolutionary creationism has in the evangelical Protestant church today) and opponents among university physicists.[19] Even so, Galileo's teaching was resisted by the church because some thought the results of his research threatened the Bible's teaching that the earth was the center of the cosmos and that the sun, moon, and stars revolved around the earth in a celestial sphere. After all, his church critics charged, the Bible says the sun rises and sets, and the Psalms proclaim that God "set the earth on its foundations; it can never be moved" (Ps. 104:5).

Today we "know better." The Bible is speaking phenomenologically (that is, from the perspective of how we perceive matters on the surface), not scientifically, about the rising and setting of the sun and metaphorically about the earth not being moved. We even use that language today. We are comfortable with the idea that the Bible is not teaching cosmology but rather assuming an ancient cosmology.

The Galileo episode should be an object lesson to the church as it responds to scientific theories that at first glance seem to conflict with the Bible. Christians should not automatically reject scientific conclusions that seem to contradict traditional interpretations of Scripture. As Calvin wisely pointed out in the sixteenth century: "If the Lord has willed that we be helped in physics, dialectic, mathematics, and other like disciplines [we might imagine that today he would add biology], by the work and ministry of the ungodly,

19. Magruder, "Galilei, Galileo," 298–300.

23

let us use this assistance. For if we neglect God's gift freely offered in these arts, we ought to suffer just punishments for our sloths."[20] I have found Pope John Paul II's statement in the same vein about the relationship between science and faith wise and illuminating: "Science can purify religion from error and superstition; religion can purify science from idolatry and false absolutes."[21]

Truth be told, science can help us read the Bible better. In the case of cosmic and human origins, I suggest that science helps us see more clearly what is obvious. The Bible teaches us *that* God created everything but is not interested in telling us *how* he created the cosmos or humanity. Even further, as we will see later, science helps us see that the Bible does not claim that humanity goes back to a single originating couple. Indeed, reading the Bible in the light of modern science helps us understand the doctrine of original sin better.

Conclusion

In this section, we have discussed the importance of biblical interpretation. As Christians, we believe that we hear the voice of God in the Bible. Therefore, the church has recognized these books as authoritative, "canonical" to use the technical term, for our understanding of God (since it is his self-disclosure), ourselves, and our world. The Bible, including the Old Testament, is the standard of our faith and practice. We believe that the Bible, as God's Word, is true in all that it intends to teach us.

We then discussed the necessity of interpretation. Yes, as the Westminster Confession of Faith states, the big picture is clear (once the text is faithfully translated), but not everything is obvious, not even some matters of importance. Thus, we must interpret the

20. Calvin, *Institutes* 2.2.15, 1:275, quoted in Zachman, "Free Scientific Inquiry," 73.

21. John Paul II to Reverend George V. Coyne, SJ, Vatican, June 1, 1988, http://w2.vatican.va/content/john-paul-ii/en/letters/1988/documents/hf_jp-ii_let_1988 0601_padre-coyne.html.

text. I suggested that the goal is to discover the author's intention (first that of the human author and then of the ultimate, divine author). As readers, we are finite and thus need to read in community. We must also recognize that the biblical books, while written for us, were not written to us. I also affirmed that our only access to the author's intended meaning is through a close reading of the text.

I also highlighted the importance of genre in order to get at the author's message. Genre triggers reading strategy. The author sends us signals as to how to take the words, raising expectations in the mind of the reader. To misidentify the genre, either formally or even unconsciously, will lead us to misunderstand what the author is trying to tell us.

Then we also considered the relationship between biblical interpretation and the interpretation of nature, which we study by way of science, by understanding that they are God's two books. When we interpret the Bible correctly, it will never conflict with science if science is correctly interpreting nature.

What Is Genesis 1–3 Teaching Us?

It is time to turn to the main text that talks about God's creation of the cosmos and human beings and provides the account of humanity's first rebellion against God. We do so in the light of all that we have said about interpretation in the previous section.

The Bible, including Genesis 1–3, is the Word of God and thus true in everything it intends to teach us. We hear the voice of God speaking to us through these chapters. Thus, it is critically important to ask what they teach, and to answer that question we have to ask what genre the author utilizes to communicate the message. In addition, we need to read this passage in the context of the original audience, since it was written to the original audience in a language (Hebrew) and cultural context (ancient Near East) that they understood. In the case of the question before us, the ancient Near Eastern background is connected to the issue of the genre, so we can treat them together.

Genre: Theological History

To read Genesis 1–3 correctly (that is, according to the intention of the author, divine and human, whose voice we want to hear), we need to pay attention to the genre. Is it history (and if so what kind)? Myth? Poetry? Legend? Most of the time people throw out these labels without justifying them. In addition, some give the impression that our choice is between a strictly historical approach that extends to the details of the passage (creation in six twenty-four-hour days; God actually breathing on dust to create Adam) or a totally nonhistorical approach. Often the term *myth* is used to identify Genesis 1–3 as nonhistorical. My view is that a close reading leads us to a third, middle way. Genesis 1–3 does make historical claims, but it describes these past events using figurative language.

First of all, let's set the context. Genesis 1–3 opens the book of Genesis, the first book of the Bible. The book of Genesis as a whole is really not a separate book in its final form but rather the first part of the Torah or Pentateuch (Genesis through Deuteronomy). The question of the genre of Genesis 1–3 (which should be considered a component of Genesis 1–11) thus needs to be seen in the context of the book of Genesis and ultimately of the Pentateuch as a whole. The Pentateuch, indeed, is part of the continuous historical narrative that runs from the creation through the postexilic period of Ezra-Nehemiah and Esther.

Thus, one important way in which the book of Genesis can be outlined is as follows:

Genesis 1–11   The Primeval History: from creation to the tower of Babel
Genesis 12–36   The Patriarchal (or if you prefer, Ancestral) Narrative: Abraham, Isaac, and Jacob
Genesis 37–50   The Joseph Narrative

Genesis 1–11 is a connected but somewhat distinctive part of Genesis. The connections with the rest of the book of Genesis lead me to conclude that chapters 1–11 are theological history—that is, a narrative that intends to impart information about past events with an emphasis on God and his relationship with his human creatures (that is what makes it theological). There is not a radical shift in genre between Genesis 11 and 12, and most scholars would affirm that Genesis 12–50 is a work of history, in that it intends its readers to understand the narrative to depict actual events in the past.[22]

But along with shared interest in the past comes an important difference between these two parts of Genesis. Genesis 1–11 covers an extraordinary span of time from creation right up to the time of Abraham. The Bible does not date the creation,[23] but from multiple lines of evidence presented by our study of the cosmos (measuring the speed of and distances between galaxies, the length of time that the light of the farthest stars took to reach the earth, and many more), scientists believe the universe to be approximately 13.4 billion years old.

Abraham, on the other hand, may be dated to approximately the first quarter of the second millennium BC. Genesis 1–11, after speaking of the creation of the cosmos, focuses on God's human creatures who are endowed with his image. We will see below that there is some question about exactly when this takes place (at the beginning of *Homo sapiens* or some later time), but we are talking thousands, maybe tens of thousands, of years ago.[24]

22. That does not necessarily mean it is history as we would write history today, but rather that it intends to be history in the sense of reporting space-and-time events (Van Seters, *Prologue to History*). We should also note that scholars who recognize a historical intention do not necessarily think that the historical depiction is accurate or reliable (Van Seters does not). For more on issues of history, see chap. 2.

23. Young earth creationists who claim that the Bible teaches that cosmos and human beings are only a few thousand years old misuse the biblical genealogies; see Longman, "Genealogy," 301–2.

24. Just the week I am writing this section, the popular press announced the discovery of human bones that extend back three hundred thousand years. Alan

No matter how you cut it, that is a long period of time to cover in eleven chapters! Compare that with the account of Abraham, which begins in Genesis 12 and ends in chapter 26, and that story doesn't even start until he is seventy-five years old. It seems the author of Genesis is more interested in detailing the story of Abraham than in recounting events from creation to the tower of Babel. And that is not even taking into account the difference in scope between Genesis 1–11, where the narrative interest extends to the whole world, and Genesis 12–26, where the narrative focuses on one man, Abraham, and his wife, Sarah.

Thus, we should not be surprised that the theological history of Genesis 1–11 covers this time period with very broad strokes. To accomplish its purpose, Genesis 1–11 speaks of these events of the deep past using figurative depictions shaped for theological purposes. For our purposes we will focus on Genesis 1–3.[25] And here the genre signals are strong, in spite of the desperate attempts of some to treat the depiction of the creation of the cosmos and humanity as a straightforward accounting. Let me give some examples.

THE DAYS OF CREATION

First of all, let's consider the days of Genesis. An initial and very superficial reading of Genesis 1:3–2:3 might lead one to think that the author intended his readers to believe that God created the cosmos and humanity in a six-day stretch and then rested on the seventh day. After all, the six days of creation each have evening and morning (1:5, 8, 13, 19, 23, and 31). But upon even a little deeper reflection, it becomes obvious that the author does not claim that these days of creation are actual twenty-four-hour days. After all, the sun, moon, and stars aren't even created until

---

Burdick, "The Oldest Human Fossils Ever Discovered Have Stories to Tell," *New Yorker*, June 7, 2017, http://www.newyorker.com/tech/elements/the-oldest-human-fossils-ever-discovered-have-stories-to-tell.

25. For a study of the stories of the flood and the tower of Babel (Gen. 6–11), see Longman and Walton, *Lost World of the Flood*.

the fourth day, and it is these celestial bodies that define days with evenings and mornings.

I'm often asked whether God could have created some other means of switching the light on and off in a twenty-four-hour period. After all, there is light and darkness that are called "day" and "night" on day one (Gen. 1:5). Of course he could have, I reply, but they still would not be a literal evening and morning. Others try to convince me that the author is speaking from the perspective of the earth and that the sun, moon, and stars were already existent right from the start but hidden by some kind of cover, which God then removed on the fourth day so that they might be seen. But why would the author write from the perspective of the earth if no one is living on the earth on the fourth day?

The insistence that the days of creation are six literal twenty-four-hour days is pretty much a modern idea. Many, if not most, of the earliest Christian readers of Genesis 1–3 recognized that the author was writing figuratively about actual events. Augustine, writing around the year 400, stated that the days of creation were not solar days.[26] As Origen (ca. 185–253) put it, "To what person of intelligence, I ask, will the account seem consistent that says there was a 'first day' and a 'second day' and a 'third day,' in which also 'evening' and 'morning' are named, without a sun, without a moon, and without stars, and even in the case of the first day without a heaven?"[27] Of course, these early theologians did not think that the cosmos was old and that humanity evolved over a long period of time. Indeed, quite the opposite. They believed that creation took place in a blink of an eye (why would God take six whole days?) and that the biblical author used the convention of a regular workweek not to claim that God took six days but as a literary device to proclaim that God created everything and to convey important and rich theological truths about the nature of

26. *Literal Meaning of Genesis* 5.5.12.
27. Origen, *On First Principles* 4.3.1, quoted in Cunningham, *Darwin's Pious Idea*, 381.

God and his relationship to his creatures, particularly his human creatures.

This understanding of the days of creation has come to be known as the "analogical day" approach. Most recently it has been championed by C. John Collins, who says, "The [creation] days are God's workdays, their length is neither specified nor important, and not everything in the account needs to be taken as historically sequential."[28] Indeed, to support the idea that the days are not claiming to state the actual sequence of the creation, we can appeal to the insights of what is sometimes called the "literary framework" view of the days (see "Lack of Sequence Concord" below on the clash of sequence between the two creation accounts).

To put it succinctly, the first three days describe the creation of realms of habitation, while the second three days describe the creation of the inhabitants of those realms. Day four (sun, moon, and stars) fills day one (light and darkness), day five (birds and fish) fills day two (sky and sea), and day six (animals and humans) fills day three (land), as the following chart indicates:

Creation of realms	Day 1 Light and darkness	Day 2 Sky and sea	Day 3 Land and vegetation
Creation of inhabitants	Day 4 Sun, moon, and stars	Day 5 Birds and fish	Day 6 Animals and humans

FIRMAMENT

Another potential genre marker is the discussion of the "firmament." This might be slightly different than some of the other

28. C. J. Collins, *Genesis 1–4*, 124.

genre signals in Genesis 1–3, since it is not clear whether the ancient readers understood the firmament in 1:6–8 literally or figuratively. In either case, though, the mention of the firmament (*raqia'*; translated "firmament" in the KJV and NKJV but "vault" in the NIV and NJB and "dome" in the NRSV) indicates that we should not take Genesis 1 as an account of how God actually created the cosmos or humanity.

As the name indicates, deriving as it does from a verb that refers to hammering in order to make a metal sheet, *raqia'* refers to a solid dome. The passage depicts God using this solid dome to separate the waters above from the waters below. He also places the celestial bodies created on the fourth day into this solid firmament (1:17).[29] Today few, if any, would argue that there is actually a solid firmament in the sky that holds the stars. Again, the Genesis description of the firmament supports the idea that we are not getting a straightforward depiction of creation.

The Third Day

While we are on the subject of the days of Genesis 1, I want to draw our attention in particular to the third day: "Then God said, 'Let the land produce vegetation: seed-bearing plants and trees on the land that bear fruit with seed in it, according to their various kinds.' And it was so. The land produced vegetation: plants bearing seed according to their kinds and trees bearing fruit with seed in it according to their kinds. And God saw that it was good. And there was evening, and there was morning—the third day" (1:11–13).

Notice what takes place during the third day: the land produces vegetation. Now we might imagine it plausible that the land would start the process of growth in an initial twenty-four-hour period, but this passage describes the land producing vegetation

---

29. For more on the firmament, including a critique of attempts to explain the *raqia'* as a reference to the atmosphere, see Longman, "Firmament," 284.

that produces fruit with seed in it within that time period. To suggest, as some do, that God produced fast-growing plants on this day in a kind of miraculous introduction of plant life goes beyond what the text is describing.[30] It is much better to take day three as yet another indication that we are dealing with a figurative description of creation.

The Seventh Day: God Takes a Break

Genesis 1 is not giving us a blow-by-blow account of how God created everything but is using the standard workweek, as known at the time the account was written, as a literary device in order to announce that God is the Creator. Just like an Israelite would work six days and rest on the seventh, so God is presented as working for six days and resting on the seventh. The seven-day week itself, like much of the Israelite calendar, is based on the movement of the moon. While the year is based on the revolution of the earth around the sun, the month, made up of four weeks, is connected to the four phases of the moon (new, waxing, full, and waning).[31]

The figurative nature of the seventh day is highlighted by the fact that God is said to *yishbot* from his work on that day (Gen. 2:2–3). The verb is from the root *shabat*, from which the noun *shabbat* (sabbath) derives, and indicates not just stopping or ceasing from work but resting from work. A human laborer needs to rest after six days to replenish energy, but we cannot imagine that God would need such rest. The conception of God taking a rest on the seventh day is furthered by the reference we find in Exodus 31:17, which looks back on Genesis 2:1–4a and says that God ceased or rested (from *shabat*) and "caught his breath" or

30. My comments on the third day were stimulated by the work of LeFeb-vre, "Calendars and Creation," 7, 173–75; now forthcoming as *The Liturgy of Creation*.

31. LeFebvre, "Calendars and Creation," 39–53.

"was refreshed" (NIV; from the verb *naphash*). Such a description must be taken figuratively, or else we are left with the awkward impression that God has limited energy.[32]

Collins summarizes the point well:

> So God's activity of preparing the earth as the right kind of place for humans to live is presented to us like an Israelite work week. You will notice that on the seventh day God rests; in Exod 31:17 it even says that on his Sabbath God "rested and was refreshed," implying that he was "weary" after a busy week. Now, any informed Israelite would first think, "Yes, I know what that is like." But then he would think, "Wait a second! God does *not* get tired!" What we are seeing is that this passage is presenting God's creation activity by way of analogy: that is, it is like human work in some ways—and, of course, it is unlike our work in other ways.[33]

LACK OF SEQUENCE CONCORD

Yet another indication that we are not getting an account of how God created the cosmos, the earth, and humanity comes with the recognition that the two creation accounts (Gen. 1:1–2:4a and 2:4b–25) do not present the same sequence of creation.

To state it baldly, the first account describes the creation of vegetation first (on the third day), followed by the animals (early on the sixth day) and finally humanity (male and female, later on the sixth day). In the second account, the sequence begins with the creation of the first man (2:7), followed by vegetation (2:8–9), the animals (2:19–20), and then the first woman (2:22–23).

The lack of sequence concord has been recognized for centuries, and there have been various reactions to it. Those who believe that the creation accounts are trying to tell the reader how God created have adopted two strategies that are based on radically different ideas of the nature of Scripture. First, some scholars have taken

---

32. LeFebvre, "Calendars and Creation," 198–99, is a very helpful discussion.
33. C. J. Collins, "Reading Genesis 1–2," 86–87.

the lack of sequence concord as an indication that the two creation accounts come from different time periods and from different hands and were placed side by side by a later editor. Indeed, the lack of concord is taken as evidence that the two creation accounts come from two different sources. Genesis 1:1–2:4a comes from a source often dated to the exilic or postexilic period (the Priestly source [P]), and Genesis 2:4b–25 comes from the tenth century BC (the Jahwist source [J]). This theory is called the Documentary Hypothesis.[34]

The second strategy adopted by some scholars is to attempt to harmonize the two accounts. They accomplish this harmonization through translating some of the verbs in the second account as pluperfect rather than simple past tense. We can see this approach at work in the NIV. Adam's creation is described using the *vav*-consecutive (or *waw*-consecutive) , and it is rightly translated in the simple past: "Then the LORD God formed a man" (Gen. 2:7). Strikingly, though, in the next verse, when the creation of vegetation is described using the same verbal form, the verb is translated not in the simple past but with a pluperfect: "Now the LORD God had planted a garden in the east" (2:8). Then later when the animals are brought into the narrative, the pluperfect is once again used: "Now the LORD God had formed out of the ground all the wild animals and all the birds in the sky" (2:19).

Why this shift? There is only one reason—to harmonize the two creation accounts and make it sound as if the creation of vegetation and animals happened before the creation of humanity. Technically such a translation is possible, but it is not likely.

That this harmonization is extremely unlikely is confirmed by Genesis 2:5, a verse that points out that before the creation of

---

34. See Friedman, *Bible with Sources Revealed*. For a further description and analysis of the Documentary Hypothesis, see Longman and Dillard, *Introduction to the Old Testament*, 40–51, or Longman, *How to Read Genesis*, 43–58.

the first man, "no shrub had yet appeared on the earth and no plant had yet sprung up, for the LORD God had not sent rain on the earth."[35] The translators of the ESV seem to understand this point, which leads them to another strategy of harmonization, to translate the noun *'eretz* as "land" rather than "earth": "When no bush of the field was yet in the land and no small plant of the field had yet sprung up—for the LORD God had not caused it to rain in the land . . ." (2:5–6).[36]

Such a translation leaves open the possibility that it had rained on the earth outside the land (the garden) and that there was vegetation on the earth outside the land, thus successfully harmonizing the two accounts.

Are the translations provided by the NIV or the ESV possible? Well, yes. The *vav*-consecutive can indicate English pluperfect, but it is much more likely that it is simple past here. The only reason to translate it pluperfect is to harmonize. Can *'eretz* mean "land" rather than "earth"? Definitely, but all other occasions in Genesis 1 and 2 are translated earth, so why "land" here? To harmonize in order to solve a perceived (but not real, in my opinion) theological problem.

There is a much simpler explanation than that provided by either those who want to use the lack of sequence concord to provide evidence for different, contradictory sources, like the Documentary Hypothesis, or those who want to use extraordinary grammatical and philological (word meanings, like on *'eretz*) arguments to harmonize the sequence of the two accounts. We should simply recognize that neither account is interested in telling us the actual sequence of creation. Other considerations (literary and theological; see the description of the "literary framework" hypothesis above) are at work here. Thus, the lack of sequence concord provides yet

35. The importance of this verse for the discussion of sequence is the subject of Kline, "Because It Had Not Rained."

36. The ESV, like the NIV, translates 2:19 as a pluperfect to harmonize the sequence of human and animal creation.

another line of textual indication that Genesis 1 and 2 are not interested in telling us the how of creation.

THE LAND OF EDEN

In Genesis 2, God places the first man in a garden named Eden. The name itself means "luxury" or "abundance" and signifies that the man lives in an environment that would meet all his material needs. But would the first readers have understood Eden as an actual location on the map? I seriously doubt it, and I do not believe that the author intended readers to take it that way.

Eden is described as having four rivers flowing from it. Granted, three of them would have been well known. The Tigris and Euphrates even today flow through Mesopotamia, from modern-day Armenia through Iraq and into the Persian Gulf. Gihon is the name used elsewhere in Scripture for a spring in southeast Jerusalem that formed a stream (1 Kings 1:33, 38, 45; 2 Chron. 32:30; 33:14). The fourth river is the Pishon, which is not mentioned anywhere else in the Bible and so is of uncertain location.

While some people take their cue from the mention of the Tigris and Euphrates to locate Eden somewhere in southern Mesopotamia, we must remember that these rivers are said to flow out of Eden, and if we were to take the description of Eden as referring to actual real estate, this would point to Armenia.

Rather than resorting to strained attempts to make these geographical references work, it is much better to understand the reference to Eden as not describing an actual place. Rather, the garden of Eden symbolizes that at the point when God endows his human creatures with his image (see "Humans in Genesis 1–3" below), they are living in harmony with creation.

THE CREATION OF ADAM

The creation of Adam comes from the second creation account found in Genesis 2:4–25. In the first account the focus is on the cosmos, in which the creation of humanity finds its place. But in the second account the interest is solidly on the creation of humanity, first the man and then the woman.

In terms of the creation of the first man, who is later called Adam, we read that "the LORD God formed a man from the dust of the ground and breathed into his nostrils the breath of life, and the man became a living being" (2:7). Picture the scene. God takes dust and breathes into it. Should this be taken at face value as the means by which God actually created the first human being? Of course not! To do so would violate our understanding of God as a spiritual being, not a physical one.

We have here an obvious case of what is called "anthropomorphism," describing God as if he were human, in this case as if he had lungs. Anthropomorphisms are a way of speaking about God figuratively, and here the creation of the first human being is being described in a figurative manner.

The author wants us to know that God created the first human, but he is not at all interested in telling us how God did it. To insist that this passage gives us God's actual method of creation is theologically incorrect. Soon we will see why the author chose to depict Adam's creation this way when we consider the ancient Near Eastern setting of the account.

The Creation of Eve

In terms of the creation of the first woman, we read, "So the LORD God caused the man to fall into a deep sleep; and while he was sleeping, he took one of the man's ribs and then closed up the place with flesh. Then the LORD God made a woman from the rib he had taken out of the man, and he brought her to the man" (2:21–22). There are clearly reasons why the creation of Eve is depicted this way, but it is not in order to tell us how God created her. Let's remember that the reason she is created is because "it is not good for the man to be alone" (2:18). Thus, we are not surprised that the description of her creation highlights her relationship with the man rather than giving us a straightforward description of how God did it. In other words, the depiction of her creation from Adam's "rib" or "side" is not intended to speak to procedure but rather to her equality and mutuality with the man. This point was well recognized by the rabbis, and it is acknowledged by modern scholars and preachers as well. Gordon Wenham, for instance, quotes the famous English preacher Matthew Henry (1662–1714): "Not made from out of his head to top him, not out of his feet to be trampled upon by him, but out of his side to be equal to him, under his arm to be protected, and near his heart to be beloved."[37]

THE SERPENT

In Genesis 3:1 we are abruptly introduced to a new character, a walking serpent. This serpent threatens the harmony of the garden by questioning God's command that Adam and Eve not eat from the tree of the knowledge of good and evil. While the introduction would have been just as sudden to ancient readers as to modern ones, ancient readers would have had a more immediate understanding of the sinister nature of the serpent.

As John Walton has pointed out, serpents, some of them walking as in Genesis 3, were symbolic throughout the ancient Near East of evil in the sense that they are antilife. He cites the eleventh tablet of the Gilgamesh Epic, in which a serpent steals a plant that might have given Gilgamesh eternal, or at least rejuvenating, life. In the Adapa Epic, a tale about how the lead character loses the chance at eternal life, we hear of a serpent-like gatekeeper named Ningishzida. Walton also points to the Egyptian religious idea that the serpent symbolizes death, as well as to the serpent-like representative of chaos named Apophis who threatened the sun god.[38] I might add another example in that Tiamat, who represents (along

37. Wenham, *Genesis 1–15*, 69.
38. Walton, "Serpent," 736–39; Walton, "Genesis," 1:33–34.

with Apsu) the primordial waters out of which Marduk makes the cosmos, is likely pictured in Mesopotamian iconography as a walking serpent. Thus, ancient readers would have quickly recognized a walking serpent as a symbolic representation of evil, another cue that the genre of these chapters includes highly symbolic language.

CONCLUSION

The Bible is totally true in everything it intends to teach. Genesis 1–3, which contains what we might consider the primary and certainly foundational creation accounts, is totally true in everything it intends to teach. And the determination of genre helps us recognize what a text like Genesis 1–3 intends to teach. We must remember that genre triggers reading strategy.

We have attended to the various signals that help us understand what genre the author uses to communicate with the audience. We have taken account of those signals that indicate to the reader that Genesis 1–3, like the rest of Genesis, indeed the rest of the redemptive history of the Bible, intends for us to understand that there is an interest in past events. We have also noticed a number of other signals (lack of sequence concord; figurative language such as days and God breathing life into dust) that inform the reader that these historical events are narrated using figurative language.

Below we will see that the relationship between Genesis 1–3 and other ancient Near Eastern creation accounts confirms the idea that here we have historical events described in a figurative manner. The result is that, while the author of the text teaches that God created everything, including humanity, he is not interested in telling us how God did it. This encourages us to turn to God's "other book," nature, to discover the how of creation.

Before moving on from genre, let me conclude by offering an analogy between the opening chapters of the Bible, Genesis 1–11 (the primordial history), and the closing chapters, the book of

Revelation.[39] In my opinion, there is a remarkable similarity between how the Bible treats the deep past (from creation to the tower of Babel) and how it treats the far-distant future (when Christ will return at the end of history). Both describe actual events, but both use highly figurative language to describe those actual events. The book of Revelation teaches that Jesus will come again in the future to save his people and judge the wicked. But will he come riding a horse (Rev. 19:11–21) or a cloud (Matt. 24:30; Mark 13:26; Luke 21:27; Rev. 1:7)? The very question is wrong. These are figurative depictions to communicate that Jesus will come back as a conquering Savior. Genesis 1–11 and the book of Revelation, though different in other respects, both speak about actual events using figurative language.

Genesis 1–2 and Other Ancient Near Eastern Creation Accounts

For well over a century, we have known about creation stories from Israel's ancient neighbors. We have literature in Sumerian, Akkadian, Egyptian, and Ugaritic that is relevant to our study of Genesis 1–2. The similarities and differences between these ancient Near Eastern creation stories and Genesis 1–2 are illuminating and give the idea that the biblical account was shaped at least in part to serve as a polemical rejoinder to their claims. Such an understanding does not depend on the biblical author being aware of these specific texts but assumes only familiarity with the general ideas that they present.

For our purposes we will use three stories, two in Akkadian and one in Ugaritic, to illustrate similarities and differences with Genesis 1–2. We do this comparison because it reveals that the shape of the biblical text is meant in part to highlight the differences between Israelite religious conceptions and those of their neighbors.

39. Of course, my comments on Revelation also apply to other parts of the New Testament that talk about the consummation of history.

Enuma Elish is a Babylonian myth composed at least by the twelfth century BC but maybe as early as the eighteenth century BC, since the text concerns the exaltation of Marduk, the chief deity of Babylon, and these are two periods of time when the city of Babylon assumed dominance in Mesopotamia.

The myth begins with an account of the birth of the gods: the primordial deities Apsu and Tiamat, representing fresh water and salt water respectively, give birth to numerous deities. The waters are simply there at the beginning, and the gods represent the beginning of the emergence of order in the cosmos.

But Apsu, the male deity, grows irate at the noise generated by the younger generation of gods and determines to put them to an end in spite of the protests of Tiamat, his consort. The god of wisdom, Ea, hears about this plot and in a preemptive strike kills Apsu. The death of Apsu is just the beginning of the conflict. Tiamat, who has more power than Apsu had, now takes up her deceased consort's intention, accompanied by a demon god named Qingu.

Ea knows that he is no match for Tiamat, so he issues a call for a hero to step forward. Marduk, his own son, accepts the invitation on the condition that if he is successful, he will become the king of the gods.

While the fight is fearsome, Marduk is ultimately successful. The text then turns to a description of creation. Marduk begins by splitting Tiamat's body (remember she represents the waters). With the upper half he creates the skies (from which rain comes), and with the lower half he creates the waters of the earth. He then pushes back the waters of the earth in order to create land. Finally, Marduk executes Qingu, and "from his blood he made mankind" (Tablet VI, 33–34).

The second story, known as Atrahasis, is also Babylonian in origin and is written in Akkadian on tablets from as early as the Old Babylonian period (eighteenth century BC) and as late as the

Neo-Assyrian period a millennium later. This text is particularly notable because it combines a creation account with a flood story, but here we are only interested in the creation story.[40]

In this myth we hear that the lesser gods (the Igigi) work for the superior gods (the Annunnake) by digging irrigation ditches. Eventually, the Igigi tire of their labors and bring their protest to the head of the Annunnake, the god Enlil. Enlil capitulates and commands Belet-ili, the divine midwife, to create humans to take over the menial labor of the lesser gods. Humans are created by killing a lesser god (We-ilu) and mixing the blood with clay from the earth. Finally, all the gods spit into the mixture.

The third story, the Ugaritic story of Baal, is only preserved on broken tablets. Nevertheless, most scholars are confident that the narrative was very similar to the Babylonian stories we have just summarized.[41] We are interested in this Ugaritic account because it concerns religious ideas that were held by people, perhaps Canaanites or related people, who were in the more immediate neighborhood of Israel.

In the relevant portion of this myth, the god Yam (the sea god) makes a play for the kingship of the gods and demands that Baal be turned over as a prisoner. While the council of the gods acquiesces, Baal refuses, storms out of the divine assembly, and goes to the craftsman god Kothar-wahasis, asking for weapons. Kothar provides him with two maces, with which he conquers Yam. It is at this point that the tablet breaks, but we assume, based on analogy with the Babylonian texts, that after the creator god defeats the god of the sea, there was an account of the creation of the world and perhaps of humanity. We should also note in this regard that Yam had allies, one of whom was a seven-headed sea monster

40. For the Atrahasis flood story and its connections with the biblical flood account, see Longman and Walton, *Lost World of the Flood*.
41. Though the eminent Sumerologist of the past generation Thorkild Jacobsen ("Battle between Marduk and Tiamat," 104–8) argued that the influence ran from the Ugaritic text to the Babylonian ones.

known by the name Lothan. This name is the Ugaritic equivalent of the Hebrew Leviathan, a name well known in the Bible as a symbol of the forces of chaos and even mentioned in a creation context in Psalm 74 (see the discussion of this text under "Other Old Testament Creation Accounts" below).

Notice, first of all, how order emerges from a watery chaos in all these creation accounts. This point holds even if Genesis 1 explicitly describes a creation from nothing, though I think that is unlikely (see the excursus "Creation from Nothing?" below). If Genesis 1 does depict a creation from nothing, the first move is from nothing to a watery mass ("Now the earth was formless and empty [*tohu wabohu*], darkness was over the surface of the deep, and the Spirit of God was hovering over the waters" [Gen. 1:2]). From this watery chaos God brings order and functionality.

Another more detailed point of comparison may be seen in the creation of humanity in Genesis 2:7. Above we commented on the obviously figurative nature of the description of God blowing on dust (does God have lungs?) to create the first man. This description tells us that humans, though creaturely, have a special relationship with God and, thus, that at their creation they are endowed with dignity. Compare and contrast that with the creation of the first humans in Enuma Elish and Atrahasis. Yes, there is a divine component and an earthly one, but the divine component—in the case of Enuma Elish, the blood of a demon god; in Atrahasis, the spit of the gods—shows that humans were evil from their origin and held in contempt by the gods.

More similarities and differences can be named between the biblical account and other ancient Near Eastern stories,[42] but my point, I believe, is made with just these. The shaping of the

---

42. For more on the similarities and dissimilarities between the biblical account and ancient Near Eastern stories, see Walton, "Genesis," and Longman, *Genesis*, 29–33, 46–47.

creation account in Genesis 1–2 is not to tell us how creation actually happened but to announce that it did happen. And here is the biggest and most obvious difference from the ancient Near Eastern accounts: it was Yahweh—the one true God of the cosmos—who did it, not Marduk or Baal. And to complete the contrast, there is also quite a different tone as to the why of the creation of humans. Yes, in both sets of accounts humans work, but in the Mesopotamian accounts humanity simply replaces the gods in the menial task of digging irrigation ditches, while in the Bible humans, created in God's image, subdue the earth and tend and guard God's garden.

Other Old Testament Creation Accounts[43]

I have said that Genesis 1–3 contains the primary and foundational accounts of the divine creation of the cosmos, the world, and humanity. But it is not the only place where the creation is described. There are numerous creation texts in the Bible—so many that we cannot adequately discuss them all.[44] Thus, I have chosen three examples from the Old Testament (Ps. 74; Prov. 8:22–31; Job 38:8–11) to show that, since there is no real interest in talking about the process of creation, God's creation work can be communicated using a variety of figurative descriptions.

PSALM 74

Psalm 74 is a communal lament written in the aftermath of the destruction of the sanctuary—presumably by the Babylonians in 586 BC, though they are not mentioned by name. The purpose of

43. Of course, there are New Testament examples as well (John 1:1–18; Rom. 1:18–20; 8:19–23; Col. 1:15–20; Heb. 1:1–4), but in this book I am keeping the focus on the Old Testament. For more on the New Testament texts, see Carlson and Longman, *Science, Creation and the Bible*, chap. 5.

44. For a fuller list of relevant passages and a detailed analysis, see Carlson and Longman, *Science, Creation and the Bible*, chaps. 4–5.

the lament is not just to express sadness but also to call God to action to restore his people. In the midst of the appeal the psalmist invokes God's great creation power:

> But God is my King from long ago;
>   he brings salvation on the earth.
>
> It was you who split open the sea by your power;
>   you broke the heads of the monster in the waters.
> It was you who crushed the heads of Leviathan
>   and gave it as food to the creatures of the desert.
> It was you who opened up springs and streams;
>   you dried up the ever-flowing rivers.
> The day is yours, and yours also the night;
>   you established the sun and moon.
> It was you who set all the boundaries of the earth;
>   you made both summer and winter. (Ps. 74:12–17)

Here the psalmist utilizes the divine conflict myth to describe creation. As we observed above, in the Mesopotamian creation story known as Enuma Elish, the creator god Marduk defeats the serpent-like sea monster Tiamat and forms the cosmos out of her carcass. Closer to Israelite culture, the Canaanites or a people closely related to them described a conflict between their chief god Baal and Yam, the Sea. In the relevant myth, the passage is broken off after the defeat of Yam, but most scholars are convinced that a creation scene follows in the missing portion. Even more interesting is that Baal is also said to fight an ally of Yam, a seven-headed sea monster named Lothan, which is the Ugaritic (the language of the myth) equivalent to Leviathan, who is described as having many heads in Psalm 74. There is no coincidence here—the Leviathan of Psalm 74 is the Lothan of the Ugaritic myth. These sea monsters represent primordial chaos, which the creator subdues and shapes into functional order.

PROVERBS 8:22–31

In the book of Proverbs, Woman Wisdom plays a pivotal role in the creation of the earth. The macrostructure of the book has two parts. In chapters 1–9, we have mainly speeches of a father to his son or of Woman Wisdom to all the implied readers of the book. In chapters 10–31, we find the proverbs, which are short observations, admonitions, and prohibitions that seek to make the reader wise.

A major goal of the first part of Proverbs, which has ramifications for how we read the second part, is to encourage the reader to form an intimate relationship with Woman Wisdom. I have elsewhere explained the significance of Woman Wisdom as representing God's wisdom and indeed God himself,[45] but for our present purpose, I want to take a quick look at Woman Wisdom's role in creation as described in Proverbs 8:22–31:

> Yahweh begot me at the beginning of his paths,
>> before his work of antiquity.
> From of old I was formed,
>> from the beginning, from before the earth.
> When there were no deeps, I was brought forth,
>> when there were no springs, heavy with water.
> Before the mountains were settled,
>> before the hills, I was brought forth.
> At that time the earth and the open country were not
>> made,
>> and the beginning of the clods of the world,
> when he established the heavens, I was there,
>> when he decreed the horizon on the face of the deep,
> when he strengthened the clouds above;
>> when he intensified the fountains of the deep,
> when he set for the sea its decree,
>> wherein the water could not pass where he said.

45. Most recently in Longman, *Fear of the Lord*, 14–23.

> I was beside him as a craftsman.
>> I was playing daily,
>>> laughing before him all the time.
>> Laughing with the inhabitants of the earth
>>> and playing with the human race. (Prov. 8:22–31)[46]

What a delightfully playful and imaginative description of creation! Woman Wisdom describes how she observed and participated in the creation. Notice again the role of the sea, which highlights the figurative language and ancient Near Eastern origins of the description of creation. The sea's material creation is not here described, but rather the sea is depicted as a rambunctious entity that needs to be commanded to assume its proper place. The sea again represents disorder that God whips into shape. It is told to stay where God commands and "not pass where he [God] said" (v. 29).

JOB 38:8–11

Our third example of a creation text treats the waters even more explicitly as a personal force that needs control. At the end of the book of Job, God speaks to Job out of the whirlwind in order to reprimand him for accusing him of injustice (40:6–8). God does not answer the question that Job poses ("Why am I suffering?"); rather, he simply asserts his power and wisdom and compels Job to bow before the mystery of his suffering.[47] He begins by leveling a series of questions at Job. He knows that Job has no answer to these questions, but he puts them to Job in order to demonstrate to him who is the Creator and who is the creature. The passage that most interests us here is Job 38:8–11:

> Who shuts the Sea with doors,
>> and who brought it out bursting forth from the womb,

---

46. For this translation and explanation, see Longman, *Proverbs*, 203–7.
47. For my approach to Job, see Longman, *Fear of the Lord*, 43–62.

> when I made the clouds its clothes,
>> and deep darkness its swaddling clothes?
> I prescribed my boundary on it;
>> I set up a bar and doors.
> And I said, "You will go this far and no more,
>> and here your proud waves will stop."[48]

God here is like a midwife to the Sea, bringing the Sea to birth and then putting limits on its natural tendency to cover everything. God created a boundary so that the land would emerge.

CONCLUSION

What are we to make of these alternate creation accounts (and there are more) in the Old Testament? At a minimum, these examples show that the biblical authors had no qualms about describing creation in highly figurative language. Indeed, they also illustrate that the biblical authors have no hesitation to invoke ancient Near Eastern mythological ideas as they do so. While it is conceivable that Genesis 1–2 is an exception, we have already examined these chapters and seen that the most natural reading recognizes the use of figurative language and the interaction with ancient Near Eastern creation accounts. There is no reason we should expect the Bible to provide us with a factual report of the process of creation, and it is a grave mistake to treat the opening chapters of the Bible as such a report.

EXCURSUS

Creation from Nothing?

I want to briefly address a controversial subject that relates to the teaching of Genesis 1–2 on creation by asking whether Genesis speaks about creation from nothing (*creatio ex nihilo*). That is,

48. Translation from Longman, *Job*, 418.

does Genesis 1 in particular talk about God starting with nothing and then creating matter and finally taking the matter and forming it into something organized and functional? Or does Genesis 1 begin the description of creation at the point when there is unformed and unorganized matter that God then shapes into something habitable for humanity? This second view would not explicitly teach that God created everything from nothing.

The debate begins at the level of translation. This is not the place to get down to the details of Hebrew grammar, so let me just start by stating that most Hebrew scholars would admit that the Hebrew could support either perspective, as might be illustrated by comparing the NIV translation with the NRSV. The NIV translates Genesis 1:1–2 as follows:

> In the beginning God created the heavens and the earth. Now the earth was formless and empty, darkness was over the surface of the deep, and the Spirit of God was hovering over the waters.

The NRSV takes a different approach:

> In the beginning when God created the heavens and the earth, the earth was a formless void and darkness covered the face of the deep, while a wind from God swept over the face of the waters.

Notice how the NRSV translation presumes that the earth was in a disorganized state at the point that ("when") God began the creation process. The emphasis is on bringing this formless void into a functional state. The NIV translation starts the description of creation before the existence of formless matter, so the process moves from nothing to disorganized matter and then finally to a functional cosmos.

Since the grammar does not definitively support one or the other of the possible translations, other considerations are operating in the minds of the translators. For those who adopt the NRSV approach, the fact that other ancient Near Eastern accounts all begin with the idea that the creator god utilizes preexistent matter indicates that in the original cultural context, what John Walton calls the Bible's "cognitive environment,"[49] the question of where the original stuff came from was not of interest. For those who instead adopt the NIV approach, later biblical teaching that God created from nothing is determinative.

I personally lean toward the NRSV understanding of the opening of Genesis and believe that one cannot dogmatically assert that Genesis 1 presents a picture of creation from nothing.[50] But it is important to remember that, after all this, it is not all that significant which approach is correct. Later biblical texts clearly teach that God created everything, so the biblical doctrine of creation from nothing stands secure. It is likely, however, that the author of Genesis 1 was simply not interested in the question of the origin of matter. That becomes a question in the later Greco-Roman environment. I imagine that if the author of Genesis were asked where the matter came from, he would answer that of course God created it.

What Does Genesis 1–2 Teach?

I don't want to leave the question of what Genesis 1–2 affirms with the impression that it teaches only that God created everything. That in and of itself is extremely important, considering all the ancient rival claims about who was the creator of the cosmos, earth, and humanity. Genesis 1–2 asserts that the creator is Yahweh, the God that Israel worshiped, and not Marduk or Baal or any other. Even so, this momentous claim does not exhaust the teaching of Genesis 1–2. After all, these chapters are foundational to the rest of the Bible. They speak of origins (Genesis means "beginnings") in a way that has ramifications for the reader's present life.

49. Longman and Walton, *Lost World of the Flood*, 6–10.
50. For the best defense of the alternative view that Genesis 1 does teach creation from nothing, see Copan and Craig, *Creation out of Nothing*.

We do not have space to review the whole scope of the message of Genesis 1–2, so here I will briefly and suggestively present the highlights.[51] Genesis 1–2 informs us about the nature of God and ourselves.

God

Modern readers often miss the unique nature of God in Genesis when examined within the context of the ancient Near East. Most radical is the revelation that there is only one God: the one God created everything else (see the excursus "Creation from Nothing?" above), and he did so through the power of his word, not through conflict with other gods.[52] This one God, the God that Israel worshiped (and identified as Yahweh in Gen. 2:4), is thus sovereign and supreme in a way that other ancient Near Eastern gods are not. He is also described in a way that demonstrates that he is not a part of creation (the creation is not an extension of his being), in that he makes it and pronounces it good. In that sense he is transcendent, but he is also involved with his creation and thus immanent. In other words, right from the start God is described in a way that we would call theistic, not pantheistic (immanent but not transcendent) or deistic (transcendent but not immanent).

Further, Genesis 1 and 2 make it clear that this God is neither gendered nor sexually active. Modern Western readers may not appreciate the radical nature of this description of God. In the ancient Near East, however, a nongendered, not-sexually-active deity is unique. That he is nongendered, neither male nor female, is indicated by Genesis 1:28, where we read, "In the image of God he

---

51. A fuller presentation of my views may be found in Longman, *Genesis*.
52. I agree largely with those who see a reference to the divine council in God's words "Let us make mankind in our image, in our likeness" (Gen. 1:26), but the idea of a divine council does not undermine the idea that there is only one Creator God ("So God created mankind in his own image" [1:27]). At most, this language is henotheistic (there may be many "gods," but only one of them deserves worship), not polytheistic.

created them; male and female he created them." In other words, both males and females reflect who God is. Indeed, for this reason later Scripture utilizes both male (king, warrior, etc.) and female (mother, Woman Wisdom, etc.) metaphors for God.

HUMANITY

The first and most obvious teaching about humanity in the creation accounts of Genesis 1 and 2 is the high place that humans occupy in God's creation. The psalmist captures the same sense when he muses:

> Yet you have made them a little lower than God,
>   and crowned them with glory and honor.
> You have given them dominion over the works of your
>   hands;
>   you have put all things under their feet.
> (Ps. 8:5–6 NRSV)

This point is communicated in a variety of ways. First of all, the sequence of creation in Genesis 1 shows the important place of humanity. While I have noted that the intention is not to tell us the actual order of creation, the depiction of humanity being created last, after everything else is put in place, is significant. Second, humans are said to be made in God's image and likeness. Though the precise meaning of image-bearing is debatable,[53] there is no question that it indicates humanity's special place in creation. In the second account, God makes the first human from the dust of the ground and his breath, which shows that humans are part of the creation like the animals and also that they have a special relationship with God.

In the figurative depiction of the creation of the first woman, we learn about gender and sexuality. Sexual activity, as indicated

53. For a discussion of the debate and my own ideas, see Longman, *Genesis*, 36–38, 42–44.

by the command to "be fruitful and increase in number" (Gen. 1:28), is an aspect of the creation, not the Creator. The emphasis is on the mutuality and equality of the genders. The woman is made from the man's side (or rib), not his head or feet. The man proclaims: "This is now bone of my bones and flesh of my flesh" (2:23). She is a helper (*'ezer*), or better an ally, "corresponding to him" (my translation of the phrase rendered "suitable" by the NIV in 2:18, 20). The term *'ezer*, no matter how it is rendered in English, does not denote subordination, as witnessed by the many times it is used to describe God (Deut. 33:29; Pss. 33:20; 89:18–19).[54]

Again, sexual activity is an aspect of the creation and not the Creator. We learn from Genesis 2 that marriage was an institution intended for humans from their creation and not a part of the fall. We also learn that God intended for humans to work; they were to "work it [the garden] and take care of [or better "guard"] it" (2:15). While marriage (and relationships more generally) and work can often feel like a struggle, we learn in Genesis 3 that such difficulties are a result of human rebellion, not God's original creation.

Indeed, if it weren't for Genesis 1 and 2, we would conclude that humans were by their created nature sinful. That was certainly the idea communicated by the Mesopotamian creation stories, in which humans were created from the clay of the earth and the blood of a demon god. Yet the Genesis creation accounts tell us not only that humans were created innocent but also that creation itself was good. "Good" here does not mean perfect, as some commonly believe, nor is it pronouncing a moral statement; rather, it means that God created everything so that it functioned well. Again, our everyday experience would not lead us to that conclusion.

Finally, Genesis 1 in particular highlights the importance of Sabbath. The creation account itself does not mandate Sabbath observance, but the choice to describe God's creation as if it were

54. For more on this teaching of Gen. 2, see "The Biblical Theology of Sexuality" in chap. 4.

a regular workweek becomes a strong rationale for Sabbath observance (see Exod. 20:8–11).

Does Genesis 1:29–30 Undermine Evolution?

Some people think that Genesis 1:29–30 contradicts an evolutionary scenario because it seems to restrict not only original humanity but also the animals to a vegetarian diet. Evolution, however, as well as the fossil record, makes it very clear that many animals ate a diet that included other animals.

Michael LeFebvre points out that it is incorrect to assume that these verses so restrict animal diet. He says that "if the purpose of Genesis 1:29–30 was to restrict all diets to vegetation, one would expect to find restrictive language (saying things like, 'shall only eat plants' or 'I give plants and not meat'). But there is no restrictive language present."[55] He quotes John Calvin, who says, "Some infer from this passage that men were content with herbs and fruits until the deluge, and that it was even unlawful for them to eat flesh. . . . These reasons, however, are not sufficiently strong. . . . I think it will be better for us to assert nothing concerning this matter."[56] Thus, it seems to me that these verses do not provide evidence that the Bible conflicts with the theory of evolution.

Creation and Providence

Genesis 1–2 teaches that Yahweh is the Creator of all things and that he has created human beings in his image to be in relationship with him. Evolution, on the other hand, posits a mechanism for the emergence of life that takes no recourse to the intervention of

55. LeFebvre, "Calendars and Creation," 191.
56. Calvin, *Genesis*, comments on Gen. 1:28–30.

a creator. If God used secondary causes such as those described in the theory of evolution to create human beings, who needs God? But I think the anxiety about evolution essentially removing God from the equation is unwarranted.

Of course, such anxiety is stoked by New Atheists like Richard Dawkins and physicist Stephen Hawking who suggest that the theory of evolution undermines religion.[57] But rather than playing into their hands by denying the strong scientific evidence in favor of evolution, we should ignore them by simply affirming that evolution, or God's use of secondary causes, does not undermine God's role as creator of humanity.[58] Ignoring Dawkins and his ilk is the best strategy of (non)engagement. Think about it. The world would have been a lot better off if Adam and Eve had simply ignored the serpent's question in the garden rather than trying to provide an answer in order to defend God. Granted I am being a bit overly dismissive here, and I earlier recommended other resources for those who want to reflect on Dawkins's arguments. But Dawkins's critiques depend on a conception of Christianity that rejects evolution, and if one understands that the Bible does not address how God created, then his arguments are without merit.

But if God used secondary causes to create humans, how do we know that God created humans? Some believe we have to have evidence that can't be explained by science in order to prove to people that only God could have done it. In other words, if we can't appeal to some "irreducibly complex" sign of design, then how can we know that God did it?

Earlier I invoked the "two books" approach to the question of science and faith and recognized that sometimes science can help us read the Bible better (and I will return to this idea below). Now we come to the other part of the "two books" doctrine, the

57. See, for instance, Dawkins, *Selfish Gene*, and Hawking and Mlodinow, *Grand Design*.
58. See Alexander, "Creation, Providence, and Evolution."

part that is reflected in Pope John Paul II's statement that "religion can purify science from idolatry and false absolutes."[59] How do we know that God created humans, even though there is no scientific evidence (or gap in the scientific evidence) to support that idea? The Bible. We know that God created humans because "the Bible tells us so." Calvin, who appreciated the work of even scientists who were not believers, also understood that to get the deepest understanding of the world, we must put on the spectacles of Scripture:

> But although the Lord represents both himself and his everlasting Kingdom in the mirror of his works with very great clarity, such is our stupidity that we grow increasingly dull toward so manifest testimonies, and they flow away without profiting us. . . . Not only the common folk and dull-witted men, but also the most excellent and those otherwise endowed with keen discernment, are inflicted with this disease.[60]

> So Scripture, gathering up the otherwise confused knowledge of God in our minds, having dispersed our dullness, clearly shows us the true God.[61]

Scripture teaches us that God's involvement in creation is just as real through his providence as through miracles. He uses both, but miracles don't trump the providential use of secondary causes. As an illustration, let's look at the book of Esther. The book is the exciting account of how the Jewish people were rescued from a genocidal plot by their enemies. If Haman and his associates had their way, the Jewish people would have been eradicated from the

59. John Paul II to Reverend George V. Coyne, SJ, Vatican, June 1, 1988, http://w2.vatican.va/content/john-paul-ii/en/letters/1988/documents/hf_jp-ii_let_1988 0601_padre-coyne.html.
60. Calvin, *Institutes* 1.5.11, 1:63–64, quoted in Zachman, "Free Scientific Inquiry," 69.
61. Calvin, *Institutes* 1.6.1, 1:70, quoted in Zachman, "Free Scientific Inquiry," 60.

face of the earth. From a Christian perspective, that would have signaled the end of the messianic hope that was realized in Jesus.

How were the Jewish people saved? Well, a woman named Esther became queen through a series of events that led to the deposing of the previous queen, Vashti. Esther's cousin Mordecai became aware of a plot hatched by Haman to pick a day when King Xerxes would allow his people to eradicate the Jewish people.

Mordecai convinced Esther to expose Haman's plot, which she did successfully, and Haman was impaled on the pole he erected to execute Mordecai. On the appointed day when the Jewish people were supposed to die, they defended themselves and killed their attackers. The end of the book announces a celebration called Purim that would be enjoyed every year to commemorate this event.

Notice that in this account God is not mentioned. Indeed, the book of Esther never mentions the name of God! However, only the most dull reader can read this book without coming away with the certain sense that, though he is never once mentioned, it is God and none other who is the hero of the day. God worked through the secondary causes laid out in the plot description above, but no one can doubt that the rescue was a divine rescue. Similarly, no one should conclude that God did not create humanity just because of the existence of secondary causes such as those described in evolutionary theory. Many of the church's most stalwart defenders of biblical authority have recognized that evolution and the Bible's description of humanity do not conflict in the light of God's providential workings. B. B. Warfield, the highly regarded theologian who helped define inerrancy, stated, over against those who thought evolution disproved the Bible, that "'evolution' cannot act as a substitute for creation, but at best can supply a theory of the method of the Divine providence."[62]

62. This appears in Warfield's classic essay "On the Antiquity and the Unity of the Human Race" (p. 1), available at http://commons.ptsem.edu/id/princeton theolog9119arms-dmd002.

Why Then Am I an Evolutionary Creationist?[63]

Since the Bible does not intend to teach us how God created humanity, we can and should, in keeping with the Belgic Confession's "two books" doctrine, derived from the Bible, and Pope John Paul II's statement that "science can purify religion," turn to science to answer the *how* question.

I want to be clear at this point. I am not a scientist, and it is not my place to put forward the argument and the evidence in favor of evolution. However, I am informed enough as a layperson to know that the evidence in favor of evolution is overwhelming. There is no serious doubt among research biologists, Christian and not, that our species emerged not through God literally blowing on dust a few thousand years ago but through a long process involving a primate past that eventually traces back to very simple organisms (common descent).[64]

Karl Giberson and Francis Collins, devout evangelicals and leading biologists,[65] present in a succinct and accessible manner the massive evidence, particularly the genetic evidence, that convinces virtually every research biologist that evolution is the best theory that accounts for human origins. They rightly assert, "When there is a near-universal consensus among scientists that something is true, we have to take that seriously, even if we don't like the conclusion."[66]

Those in the Christian community who suggest that the theory of evolution is in crisis are misleading their audiences. While there

63. For a more anecdotal account, see Longman, "Old Testament Professor Celebrates Creation."

64. For my Christian friends, I recommend the work of Christian biologists like Francis Collins, Dennis Venema, Jeffrey Schloss, Praveen Sethupathy, and Joshua Swamidass that can be accessed at the BioLogos website (www.biologos.org).

65. Collins is particularly well known as the former head of the Human Genome Project and also the director of the National Institutes of Health (2009 to present); see Falk, "Francis Collins," 100–101.

66. Giberson and Collins, *Language of Science and Faith*, 28. An even more recent excellent and accessible presentation of the genetic evidence may be found in Venema and McKnight, *Adam and the Genome*.

are still questions about the details of the process, there is no doubt about the overall theory itself. The theory has been out there for a century and a half, and the evidence, both the fossil and especially the genetic evidence, powerfully attests to its veracity. It's not going to be overturned in a dramatic way.

To try to deny evolution because one is trying to defend the Bible is unnecessary because the Bible is not at odds with evolution. To do so in the light of the overwhelming evidence in favor of evolution is putting an unnecessary obstacle to faith. Augustine's admonition is telling:

> Usually, even a non-Christian knows something about the earth, the heavens, and the other elements of this world, about the motion and orbit of the stars and even their size and relative positions, about the predictable eclipses of the sun and moon, the cycles of the years and the seasons, about the kinds of animals, shrubs, stones, and so forth. . . . Now, it is a disgraceful and dangerous thing for an infidel to hear a Christian, presumably giving the meaning of Holy Scripture, talking nonsense on these topics; and we should take all means to prevent such an embarrassing situation . . . and [that], to the great loss of those for whose salvation we toil, the writers of our Scriptures are criticized.[67]

But let's say that through some totally unexpected happenstance, it turns out that evolution is not the best model to understand the emergence of our species. What would that do to my understanding of Genesis 1–2? Absolutely nothing, or at least not in a substantial way. If the evidence started supporting a sudden emergence of humanity (not likely) or some more complicated understanding of the natural process that brought humans into existence, it would make no difference to our interpretation of Genesis 1–2, since it does not teach evolution—indeed does not teach anything about how God created the universe. That is not its purpose.

67. Augustine, *Literal Meaning of Genesis*, 42–43.

The Christian has no reason to feel a threat from science at all. We should support and rejoice in the marvelous work scientists are doing to uncover the process God used to bring us into existence. After all, we rejoice in the fact that God brought us into being. We thank God for our life and the lives of those dear to us, even when we can explain quite well the secondary causes that led to our births.

Evolution and the Historical Adam and Eve

As we turn our attention to what God's two books teach us about human origins, we must remember what we observed above: the Bible has no interest in answering the *how* question, so we turn to the book of nature to explore that question. We must also remember that the book of nature does not answer the *who* or *why* questions, so we turn to the Bible to answer those questions.

The answer to who created everything including human beings is absolutely clear according to the Bible. God did it, the God called Yahweh in the Old Testament, whose triune nature becomes increasingly clear as the canon progresses, so that the New Testament speaks of the creative activity of the Father, Son, and Holy Spirit (John 1:1–5; Rom. 1:18–20; Col. 1:15–20).

The *why* question is not answered as directly. Some theologians make a big point of the fact that God is self-sufficient and does not need anything or anyone (classic theology calls this the "aseity" of God). While it might well be true that God does not *need* creation, it's hard to make sense of the biblical narrative without concluding that God *delights* in his creative work and *desires* relationship with his creatures. Indeed, the biblical text makes it clear that, while God loves all his creative work, he in particular loves his human creatures, whom he created in his own image. Why else would he have created us? And, more to the point, why would he have continued to pursue relationship with us so passionately after humanity rebelled against him?

We now turn to the book of nature to explore the question of how. Science has proposed a theory, evolution, that has been supported by abundant evidence provided by the fossil record and, more recently and pointedly, by genetic evidence. The evidence is so consistent with the theory that only outlier scientists doubt that humanity was created through an evolutionary process that involves common descent. As discussed above, these scientists have an unnecessary and misplaced motive of defending the Bible, which they believe teaches that God created human beings by a special act of creation and not through the providence-guided means of evolution.

Of course, we want to ask how these two truths might relate to each other: How can humans who emerge from an evolutionary past be said to be created in the image of God? What about Adam and Eve? Were they actual people? And then there is the biblical claim that humans were "good" or "innocent" at the time of their creation: How does that square with the narrative provided by evolution, which operates through "nature, red in tooth and claw,"[68] which also raises the question of death before the fall? And then there is the fall: Was there a historical fall that introduced sin and death into the world as Paul claims (Rom. 5:12–20)? This also leads to the question of original sin: In what way (if any) does Adam and Eve's sin relate to us today? To answer these many questions, let's look at what Genesis 1–3 teaches about human beings.

Humans in Genesis 1–3

In my view, the Bible teaches clearly that human beings were created by God and that they were created in the image of God. The Bible also teaches clearly that at the time of their creation as image-bearing creatures, humans were morally innocent and

68. This oft-quoted phrase comes from Alfred, Lord Tennyson, "In Memoriam A.H.H.," canto 56, p. 118.

capable of moral choice. And the Bible makes it clear that human sinfulness and death as we know them today are not the result of how God made us but came about because of humanity's willful rebellion against him. Are any of these important biblical teachings undermined by the theory of evolution? I suggest not. If we see Genesis 1–3 (indeed 1–11) as theological history that depicts the deep past using figurative language, then, indeed, there is more than one way to understand how the theory of evolution is compatible with biblical truth.

Let me begin with the perspective that I find most persuasive, followed by certain possible variations of that view. It is not at all important that we have hard and fast formulations for issues that the Bible neither directly addresses nor has strong implications toward.

In the first scenario, we might imagine that God used the evolutionary process to produce the first *Homo sapiens*. Evolution does not work by producing a single couple out of a previous population; rather, a certain group of the previous population becomes isolated from the larger group, and their distinctive gene pool leads to the new species. This process is complex—and it is not as if a new group emerges all of a sudden—but the bottom line is that the genetic evidence is clear that humanity does not go back to a single couple from which all later *Homo sapiens* descended.

The complexity of the emergence of *Homo sapiens* is not really a problem, since the biblical account speaks not just of *Homo sapiens* but of humans who have the status of divine image bearers. Thus, we can have *Homo sapiens* who were not endowed with that status.

Here it is important to realize that the image of God is not a quality or an attribute of human beings but rather a status that comes with responsibility. Recent studies have shown that the best route to understanding the meaning of humans' status of image bearers (which is never clearly defined or described by Scripture) is by examining how the words "image" (*tselem*) and "likeness" (*demut*), found in Genesis 1:26–27, are used elsewhere in the Bible and in the broader ancient Near East.[69] In the Bible we see the use of the term (actually its Aramaic cognate) in Daniel 3, where Nebuchadnezzar erects a gigantic statue of himself to which he demands that everyone bow.

Perhaps the most striking confirmation of this understanding of the image of God can be found in the ninth-century-BC Aramaic-Akkadian inscription on a statue from Tell Fakhariyeh in Syria, which refers to the statue as the "likeness" and "image" of King Hadad-yis'i.[70] As Walter Brueggemann puts it, "It is now generally agreed that the image of God reflected in human persons is after the manner of a king who establishes himself to assert his sovereign rule where the king himself cannot be present."[71]

At a certain point, then, when humans became capable of moral choice and were morally innocent, God conferred on them the status of being his representatives. Thus, they reflect the divine glory like the moon reflects the light of the sun (see Ps. 8:3–5). This status came with responsibility, as God instructed them, "Be fruitful and increase in number; fill the earth and subdue it. Rule over the fish in the sea and the birds in the sky and over every living creature that moves on the ground" (Gen. 1:28). In other words, humans created in the divine image were to be God's royal representatives to the rest of creation, acting with benevolence toward the creation, not exploiting it.

Neither the Bible nor science has anything to say about the moment that God so endowed humans. Thus, some understand this to have happened toward the emergence of humanity (over one hundred thousand years ago), while others—and this view strikes me as more persuasive—place this moment much later,

69. See discussion and citations in Longman, *Genesis*, 37–38.
70. Garr, "'Image' and 'Likeness,'" 228, as well as his full study, *In His Own Image and Likeness*.
71. Brueggemann, *Genesis*, 32.

at the time that humans start showing signs of divine awareness through burial practices, cave paintings, and so forth.

Another variation in perspective among those of us who accept the findings of evolutionary creationism has to do with what Adam and Eve represent in the account of Genesis 1–3. One possible view is that they represent the whole population endowed with the image of God. After all, Adam's name means "humanity." But another view takes Adam and Eve as a representative couple within the larger population.[72] The royal language of Genesis 1:28 suggests that the couple might be considered the kings of this original population, while others point to Genesis 2, which in describing the creation uses language that is similar to the construction of the Israelite tabernacle and also includes the charge to Adam to "work" and "take care of" (Heb. *shamar*, better "guard") the garden, and consider them more like priestly figures.

We don't need to decide between these variant scenarios. The Bible is not interested in answering all our questions, but what is important is that what the Bible does teach is not undermined or contradicted by the findings of modern biology. As I have said more than once, God's two books, Scripture and nature, will not contradict each other when properly interpreted.

But what about Genesis 3? How are we to understand the account of humanity's rebellion against God in the light of evolution? The first point we need to emphasize is that, while the account in Genesis 1–3 describes past events in figurative language, these chapters *are* talking about past events. Interpretations that assert that human beings created in the image of God were never morally innocent, or state that the sinfulness of human beings is an inherent trait of humanity rather than the result of human rebellion against God (thus denying a historical fall),[73] do not take the biblical account seriously, denying an essential

---

72. Wright, *Surprised by Scripture*, chap. 2.
73. See Enns, *Evolution of Adam*, and Schneider, "Fall of 'Augustinian Adam.'"

theological teaching of the Bible. These interpretations attribute human sinfulness and death to divine creation rather than human willfulness.

Such views are typically supported by appeal to science, which only bears witness to "nature, red in tooth and claw."[74] But we would not expect scientific evidence for a period of moral innocence or a historical rebellion. For one thing, if we take the Bible seriously, the period of time between the endowment of humans with the image of God and the rebellion was short-lived, to be sure. We learn about it only from the Bible. Again, remember that while science can help us read the Bible better, the Bible reveals matters that are not accessible through scientific investigation.

That said, the figurative nature of the account of humanity's rebellion in Genesis 3 has been patently obvious to many since the time of the early church. Consider the feisty assessment of the church father Origen:

> And who will be found simple enough to believe that like some farmer "God planted trees in the garden of Eden, in the east" and that he planted "the tree of life" in it, that is a visible tree that could be touched, so that someone could eat of this tree with corporeal teeth and gain life, and further, could eat of another tree and receive the knowledge of "good and evil"? Moreover, we find that God is said to stroll in the garden in the afternoon and Adam to hide under the tree. Surely, I think no one doubts that these statements are made by Scripture in the form of a figure by which they point to certain mysteries.[75]

One does not have to agree with Origen's overall hermeneutical approach (or his sarcastic tone) in order to agree with his recognition of the figurative nature of the chapter. But again, what is

74. But note that scientists more recently have been giving "altruism" a larger role in the evolutionary process. See Fuentes, *Creative Spark*.

75. Origen, *On First Principles* 4.3.1, cited and discussed in Cunningham, *Darwin's Pious Idea*, 381–82.

the figurative language pointing to? Whatever we conclude, our interpretation must be consonant with the nature of the figures. Specific figures are chosen for a purpose.

These first human beings (or possibly a representative couple among them) endowed with the status of divine image bearers had an intimate relationship with God. They did not have to seek holy (set apart) places in order to meet God or offer sacrifices in anticipation of that meeting. There was no barrier between them and God. But they were called to obey God out of their own volition. God would not compel them to obey him. And rather than obey, they rebelled against him, thus introducing sin and death into the human experience.

What many Christian readers, who tend to focus on the New Testament, fail to realize is that this arguably foundational story is never back-referenced in later Old Testament texts to explain Israel's sin, guilt, and death. There is no concept of "original sin" in the Old Testament, nor did any Israelite think that "sinful nature" was inherited or in any way a result of Adam and Eve's first sin. Nor does the New Testament, for that matter, though it is true that the New Testament makes more of Adam and Eve's sin than does the Old Testament. To that topic we now turn.

Romans 5 and the "Historical Adam"

As Christians who take the New Testament seriously, we must pay close attention to passages like Romans 5:12–21:[76]

Therefore, just as sin entered the world through one man, and death through sin, and in this way death came to all people, because all sinned—

To be sure, sin was in the world before the law was given, but sin is not charged against anyone's account where there is no law.

76. One of the very best treatments of Rom. 5:12–21 is that of Scot McKnight in the book he coauthored with the biologist Dennis Venema, *Adam and the Genome*, 171–91.

Nevertheless, death reigned from the time of Adam to the time of Moses, even over those who did not sin by breaking a command, as did Adam, who is a pattern of the one to come.

But the gift is not like the trespass. For if the many died by the trespass of the one man, how much more did God's grace and the gift that came by the grace of the one man, Jesus Christ, overflow to the many! Nor can the gift of God be compared with the result of one man's sin: The judgment followed one sin and brought condemnation, but the gift followed many trespasses and brought justification. For if, by the trespass of one man, death reigned through that one man, how much more will those who receive God's abundant provision of grace and of the gift of righteousness reign in life through the one man, Jesus Christ!

Consequently, just as one trespass resulted in condemnation for all people, so also one righteous act resulted in justification and life for all people. For just as through the disobedience of the one man the many were made sinners, so also through the obedience of the one man the many will be made righteous.

The law was brought in so that the trespass might increase. But where sin increased, grace increased all the more, so that, just as sin reigned in death, so also grace might reign through righteousness to bring eternal life through Jesus Christ our Lord.

I have quoted this passage in full because for many people Paul's statement here constitutes the largest stumbling block to seeing how contemporary evolutionary biology can be compatible with biblical theology.[77] Some people today believe that Paul's statement here is totally incompatible with evolutionary biology's conclusion that humanity does not go back to an original single pair—there was never a time when there were only two humans, a male and a female.[78] But such a negative conclusion

77. In what follows I have found C. M. Hays and S. L. Herring ("Adam and the Fall") very helpful.

78. The evidence is nicely cited in Venema, "Genesis and the Genome," 166–78, as well as his contribution to McKnight and Venema, *Adam and the Genome*.

involves an overreading (and a rather modern one) of Paul's words here.

In the first place, a common view is that Paul here must understand Adam to be a historical individual.[79] He talks as if he is, and he draws an important analogy between Adam and Jesus, whom Paul clearly believes was a historical individual. Indeed, it is not uncommon to hear the charge, which is a non sequitur, that if one does not think Adam is a historical character, then Jesus is not a historical character.

This viewpoint is effectively countered by James Dunn, whose insightful comment I largely agree with, though I prefer slightly different language, as I will make clear below.

> It would not be true to say that Paul's theological point here depends on Adam being a "historical" individual or on his disobedience being a historical event as such. Such an implication does not necessarily follow from the fact that a parallel is drawn with Christ's single act: an act in mythic history can be paralleled to an act in living history without the point of comparison being lost. So long as the story of Adam as the initiator of the sad tale of human failure was well known, which we may assume (the brevity of Paul's presentation presupposes such knowledge), such a comparison was meaningful. Nor should modern interpretation encourage patronizing generalizations about the primitive mind naturally understanding the Adam stories as literally historical. It is sufficiently clear, for example, from Plutarch's account of the ways in which the Osiris myth was understood at this period that such tales told about the dawn of human history could be and were treated with a considerable degree of sophistication with the literal meaning largely discounted.[80]

79. By the way, it is not only more conservative readers of Rom. 5 who come to this mistaken conclusion. Enns (*Evolution of Adam*, 120–21) also asserts this reading of Rom. 5 and then concludes that Paul was "wrong" about this historical conclusion while still affirming Paul's theology. I don't believe that Enns's conclusion is necessary or correct.

80. Dunn, *Romans 1–8*, 289.

The first point to make is that Paul here is referring back to the theological history found in Genesis 3,[81] which, as a figurative depiction of an event, presents Adam as a literary representative of the first humans who had the status of image bearers. The second point is that an analogy between a literary figure like Adam and a historical individual like Jesus is neither surprising nor unprecedented in the time period in which Paul wrote Romans. The analogy does not depend on them both being historical individuals, but I would say that the analogy does depend on there being a historical reality behind the literary figure of Adam and—at this point I disagree with Dunn—a historical reality behind an act of original disobedience.

While Dunn's citation of ancient precedents is most important, I would also draw our attention to the fact that we too create similar analogies between literary and historical figures. For instance, after a long frustrating day, when my wife asks me how my day went, I might respond, "I've been tilting at windmills all day!" Of course, I am drawing an analogy between myself and Don Quixote, a fictional character in Cervantes's famous novel by that name. My wife, being aware of the analogy, understands the point I am making and still considers me a historical character. She might even give me an encouraging hug.

In a critical review of my work in this area, Todd Beall, a self-professed young earth creationist (and, I might add, one of its best and most able proponents), accused me of changing my mind on the historical Adam from the time I wrote *How to Read Genesis* (2005) to the time of our interaction in *Reading Genesis 1–2*

81. I prefer "theological history" to Dunn's "mythic history," though I am pretty sure we mean the same thing. The reason I avoid the term *myth* is that it is so often taken in its popular rather than in its academic meaning. The popular meaning implies for many people that the story is false, while the academic meaning would defend the idea that *myth* does not make clear whether or not there is some kind of historical reference behind the story but emphasizes the fact that these are important foundational stories telling the reader truths about ourselves and our world, including the divine realm.

(2013).[82] Why? Because he believed I spoke in *How to Read Genesis* "as if" Adam were a historical individual. But actually, as I pointed out to him in my response, I hadn't changed my mind. I was not addressing the issue of the historical status of Adam as an individual in the earlier book, and if I had, I would have made my view clear. I was rather simply appealing back to the story found in Genesis 1–3.

Indeed, if I preached on Genesis 1–3 or Romans 5, I would not make a point of the fact that Adam and Eve are literary representatives of a historical reality rather than historical individuals. It would be unnecessary and distracting to do so. But if I were teaching a Sunday school class on the subject or if the issue came up in some other context where it was relevant, I would make my viewpoint clear. After all, a Sunday school class allows for questions and nuanced answers in a way that a sermon doesn't.

Romans 5 and Original Sin

Romans 5 is rightly taken to be one of the main texts, if not *the* main text, that teaches the important biblical truth that all humans are sinful from birth and that we all have some type of connection to the first sin perpetrated by Adam.[83] Paul presents Adam (whom we are taking as a literary representation of the first humans endowed with the divine image) as the one who introduces sin and death into the world.

Notice, however, that Paul is not explicit about how Adam's sin affects us, and so theologians have stepped into the breach to explain this. My point in what follows is that the Bible clearly teaches that humanity's first sin does relate to all subsequent humans including ourselves, telling us that we are all sinners and that we all experience death, but there is room for talking about

82. See our presentations and interaction in Charles, *Reading Genesis 1–2*.
83. Paul focuses on Adam, though Gen. 3 makes it clear that Adam and Eve are both culpable.

the exact nature of the relationship between Adam and Eve and ourselves.

Indeed, here again I think science can help us read the Bible better, not by undermining the doctrine of original sin but rather in disqualifying certain theological models of original sin, particularly the "inheritance" model (that we inherit sin from Adam like a genetic disease). Such a view necessitates a genetic connection with Adam.

But first let's make one thing absolutely clear, because it is frequently misunderstood. Paul asserts that Adam's sin introduces sin and death into the world. Notice that he says nothing about guilt. Paul's point here is not that we are all guilty because of Adam's sin but that we are guilty because "all [including you and me] sinned" (Rom. 5:12).

It is important to point this out, because many have a contrary view that goes back to a grave misunderstanding handed down from Augustine. Augustine, the rightly revered theologian who lived around AD 400, was not so accomplished a Greek scholar. He mistranslated the Greek of Romans 5:12 so that it read (in Latin), "Therefore, just as sin entered the world through one man, and death through sin, and in this way death came to all people, *in whom* [rather than "because"] all sinned . . ." This misunderstanding led to the idea that Paul explicitly stated that Adam's sin is counted as our sin, that we inherit our sinful nature from Adam's act.[84]

As many have pointed out, such a view attributes an alien guilt to us. But if the Greek is translated correctly (as in the NIV and all other modern translations), it is clear that, while Adam (who we believe represents the first humans holding the status of divine image bearers) introduced sin and death into the world (by being the first), our sin is our sin (not his), and our death is the result of our sin (not his).

84. C. M. Hays and S. L. Herring, "Adam and the Fall."

Some people believe that unless one holds a view of original sin similar to Augustine's, entailing the idea that Adam's sin is in some sense counted as our sin, then one somehow denies original sin. But the truth is that there are other ways to account for our relationship to Adam's first sin. Again, remember the Bible is not explicit about the nature of that relationship, so at this point we are engaged in second-order theological reasoning, not something the Bible directly teaches.

The view that I find most satisfying in terms of accounting for the biblical material while also recognizing the validity of contemporary scientific understanding (remember, "Science can help us read the Bible better") is as follows. In the first place, the story of Adam and Eve tells us what we would all do if we were in their circumstance. Indeed, it tells us what we all do from birth. We turn in on ourselves and act out of our own selfish pride and desires rather than out of obedience to God. In this sense, Adam and Eve, whether standing for the first humans created in the image of God or a representative couple in that group, are our representatives.

Adam and Eve's sin was to assert their moral autonomy over against God's clear command. God said not to eat of the fruit of the tree of the knowledge of good and evil. The fruit does not represent simply the intellectual apprehension of what is good and evil. In that sense, they already knew what was evil (eating the fruit). By eating, they gained a different kind of knowledge, the experiential type, and evil became part of who they were. They thought they knew better than God, but they were wrong and suffered the consequences. And, in a sense, we all suffer the consequences, not because we inherit Adam and Eve's guilt for their sin, but because their sin so disrupted the cosmic and social order that it is not possible for those who come after them (who, remember, would do what they did in the same situation) not to sin.[85]

85. My views are indebted to Walton, "Human Origins and the Bible." See more recently the viewpoint presented by Smith, "What Stands on the Fall?"

One frequently hears a specious argument made by those who want to defend the idea that Adam and Eve were historical individuals and the first and sole progenitors of humanity (over against overwhelming scientific evidence) that if Adam was not a historical individual, then there was no need for Jesus to come and redeem humanity. It is certainly not necessary for Adam to be a historical individual for all of us sinners to need Jesus if we are to be reconciled to God. No one I know is trying to make the argument that humans are not sinners in need of a savior.

EXCURSUS

Critiquing a Last-Gasp Effort to Undo Evolutionary Creationism

Just around the time I turned in this manuscript, a massive (almost one thousand pages) critique of evolutionary creationism, the view that I hold, appeared: *Theistic Evolution: A Scientific, Philosophical, and Theological Critique.*[86] When I first heard about this volume, I thought, Oh no, I am going to have to rewrite or even change some of my views if the authors came up with new ideas or critiques of the views that I hold and express here (yeah, that is what it is like when you finish a manuscript). I determined, as I told one of the editors in an email, that I would read it with openness.

Fortunately (at least for my time budget), I found little new or particularly challenging to what I have already written. Part of this may be because I was one of the editors of the recent *Dictionary of Christianity and Science,*[87] and many of the contributors to *Theistic Evolution* wrote articles for that work and expressed the same ideas there. Still, from what I can tell, *Theistic Evolution* is getting a wide hearing in certain sectors of the evangelical church.

86. Moreland et al., *Theistic Evolution.*
87. Copan et al., *Dictionary of Christianity and Science.*

For this reason, I have provided a short critique for those who might be interested.

I do want to admit that *Theistic Evolution* fairly critiques some ideas held by a few evolutionary creationists, but then again I also critique those ideas in this book (e.g., those who deny a historical fall or original sin). But even while they do this, the authors give the impression that they are imploding the whole evolutionary-creationist approach. Indeed, they associate evolutionary creationism as a whole with some of its, shall we say, more careless articulations.

Let's begin with the false dilemma set up by Wayne Grudem, that we have a choice between historical and figurative interpretation of Genesis 1–3.[88] My previous comments point out that the best reading of Genesis 1–11 is that it is history that uses figurative language.

In regard to biblical interpretation, I would also contest what one author claims is a "natural reading of the Genesis account," which he associates with a reading that takes Genesis 1–2 as a straightforward depiction of how God created things, including the indefensible understanding of the "kinds" of Genesis 1 that precludes the idea that there could be common descent.[89] There is nothing natural about a reading that is not aware of the proper genre of the account nor of its "cognitive environment," as we discussed earlier.

We also hear frequently in this volume, for instance from Stephen C. Meyer, that the theory of biological evolution is failing. Such a perspective can only be had if one reads only the intelligent design literature. And the same author makes the astounding charge that evolutionary creationists have entered "a hasty marriage" between the Bible and biology.[90] Hasty! It has been 150 years of repeated confirmation of the theory of evolution.

88. Grudem, "Biblical and Theological Introduction."
89. Meyer, "Scientific and Philosophical Introduction," 41.
90. Meyer, "Neo-Darwinism," 106.

Many of the contributors in this volume make much of what they think is a contradiction within the idea of evolutionary creationism. That is, if God is involved as evolutionary creationists insist, then how can the process of natural selection be random as the theory of evolution claims? However, we should not think that though the process of creation appears to us to be random, this means that it is actually random. Remember what we said about the book of Esther. It sure seems "random" or pure chance that on a sleepless night Xerxes had his people read about Mordecai's efforts to foil an assassination plot, but we all know that a deeper plan was at work. These critics of "randomness" in evolution again show an anemic view of providence.

Further, we get the idea from these contributors that whenever a later biblical author refers to Adam and Eve or to the story of Genesis 1–3, they believe they were historical individuals. As I earlier said, this is a patronizing comment on the biblical authors. When they refer to Adam and Eve, they are referring to the characters of the story; they are not commenting on their individual historical existence.

I must also say something about the scientists who contribute to the book. Their credentials are impressive, to be sure. They are extremely intelligent people, as are all the contributors to this volume, but it is striking to note how few of them are biologists. Even if one is a brilliant mathematician or paleontologist, one is not in a privileged position to offer special insight into biology. It would be like me, something of an expert in Hebrew and other ancient Semitic languages (and therefore linguistics), offering comments on modern Slavic. The fact that there are hosts of Christian PhDs in biology who are evolutionary creationists and so very, very few who are not is remarkable, if not telling. In my private conversations with a couple of Christian biologists who do not accept evolution (not contributors to this volume), they acknowledge the extent to which they are outliers in their field and how strong the evidence is for evolution. They choose not to accept the theory, however, because they have been told or have come to believe that the Bible teaches otherwise. I commend their faith, but this is a sacrifice I feel they don't have to and shouldn't make, because it defends an interpretation of the Bible that is not sustainable.

In the spirit of cooperation, let me make a concession of sorts—not about evolution per se, but about the emergence of life out of inanimate matter and the rise of consciousness and a moral sense. Perhaps these will never be explained through secondary physical processes. These may be lacunae *naturae causa* (gaps due to nature) and not lacunae *ignorantiae causa* (gaps due to ignorance). But we can't insist that the emergence of life will never be given a natural explanation, and if such matters are given a scientific answer, it won't be a problem for what the Bible itself claims.

Conclusion

It is my conclusion that evolution and all its entailments are no threat to the biblical account of creation, which has no interest in telling us about God's method of creation. In my opinion, to argue against evolution is not a defense of the Bible but rather brings embarrassment to the gospel (in the sense that Augustine describes those who try to argue that the Bible differs from the conclusions derived from the honest research of even non-Christian thinkers). That is not to say that every contemporary Christian, or even evangelical, interpreter who accepts evolution is correct on every account. For instance, those who use science to deny the historical nature of the fall or who believe that Paul was mistaken about the historical character of Adam and Eve go against the grain of what the Scriptures teach.

While the Bible does not teach evolution, our awareness that God used evolution to create humanity and also the scientific conclusion that humanity does not go back to a single couple, while not undermining any teaching of the Bible, do lend evidence about certain theological implications from what the Bible teaches. As we saw above, for instance, while evolution does not contradict the idea of original sin nor its effects on all humanity, it does disqualify at least one theory often presented for how we relate to that original sin—namely the so-called inheritance model. In this way, we saw that science can actually help us read the Bible better.

Another benefit of understanding that the Bible does not teach us how God created humans is to get readers to really pay attention to what the Bible does teach about God and humanity. Above, we pointed out that Genesis 1–3 is profound in its foundational teaching about the nature of God and who we are as humans. To obsess over something the Bible does not teach makes us blind to what it does teach.

The issue of creation and evolution has already in an important sense raised the issue of historical reference in the Bible. I have argued that Genesis 1–11 is neither straightforward historical narrative nor nonhistorical myth but rather is describing actual events using figurative language. We now turn to a continuation of the issue of historical reference in relation to the rest of the Old Testament. As we will see, some evangelical Protestant scholars raise the question of the historicity of redemptive acts in the rest of the Old Testament. We will focus this discussion in what is perhaps the most discussed moment of that redemptive story—namely, the exodus and the related conquest. Did the exodus and conquest happen, and does it matter whether they did?

DISCUSSION QUESTIONS

1. What were your opinions about creation and evolution before reading this chapter? Have they changed, and, if so, how?

2. Do you think it is fair to say that Genesis 1 and 2 are about the who of creation rather than the how? Why or why not?

3. Does knowledge of ancient Near Eastern creation stories help us understand the biblical account. If yes, how so?

4. What do you think about the "two books" theology of the Belgic Confession, where God speaks truly through Scripture and nature?

5. Describe in your own words what this chapter calls "theological history." Would you agree that Genesis 1–3 (and even 1–11) is theological history?

6. What do the two opening chapters of Genesis teach us about God? About ourselves?

7. Are you convinced that the description of God's creation of the cosmos, the world, and humans is largely figurative? Which are the most persuasive examples of figurative depiction? Which examples are not as convincing?

8. What does it mean to be created in the image of God?

9. What is the fall? Is it a historical event according to Genesis 3 or Romans 5:12–21?

10. What is original sin? Does the Bible teach it? Is it compatible with evolutionary theory?

2

History

Did the Exodus and Conquest Happen,
and Does It Matter?

I remember it as if it were yesterday, though it happened a little over fifty years ago. My family was attending a large community church in our rather affluent neighborhood. I was about fourteen or fifteen years old, the age to become a member. A final step in the membership process was a meeting with one of the pastoral staff. My interviewer was one of the older ministers who was nearing retirement. The only specific memory that I have of the meeting was when he asked me at the end, "Do you have any questions before you become a member?" While I forget what led me to say it, I remember saying rather sheepishly, "Well, I am having a hard time believing that the stories that I read in the Bible actually happened." My minister responded without missing a beat, "Don't worry about it. We don't think they happened either." To be honest, I didn't worry about it, and I became a member. If it didn't bother him that the story of the gospel wasn't historical, then why should I worry about it?

When I was seventeen, however, a young Baptist minister who moved into the area befriended our high school football team and presented the gospel to me in a clear way that affirmed the historical nature of Jesus's life, crucifixion, and resurrection. It was then that I became a Christian. And from that moment on I realized it was important to affirm that the biblical story had a connection with real events and wasn't "just a story."

The Controversy

Historicity has become a controversial issue in some sections of the evangelical Protestant church in a way that it hasn't been before.[1] And I think the best way to understand this challenge is to engage with the work of four scholars who make an evangelical case for questioning the historicity of Old Testament narratives such as the exodus and the conquest—Kenton Sparks, Peter Enns, Megan Bishop Moore, and Brad Kelle.[2] I will then raise what I believe are theological problems with their views before presenting an argument in favor of affirming the historicity of what I call the redemptive history of the Old Testament. Sparks, Enns, and Moore and Kelle will be my main dialogue partners here, but I think it is important to consider their works within a broader context.

When I first began my serious academic study of the Bible in the 1970s, there were essentially two major schools of thought when it came to the question of history and the Old Testament. There were differences among those within these two schools, to be sure, but scholars could generally be divided into those who felt comfortable defending the historicity of the main contours

1. That this issue also sparks different opinions among Jewish scholars may be seen by comparing Cline, *From Eden to Exile*, and Friedman, *Exodus*. I will have more to say about Friedman's interesting proposal below.
2. Sparks, *God's Word in Human Words*; Enns, *Bible Tells Me So*; Moore and Kelle, *Biblical History and Israel's Past*.

of the biblical story (today this group would be called "maximalists") and those who questioned the veracity of the early history of Israel (typically until the period of the monarchy) but still felt that later Israelite history was generally reliable, at least in the main points. Evangelical Protestants as well as some conservative Jewish and Catholic thinkers constituted the bulk of the first group, while most other scholars positioned themselves in the second.

The difference between the two groups was largely due to their different stances toward the Bible itself. The first group's perspective was shaped by its belief that the Bible holds a special status as the Word of God and would not mislead its readers. Thus, when it makes historical claims, these statements could be taken as reliable testimony to past events. The other school of thought believed that the Bible needed to be treated as any other ancient document and be subject to the same kind of historical-critical analysis. Since, according to this second group, scholarly analysis of the Bible needed to proceed by means that were acceptable to believers and unbelievers alike, one could neither accept the special status of the Bible's claim to be the Word of God nor accept the worldview that the Bible itself reflects.

Let me offer a personal illustration. I remember distinctly what a very close scholarly friend of mine said when I told him that I was coauthoring a history of Israel during the biblical period.[3] He responded immediately, "You can't believe in God and write history." Of course, I disagreed with him, but I understood where he was coming from. To take the biblical accounts seriously, accounts that describe God's intervention in history, one needs to think there is a God who can so intervene. If you don't think there is such a God (or if you think that you can't introduce God into the discussion for some other reason), then you won't write a history

---

3. The finished project was Provan, Long, and Longman, *Biblical History of Israel*.

that speaks about God's involvement (and you won't take a history written with such a presupposition seriously).

So again, that was the lay of the scholarly landscape up until about 1980. In the past few decades the situation has grown more complex, and I will highlight two trends that have led to our present intra-evangelical controversy. The first is the rise of what many call "minimalism." The name rightly implies that minimalist scholars are the opposite of maximalists, asserting that the Bible contains very little reliable historical information.[4] Such scholars obviously differ from evangelicals, who tend to be maximalists. But they also differ from many of their historical-critical colleagues, since they think that not only the early history of Israel but also much of the later history is unreliable. After all, they argue, the historical claims made in the Old Testament were fictions created by a people who first came into the land in either the Persian or the Greek period. The purpose of these "histories" was to lay claim to the land by devising a story about their God giving them the land. The Bible is an ideological document that can't be trusted for historical information, and those who do trust it are themselves ideologues either for religious purposes or, in the case of those who believe that the Hebrew Bible gives present-day Israel the divine right to the land, for political purposes.

The second relevant development is the acceptance by some evangelical scholars of the arguments of historical critics and, in the case of some, even minimalists. It is this development in particular that I am responding to in this chapter. So let's turn to the works of Sparks, Enns, and Moore and Kelle. I will provide a summary of their arguments, and then in the following sections I will engage more deeply many of the topics that the summaries introduce.

4. While the minimalist literature is extensive, some of the best-known works include Davies, *In Search of "Ancient Israel"*; Whitelam, *Invention of Ancient Israel*; Grabbe, *Can a "History of Israel" Be Written?*; Lemche, *Israelites in History and Tradition*; and Thompson, *Mythic Past*.

Kenton Sparks

In his book *God's Word in Human Words*,[5] Kenton Sparks, discussing the exodus, chides a number of fellow evangelical scholars (including *moi*) for our failure to embrace historical-critical scholarship. He provides an argument in favor of doing so. At this point, I want to look particularly at how he views the exodus, as this is a pivotal event in salvation history, a key test case with regard to the historicity of the Old Testament narratives, and a useful window into the broader issues.

Sparks concludes that there is no justification for affirming a historical basis to the exodus story. After all, he says, there is no evidence for such an event. Of course, many of us would point to the Bible itself as testimony to the event, but he challenges the use of the Bible in this way. Should we uncritically accept all ancient testimonies? My response would be, "Of course not," but we should at a minimum respect the Bible (and other ancient documents) as a testimony, and to reject it we would need to provide arguments against it.[6]

What concerns Sparks and what constitutes for him an argument against the biblical account of the exodus is that there is no *Egyptian* evidence. Wouldn't such a dramatic moment in Egyptian history, as described in the Bible, leave some trace in Egyptian sources? A whole generation of firstborn dead, a defeat at the sea, and the loss of slave labor? We will deal with this specific objection at greater length below. Suffice it to say here that the Egyptians did not mention this moment in their records likely because they weren't in the habit of recording their humiliating defeats, particularly since most of the records we have of this time period in Egypt are on monumental architecture or steles.

5. In the following discussion, page references will be given in the text.
6. Yes, this is an appeal for a principle of falsification rather than verification. For a lengthy presentation and argument in favor of treating the Bible as historical testimony, see Provan, Long, and Longman, *Biblical History of Israel*, 3–152.

Sparks is aware of this defense, and his comeback is that they had other defeats that we do know about: What about the Hyksos (a Semitic group that came in and took over Lower Egypt for much of the sixteenth century BC)? What about the Sea Peoples who attacked the Delta area around 1200 BC? My response to this rejoinder is that these events are not similar to the situation with the exodus story. We know about the Hyksos because a native Egyptian dynasty eventually booted them out of the land and chased them up into Palestine. We learn about the Sea Peoples because the Egyptians did not suffer a serious defeat at their hands but rebuffed them so that they had to go up the Mediterranean coast to find a place where they could land (heard of the Philistines?). So the exodus account is not similar to these two proposed analogies. There is no happy ending for the Egyptians in the story of the exodus as there is for Sparks's examples.

That said, it's not as if Sparks feels that there is no historical background to the exodus story. He writes:

> It requires only a little imagination to see how the biblical story might dimly reflect actual events in ancient Egypt. Many of the motifs in the exodus story have an historical flavor—not in the sense of specific events but rather as recurring historical patterns in ancient Egyptian history. Good examples include the motifs of Pharaoh and his Asiatic slaves, of the Egyptian oppression of Palestine, of travel and trade between Egypt and Palestine, and of the great plagues that commonly wreaked havoc in ancient Egypt. These kinds of things certainly did happen. So it is quite possible that the exodus tradition is historical, at least in the sense that it summarizes as one story what were actually the repetitive patterns of life in ancient Egypt and Western Asia. (99–100)

It is my fear, however, that this sense of the historical background of the exodus story cannot carry the weight of the Bible's theological use of it, as I will argue below. Indeed, that fear is not assuaged when he says, "Nevertheless, even if we grant the possibility of miracles like the Passover and the parting of the Red Sea—as thoughtful Christians should—we must admit that the expected historical evidence for these miracles is wanting" (100).

Let me be clear. Sparks does not deny that miracles and supernatural events happen. He strongly affirms the resurrection of Jesus. He wants to be historical-critical, to be sure, but he rejects the philosophical presuppositions of traditional historical criticism, which denies the possibility of the supernatural.[7] But he says that even though there is no direct historical evidence for the resurrection (as he believes there isn't for the exodus), there is a long historical reverberation for Jesus's resurrection as evidenced by the growth and dedication of the church (unlike the exodus, which he says left nothing in its wake). But we might ask, What about Israel? What about the impression that the exodus made on Israelites as their founding event as a nation and on the nation's hopes for the future? We will come back to this question below.

Peter Enns

In his book *The Bible Tells Me So*,[8] Peter Enns says so much that is right and good on the subject of biblical historiography. Much of it sounds very familiar (oh yeah, I was his professor; but so was Raymond Dillard, from whom we both learned a lot about biblical history). Enns is right to point out that accounts of the past are not objective but rather shaped in order to depict the past in ways that are relevant to issues in the author's present. Historical accounts are always selective and interpretive. Enns appropriately uses the contrast between Samuel-Kings and Chronicles to illustrate this point. But he is wrong to suggest that there are contradictions

7. The philosophical underpinnings of the historical-critical method are provided by Ernst Troeltsch (see J. J. Collins, *Bible after Babel*, for this point). Sparks rejects these Troeltschian ideas (which makes one wonder whether he truly is historical-critical). For my views on historical criticism, including interaction with Troeltsch, see Longman, "History and Old Testament Interpretation."
8. In the following discussion, page references will be given in the text.

between them when rightly understood. He is also right to talk about the story-like character of the depiction of the past and to remind us of the power of story. As I said, there is a lot that I like about his treatment of history.

But some elements of his discussion and suggestions and the way he states things make me uneasy, particularly when it comes to early history—that is, the time before the monarchy. I will focus on what he says about the exodus and conquest because that is the period that I am concentrating on here.

Enns, like Sparks, points out the lack of what we will call "direct evidence" for the exodus and conquest. There is no mention of Israel's presence in Egypt, nor are there remnants in the wilderness of people who traveled there for forty years. Archaeology has not provided evidence of a violent intrusion into the land of Canaan in either the fifteenth or thirteenth century BC (the two possible dates for the exodus and conquest). In his inimitable way, Enns makes light of attempts to understand this lack of evidence. We will deal with these issues later. For now we are interested to see how he deals with the question of the historicity of the exodus and conquest.

In my opinion, he makes a gesture in the right direction when he says, "I feel pretty strongly, actually, that the exodus story has some historical basis; it wasn't made up out of thin air. A story of national origins that begins 'we were slaves' doesn't sound like the kind of thing people would try to come up with to make an impression. Perhaps a much smaller number of 'Asiatic' slaves—a few hundred or so—left Egypt under the leadership of a charismatic figure and made their way to Canaan" (117–18). But, though he feels strongly, he doesn't develop this point or talk about why it is theologically important that there is a historical core here. And why a "few hundred or so"? Why not a few thousand? The biblical text can be read to support his (and my) idea that it is not describing a couple million slaves making the trip, so one does not even have to appeal to hyperbole, though that is also a possibility. The rest of Enns's discussion surrounding the exodus and the conquest (on which he has only strong opinions that it didn't happen as described in the book of Joshua) is about what really matters in the story. As he later states, "Whatever historical echo there is in the exodus story, Israel's storytellers clearly exerted a lot of effort to dress it up in unhistorical clothing" (119). I will question this below.

Megan Bishop Moore and Brad Kelle

The most mystifying approach to these issues from within evangelical circles[9] comes from Megan Bishop Moore and Brad Kelle's *Biblical History and Israel's Past*. Deferring to what they consider to be the scholarly consensus (more on this below), Moore and Kelle point out that there is no direct extrabiblical evidence that supports the idea of an exodus and wilderness wandering, so it is futile to make the case that the exodus and conquest happened as described in the Bible. They "discount" the attempts by some (most notably Kitchen and Hoffmeier) to suggest that the indirect evidence provides support for seeing a historical connection in these stories.

What confuses me is how the authors uncritically accept the consensus approach and conclusions of the historical-critical method. Their whole approach is to present what they say is the consensus scholarly view on matters of history and criticize others simply for not accepting that viewpoint. In the afterword, they conclude, "It will no longer be acceptable for a credible history to proceed with a traditional presentation that discounts positions that have come to occupy a central place in the broader scholarly

9. I am not sure exactly how the authors would react to the "evangelical" identifier, but I am basing this assessment on Kelle's institutional affiliations as a professor at Point Loma Nazarene University and as a visiting professor at Fuller Theological Seminary.

conversation."[10] They seem to be advocating an uncritical reading of the broader scholarly community, an approach that is unreasonable and a bit naive.

This leads to another criticism of their approach: what they present as the viewpoints and methods of the broader scholarly community misrepresents the situation in the scholarly community. Or perhaps they define as "scholar" only those who operate by their methods and come to certain conclusions with which they agree. If one assesses the viewpoints on these issues from scholars who are teaching at schools across the country (not just Ivy League schools or state universities)[11] and who have bona fide doctorates in biblical studies and are engaged in research, my guess is that by head count the "consensus" would go in the direction of finding historical validity for the broad outline of events in the biblical account of Israel's history, not in the direction of the more skeptical conclusions of Moore and Kelle.

My point here is not to say that such matters are decided by a vote (my apologies to the Jesus Seminar) but to push back on Moore and Kelle when they make it sound like those who have a more appreciative view of the historical reliability of the biblical texts are some kind of minority outliers. My reaction to their

10. Moore and Kelle, *Biblical History*, 467. This statement can be challenged on a whole host of fronts. Since they cite *A Biblical History of Israel*, which I coauthored with Iain Provan and V. Philips Long, it is clear that they don't mean "ignores" when they say "discounts," since we interact with other positions on the central questions of biblical history, including those of historical-critical scholars and minimalists. They must, therefore, mean by "discounts" that we "disagree" with these views. And this understanding of "discounts" is consistent with the way they simply assert rather than argue for these viewpoints that they claim come from the broader scholarly community. This interpretation of their statement is similar to that provided by Iain Provan, who wrote a lengthy critique of *Biblical History and Israel's Past* in the most current edition of Provan, Long, and Longman (*Biblical History of Israel*, 435–39).

11. According to friends who teach at such schools, many of them would not hire a professor who shows an evangelical Protestant connection. I don't even say this critically. After all, Westmont College, where I taught before my recent retirement, and many other schools would not hire a non-evangelical.

comments on the broader scholarly community is similar to that of Kenneth Kitchen, known as one of the greatest Egyptologists of this generation, who wrote about twenty years ago, "Any 'scholarly consensus' that 'early Israel was never in Egypt' or did not exit Egypt is (on the total evidence available) a palpable nonsense and must be scrapped."[12]

And finally, what do Moore and Kelle mean by "it will no longer be acceptable" to write a history that finds historical referents for the key events in the biblical account of Israel? Acceptable to whom? To them and those who agree with them? Again, I would guess that the scholarly consensus is not what they make it out to be, so the teaching in countless schools (and the writings of numerous scholars) doesn't bear this out.

I would have liked to see at this point in their work a robust discussion of the issues of faith and history, but the closest we come is in the afterword. There the discussion is centered on whether the faith of the interpreter ought to affect their approach to the text, but not, as far as I could see, whether one could still claim a theological significance to the exodus and conquest if there were no historical background to the stories. My own view, as I will make clear below, is that if there were no exodus and conquest, then these stories would be theologically uninteresting or irrelevant.

Conclusion

While there are similarities between the evangelical scholars I described above and minimalists, there is also a very important difference between them that we need to bear in mind. While skeptical of the Old Testament's historical claims, these evangelical scholars fully embrace its theological message. We will return to an evaluation of their thinking in a moment, but first we need

12. Kitchen, "Egyptians and Hebrews," 121.

to address the question of genre and history, which serves as a background for our discussion.

The Question of Genre and History

Genre triggers our reading strategy. Authors write in such a way as to signal to their readers "how to take" their words and receive the message that they are communicating. I have already introduced the concept of genre in regard to the evolution/creation controversy in a way that anticipates this broader discussion of its relationship to issues of history, and those readers who may have skipped to this chapter before reading chapter 1 would do well to go back and read the relevant section.[13] But, in short, not every biblical book or part thereof has an equal interest in or uniform approach to the narration of past events. It's very important to examine a book's genre to see what claims the author is making concerning the past and just how important the historicity of a story is to the author's message.

Evangelicals do have a way of "overhistoricizing" the Bible—that is, treating every book as if it recounts events that occurred in space and time. I think this tendency is the result of a mistaken idea of inerrancy and apologetics. I have already affirmed the concept of inerrancy but again want to note that a proper understanding of that doctrine is that the Bible is true in everything it intends to teach. If a book does not intend to communicate that the story is historical, then to insist that it is historically true is a mistake.

Take the book of Job. The message of the book of Job is not dependent on Job being a real person or the book describing actual events. For one thing, Job's suffering is didactic—that is, it teaches us about wisdom and suffering—not redemptive, part of the account of God's work in space and time to reconcile his sinful

13. See "Genre Triggers Reading Strategy" in chap. 1.

people to himself. Like a parable, a story can teach us important lessons, but the story of redemption tells us how God actually entered into space and time to save us. The story of redemption, of course, culminates in Jesus's death and resurrection, which is why Paul makes such a big deal about the necessity of Jesus's actual resurrection in history ("If Christ has not been raised, our preaching is useless and so is your faith" [1 Cor. 15:14]). Job is not historical narrative. It is rather a "thought experiment" using Job's suffering to reflect on important issues of theology.[14]

Again, we evangelicals have a tendency to treat the Bible as if it were all one genre. But even evangelicals recognize, in principle, that parts of the Bible are not historical, most especially the parables, which constitute such a large part of Jesus's teaching. There may be someone somewhere, maybe even a scholar I am unaware of, who thinks otherwise, but the vast majority of readers, and certainly evangelical scholars, do not think that even the parable of the good Samaritan (Luke 10:25–37) has to represent an actual event for it to communicate its message to its readers. They may disagree about the message, but they recognize that the genre of parable is best understood as a fictional story that addresses issues of theology and ethics.

But beyond the issue of historical and nonhistorical genres, there is the question of how genres interested and grounded in history portray the past. Here I want to address the misconception that when the Bible talks about the past, it does so objectively and in what we might call plain language. "Just the facts, ma'am, just the facts."[15]

Once again, we have already dealt with this issue in regard to the creation/evolution question, where we put forward the argument that although Genesis 1–3 intends to speak about the past, it

14. Walton and Longman, *How to Read Job*.
15. The reference is a common statement from Detective Webb in the television series *Dragnet*, popular in the 1950s. My apologies to the generations after the baby boomers.

does so using figurative language since it is covering the far distant past with a worldwide focus. Genesis 12 and following continues to present space-and-time events, but now with a sharper focus and closer attention to detail.

As we deal with the issue of historicity in the following section, we will focus on the exodus and conquest, which continue the account of redemptive history begun in Genesis 12–50 and therefore are more closely related to that part of Genesis than to the first eleven chapters. Even so, as we will see concerning the use of hyperbole in Joshua 1–12, we encounter the use of figurative language even here.

The Historicity of the Exodus and Conquest

With this background on genre and history, we return to the controversy over historicity that has recently arisen within evangelical circles. Let's begin with the exodus from Egypt as an example.

Sparks is very clear that, as historians, we cannot believe that anything like the biblical account of the exodus took place. There is no extrabiblical evidence for it. No Egyptian source or monument talks about it or the presence of Israel in that nation. No archaeological remains of Israel's wandering are found in the wilderness. And, perhaps most fatally, the archaeology of the conquest, which the Bible says took place forty years after the exodus, does not comport well with the biblical description, whether the exodus is dated to the fifteenth century or the thirteenth century BC. All we have is the Bible with no corroborating evidence.

But Sparks also believes that the exodus retains its power in telling us about the nature of God as a redeemer, one who can rescue his people from slavery. Such a message does not need to be communicated by the account of a historical event—a story will do just as well. Stories are compelling and can tell us something true about God. We should not worry about whether the exodus actually happened because we lose nothing of importance about its message if it didn't.

But is this really the case? Is the theological message of the exodus independent of its historicity? I would have to answer this question in the negative. If the exodus did not happen, then there would be *no* theological value to the story. Why? Because the power of the story of the exodus is that it establishes a track record for God.

Let me illustrate my point by looking at Psalm 77, a psalm that looks back on the exodus event as a source of comfort in a difficult present and hope for an uncertain future. The composer, identified in the title as Asaph, the Levitical temple musician, starts his lament by explaining his sorry situation to the congregation:

> I cried out to God for help;
>   I cried out to God to hear me.
> When I was in distress, I sought the Lord;
>   at night I stretched out untiring hands,
>   and I would not be comforted. (77:1–2)

As is typical for psalms, Asaph does not specify his problem. We don't know whether he or a loved one was ill or he or his community were under attack or threatened in some way. What we do know is that the psalms, while written out of personal experience, were composed so that people who came afterward could use the psalms for their own similar, though not necessarily identical, situations.

John Calvin called the psalms a "mirror of the soul": "What various and resplendent riches are contained in this treasure, it were difficult to find words to describe. . . . I have been wont to call this book not inappropriately, an anatomy of all parts of the soul; for there is not an emotion of which any one can be conscious that is not here represented as in a mirror."[16] As we look into a physical mirror, we see how we are doing on the outside. As we read the psalms, we find words that help us articulate what is going on in our hearts. In other words, we find ourselves identifying with the psalmist as he speaks, and his words help give words to what we are thinking and feeling.

In the next verses, the psalmist addresses his anger and disappointment directly to God:

> I remembered you, God, and I groaned;
>> I meditated, and my spirit grew faint.
> You kept my eyes from closing;
>> I was too troubled to speak.
> I thought about the former days,
>> the years of long ago;
> I remembered my songs in the night.
>> My heart meditated and my spirit asked:
>
> "Will the Lord reject forever?
>> Will he never show his favor again?
> Has his unfailing love vanished forever?
>> Has his promise failed for all time?
> Has God forgotten to be merciful?
>> Has he in anger withheld his compassion?" (77:3–9)

The "former days" were the good days of the past. Days of celebration and of singing songs, presumably hymns. After all, those are the types of songs we sing when life is going great. Laments are for times when life is full of difficulties. The psalmist is right. When we are in a time of lament, remembering the times when we sang hymns just makes us feel worse.

The psalmist's angry disappointment then escalates to the next stage, which we see in the series of six questions directed straight

---

16. John Calvin, *Commentary on the Psalms*, vol. 1, p. vi, quoted in Lockyer, "In Wonder of the Psalms," 76.

at God. When we look closely, we can appreciate the bitterness behind these questions. They are rhetorical questions that aren't really looking for answers. They are veiled accusations. Words like *favor, unfailing love, promise,* and *compassion,* as well as the reference to God's mercy, are all related to God's covenant with his people. God had entered into a covenant, a solemn and legal commitment, to treat his people with favor, compassion, mercy, and love. The psalmist is questioning God's truthfulness. "You said you would be our God and take care of us, but with the way my life is going, I think you were lying!"

But the psalm does more than help readers pour out their feelings to God; it also directs them back to him. Notice how the psalm, like many laments (compare, for example, Psalm 69), ends on a positive note:

> Your ways, God, are holy.
>> What God is as great as our God?
> You are the God who performs miracles;
>> you display your power among the peoples.
> With your mighty arm you redeemed your people,
>> the descendants of Jacob and Joseph. (77:13–15)

But unlike the bulk of the laments, Asaph informs us about what led to his change of attitude:

> Then I thought, "To this I will appeal:
>> the years when the Most High stretched out his right
>> hand.
> I will remember the deeds of the LORD;
>> yes, I will remember your miracles of long ago.
> I will consider all your works
>> and meditate on all your mighty deeds." (77:10–12)

"I will remember the deeds of the LORD!" The psalmist looks to the past in order to live in the present with confidence and to

approach the future with hope. But why? Why does remembering the past help us now? At the very end, the psalmist gives us a
concrete example:

> The waters saw you, O God,
>> the waters saw you and writhed;
>> the very depths were convulsed.
> The clouds poured down water,
>> the heavens resounded with thunder;
>> your arrows flashed back and forth.
> Your thunder was heard in the whirlwind,
>> your lightning lit up the world;
>> the earth trembled and quaked.
> Your path led through the sea,
>> your way through the mighty waters,
>> though your footprints were not seen.
>
> You led your people like a flock
>> by the hand of Moses and Aaron. (77:16–20)

Asaph, of course, is referring to the climax of Israel's exodus
from Egypt, the crossing of the Reed Sea[17] (Exod. 14–15). He pictures the event as a battle between God and the waters of the sea
itself. By personifying the waters, the poet evokes the picture of the
waters as standing for evil. God fights the waters of chaos in order
to open up a path of safety for his people. The Israelites themselves
are pictured as God's flock, whom he, through the agency of Moses
and Aaron, leads through "the darkest valley" (Ps. 23:4) to safety.

What is it about the Reed Sea crossing that so encourages the
suffering psalmist (and us as we identify with the speaker)? The

---

17. Many English translations speak of the Red Sea, even though the Hebrew
is very clearly "Reed Sea" (*yam sup*). While that is beyond dispute, some scholars
take their cue from the Greek and identify the Reed Sea with what today we call
the Red Sea. While I disagree (see my thinking in *How to Read Exodus*, 113–14),
the issue does not bear on my present point. Here I only want to explain my use
of Reed Sea rather than the more common Red Sea.

psalmist can't sleep because he cannot see any way out of his predicament. There is nothing he can do to help himself. And it is here that he sees the analogy between his situation and that of those who found themselves on the shore of the sea. The Israelites had no possibility of escape from a gruesome fate. They had an impassable sea at their back as a humiliated and furious Pharaoh charged toward them with his army of "six hundred of the best chariots, along with all the other chariots of Egypt, with officers over all of them" (Exod. 14:7). It was in the face of what looked like certain destruction that God opened up the sea and provided a surprising means of escape.

It was in the light of the exodus that the psalmist remembered that his God was a God who could rescue his people even when it appeared humanly impossible. If he did it in the past, he could do it in the present. Life did not appear as impossible to him as it previously had.

The exodus event so imprinted itself on the memory of later Israel that its theme reverberates throughout the Old Testament and into the New Testament. Not only do we get echoes of the event in psalms like Psalm 77, but the prophets also refer to it as a paradigm for a future restoration after the coming judgment that is the main focus of their oracles. Listen to the echo of the exodus event in Hosea 2:14–15:

> Therefore I am now going to allure her;
>   I will lead her into the wilderness
>   and speak tenderly to her.
> There I will give her back her vineyards,
>   and will make the Valley of Achor a door of hope.
> There she will respond as in the days of her youth,
>   as in the day she came up out of Egypt.

Hosea is writing in the eighth century BC, centuries after the exodus. He envisions the coming judgment, which will be realized in the Assyrian conquest of the Northern Kingdom and the Baby-lonian conquest of the Southern Kingdom as a return to captivity. But that is not the end of the story. God will deliver his people, and they will return from the wilderness ("as in the day she came up out of Egypt"). The Valley of Achor will this time be a "door of hope" (Achor means "trouble" and was named because of the sin of a man named Achan after the battle at Jericho [see Josh. 7]).

While Ezra-Nehemiah reflects an understanding that this sec-ond exodus comes to at least a partial fulfillment at the time of the return from the exile, the Gospel writers make it abundantly clear that the ultimate fulfillment of the anticipated second exodus comes in the ministry of Jesus. The Gospels go to great lengths to show us that Jesus's life and work follow the pattern of the exodus event. We Christian readers often miss it because we are not as familiar with the Old Testament as we should be.

Indeed, the parallels between the exodus and Jesus are so exten-sive that we can only scratch the surface here. Let's begin with his baptism. Jesus's baptism relates to the Israelites' crossing of the sea; what follows, Jesus's forty days in the wilderness, relates to what follows the crossing of the sea—namely, Israel's forty years in the wilderness. Paul, after all, tells us that Israel's Reed Sea crossing was their experience of baptism (1 Cor. 10:1–6); therefore, Jesus's baptism can be compared to their crossing of the sea.

At the end of his forty days in the wilderness (Matt. 4:1–11), Jesus experiences the same temptations that Israel did in its wil-derness wanderings. The only difference is that Jesus does not succumb to the temptations. The first temptation for Jesus is to turn the stones into bread. The Israelites in the wilderness were constantly grumbling about food, but Jesus resists the devil's temp-tation by citing the book of Deuteronomy: "It is written: 'Man shall not live on bread alone, but on every word that comes from the mouth of God'" (Matt. 4:4, quoting Deut. 8:3). The second temptation is for Jesus to test God by throwing himself down from the pinnacle of the temple. Jesus quotes Deuteronomy a second time: "It is also written: 'Do not put the Lord your God to the test'" (Matt. 4:7, quoting Deut. 6:16). His final test is the call to bend the knee and worship the devil, but quoting Deuteronomy a third time, he responds, "Worship the Lord your God, and serve him only" (Matt. 4:10, quoting Deut. 6:13). Jesus cites Deuteronomy three times knowing that that book contains Moses's final sermon to the children of the exodus generation, who had disobeyed God in the wilderness and had died there. Jesus is the obedient Son of God in contrast to the disobedient sons of God.

The comparisons continue throughout the Gospels. Jesus chooses twelve disciples to reflect a new people of God. He gives a sermon on a mountain where he discusses the law (Matt. 5–7), which evokes the memory of God giving the law on Mount Sinai. And the parallels go on and on. This analogy culminates with Jesus's death by crucifixion on the eve of the Passover, the annual celebration of Israel's deliverance from Egypt.

Our point is that the exodus reverberates throughout the Old Testament into the New in a way that shows its pivotal importance not only as a literary theme but as an actual redemptive event that anticipates an even greater redemptive event.

The conquest plays a similar role in later Israel's thinking in a psalm like Psalm 136, which celebrates the exodus:

> [Give thanks] to him who struck down the firstborn of
>   Egypt
> > *His love endures forever.*
> and brought Israel out from among them
> > *His love endures forever.*
> with a mighty hand and outstretched arm;
> > *His love endures forever.*
>
> to him who divided the Red Sea asunder
> > *His love endures forever.*

and brought Israel through the midst of it,
> *His love endures forever.*
but swept Pharaoh and his army into the Red Sea;
> *His love endures forever.*

to him who led his people through the wilderness;
> *His love endures forever.*
> (136:10–16)

The psalmist then moves on to the conquest:

to him who struck down great kings,
> *His love endures forever.*
and killed mighty kings—
> *His love endures forever.*
Sihon king of the Amorites
> *His love endures forever.*
and Og king of Bashan—
> *His love endures forever.*
and gave their land as an inheritance,
> *His love endures forever.*
an inheritance to his servant Israel.
> *His love endures forever.*
> (136:17–22)

Though not as widely recognized, some prophets looked forward to a future conquest as well as a future exodus. By the time of Daniel, Zechariah, and Malachi, Israel had been both the benefactor of the divine warrior and the object of his judgment. These exilic and postexilic prophets lived during a time when Israel lived under the thumb of a foreign oppressor. They looked forward to the intervention of the divine warrior, the God who had fought on their behalf in the past.

In his first apocalyptic vision, for example, Daniel sees four terrifying beasts arising out of the chaotic sea (Dan. 7:1–8). According to an interpreting angel, these beasts represent evil human kingdoms that threaten the people of God. The second half of the vision shifts from the beasts that represent human kingdoms to human figures that stand for the divine realm. Into the presence of a figure that symbolizes God the judge ("the Ancient of Days" [7:9]) comes "one like a son of man, coming with the clouds of heaven" (7:13). While this figure is "like a son of man," meaning "like a human being," he rides the clouds, the divine war chariot, thus clearly showing that he is not really human.

This vision with two figures that represent divine beings is quite radical for the Old Testament and explains why this passage is quoted so often in the New Testament in reference to Christ (Matt. 24:30; Mark 13:26; Luke 21:27; Rev. 1:7). What is clear is that this passage and others in the writings of the exilic and postexilic prophets lead to a strong expectation of a warrior-messiah who will save God's people from their oppressors.

This expectation stands behind John the Baptist's statement, "After me comes one who is more powerful than I, whose sandals I am not worthy to carry. He will baptize you with the Holy Spirit and fire. His winnowing fork is in his hand, and he will clear his threshing floor, gathering his wheat into the barn and burning up the chaff with unquenchable fire" (Matt. 3:11–12). In the next chapter, on divine violence, we will develop further how Jesus meets John's expectations in a rather surprising way, revealing himself as the warrior God who fights on behalf of his people. In this way, not only the exodus but also the conquest anticipates Jesus.[18]

It is hard to escape the conclusion that the biblical authors certainly believed that the exodus and conquest were space-and-time events as well as the conclusion that the historicity of these events is important for their theological significance. Christopher

18. As a side note, I think we have here a further motivation for wanting to do away with a historical exodus and conquest: a distaste for the theme of divine violence that has entered the scene after 9/11 (see more on this in chap. 3).

Ansberry gets it right when he says, "If Yahweh never intervened on Israel's behalf to deliver her from Egypt, then the nation's identity as the elect people of God is deprived of its foundation. What's more, if Yahweh never intervened on Israel's behalf to save her from Egypt, then her hope that Yahweh would again intervene in history to exact her deliverance from exile is largely baseless."[19]

Why Do Some Doubt the Historicity of the Exodus and Conquest?

THE LACK OF DIRECT EVIDENCE

As I pointed out above, Sparks, Enns, and Moore and Kelle argue that there is no direct evidence to support the story of the exodus and conquest. They are correct in reference to extrabiblical textual or archaeological attestations. But they buy into the minimalist arguments and wrongly dismiss the Bible itself as an example of direct evidence to these events. The biblical text itself should be taken seriously as historical testimony.[20] While even those who think the Bible is just like any ancient text need to reckon with it as testimony, those of us who take the Bible as the Word of God must take it even more seriously. If the Bible is God's self-revelation, then it is, as the various evangelical Protestant statements put it, true in all that it teaches, including in terms of history.

Of course, my comments assume that the books of Exodus and Joshua are works of history, a point widely accepted even among those who think the history is unreliable. But we also need to read these books not as modern history but rather as ancient Near Eastern history. We need to not only explore what I will call "indirect evidence" for the exodus and conquest but also come to grips with the nature of the events themselves as described in

19. Ansberry, "Exodus," 70.
20. For a thorough defense of this view, see Provan, Long, and Longman, *Biblical History of Israel*, 3–152.

the biblical text. But before proceeding further, we must take a moment to do our best to situate the time period in which these events purport to take place.

Excursus

The Dates of the Exodus and the Conquest[21]

As we turn to the question of the historicity of these events, we must first enter the contentious debate about the dating of these events. This debate, of course, only takes place among those scholars who believe that the exodus and conquest actually occurred in space and time. Among these scholars, the issue is whether these events happened during the Late Bronze Age, specifically the fifteenth century BC, or during the Early Iron Age, specifically the thirteenth century BC.

The Bible does not date things the way that we do today (BC and AD), nor does it use any kind of absolute dating system. Instead, it employs a system of relative dates (such and so happened x number of years after such and so; A became king in the third year of King B). One obstacle, then, has to do with converting the Bible's relative dates into our absolute dates. More on this later.

One problem (at least to us with our present interests) is that the biblical account of the exodus never mentions the Egyptian pharaoh by name. If the story had referred specifically to Ramesses or some other pharaoh, we would immediately be on solid ground in terms of dating the period in which the exodus took place, but it does not. Jim Hoffmeier suggests that the avoidance of the personal name of the pharaoh mimics the Egyptian practice of never mentioning the name of an enemy king. In this way, it discourages the memory of the king.[22] But no matter the reason, we do not

21. For a recent and extensive review of the two proposed dates for the exodus, see Hawkins, *How Israel Became a People*, 49–90.
22. Hoffmeier, *Israel in Egypt*, 109, 112.

have the name of the pharaoh, so we have to use more indirect means to situate the story.

As has long been recognized, the most important statement about the date of the exodus is found in 1 Kings 6:1, and here is where the debate begins. In this passage the narrator tells us, "In the four hundred and eightieth year after the Israelites came out of Egypt, in the fourth year of Solomon's reign over Israel, in the month of Ziv, the second month, he began to build the temple of the LORD." This verse looks simple enough, at least at first glance. If we can figure out which year was Solomon's fourth year and add 480 years to it, we would be golden. As it turns out, we can come to a pretty solid date, but first we have to talk about turning those relative dates into absolute dates. The details are tedious, but we can rehearse the basic principles that allow such a conversion.[23]

We start by realizing that all dating in the ancient Near East, not just in Israel, was relative dating, including in ancient Assyria. The Assyrians kept what they called *limmu* lists. These *limmu* (or eponym) lists note each year by the name of a prominent person who was chosen to be the eponym of that year. Some also mention a prominent event of that year. Here is an excerpt from a *limmu* list that proves relevant for our topic:

> (In the eponymate of) Ninurta-mukinnishi, of Habruri, to Hatarikka; plague.
> (In the eponymate of) Sidqi-ilu, of Tushan, the king stayed in the land.
> (In the eponymate of) Bursagele, of Guzan, revolt in the citadel of Ashur; in the month of Siwan the sun had an eclipse.[24]

Notice that an eclipse is mentioned in the year in which Bursagele was the eponym. We have two such mentions of eclipses in

23. The classic work on Old Testament chronology is Thiele, *Mysterious Numbers of the Hebrew Kings*. For a recent concise survey, see "Chronology of the Biblical Period," in Longman, *Baker Illustrated Bible Dictionary*, 301–6.
24. Translation by Millard, *Eponyms of the Assyrian Empire*, 57–59.

the Assyrian dating system. The beautiful thing about an eclipse is that we can give it an absolute date, since eclipses happen on a regular cycle. Astronomers can tell us when an eclipse happened in Mesopotamia, and so we can convert this date into an absolute date: 763 BC. *Voilà*! Since there are relative dates in the Bible that connect the histories of Assyria and Israel (examples include 2 Kings 15:29; 16:7, 10), we have enough to work with to establish a fairly, but not completely, solid chronology for at least the first millennium BC (about the time of the united monarchy and after), while the matter is a little more tenuous for events that take place before the monarchy.

After all the computations have been completed, the result is that Solomon's fourth year is 966 BC (give or take a year or two). With this datum, it seems that all we have to do is to add 480 (the number of 1 Kings 6:1)[25] and presto, we have the date of the exodus: 1446 BC, the mid-fifteenth century. The conquest then would be forty years later.

Unfortunately, the archaeology of the twentieth century failed to corroborate this date and even, according to traditional interpretations of the remains, provided contrary evidence (more on interpretation in archaeological research later). Jericho (identified with Tell es-Sultan) was not occupied during the Late Bronze Age (1550–1250 BC) according to Kathleen Kenyon, who dug there in the 1950s, nor was Ai (identified with Et-Tell), the second city Joshua attacked. There was precious little evidence in this time period of a violent intrusion into the region, and the pottery typology did not reveal a change that might signal a shift of cultures from Canaanite to Israelite.

There were two reactions to this seeming tension between text and archaeology. The first was to reinterpret the archaeological evidence and maintain confidence of a fifteenth-century-BC date. Like the biblical text, archaeological remains require interpretation.

25. The early Greek translation of the passage has 440, but for our purposes this variation is insignificant.

Some methods of archaeology utilize scientific methods (like carbon-14 dating, which is not helpful for our question because the margin of error is too large for something this recent), but, really, archaeology is a soft science and more like an art. Thus, there are those who look at the same evidence as Kenyon did but come to a different conclusion. The most sustained and scholarly reinterpretation of the evidence in support of a fifteenth-century date was given by John Bimson.[26] While failing to convince the field at large, Bimson does show that a reading of the archaeological evidence that supports a fifteenth-century date is possible.

The other reaction among those who believe that the Bible gives a reliable report of the exodus and conquest is to reinterpret the biblical material in order to arrive at a date that conforms better with the archaeological evidence.[27] In principle, I have no problem with this approach. As we discussed in the section on creation and evolution, science can help us read the Bible better, but here I would add the caveat that, as I just mentioned, we are dealing at best with soft science that does not deliver conclusions with the same measure of confidence as the hard sciences (or shouldn't).

I would hazard to say that the vast majority of evangelical[28] (and other)[29] scholars of the Old Testament and the ancient Near East would argue as follows. The 480 years of 1 Kings 6:1 is not a literal number but a figurative one. After all, it is divisible twelve times by forty, the figurative number for a generation (presumably because of the forty years in the wilderness in which the adult generation that left Egypt died out). But while forty is a figurative number for a generation, a more accurate number for a generation would be twenty-five years (the average age when adults start having babies). Thus, getting the actual number of years between the exodus and Solomon's

26. Bimson, *Redating the Exodus and Conquest*.
27. The following approach to late-dating the exodus had James Jack (*Date of the Exodus*) as an early precursor.
28. A partial list includes K. Kitchen and J. Hoffmeier.
29. See, for instance, Bright, *History of Israel*.

fourth year requires multiplying twelve by twenty-five, which is three hundred years, and now, *voilà* for a second time, we come to 1266 BC for the date of the exodus, a thirteenth-century date.

The benefit of a thirteenth-century date (Early Iron Age) is that it works much better, though not perfectly (Ai remains a problem, for example),[30] with the archaeology. And Ramesses II, who reigned during this time, makes for a good pharaoh of the exodus,[31] particularly since one of the two store cites built by the Israelites was given the name Rameses (Exod. 1:11).[32]

Surprisingly, the debate between those who advocate a fifteenth-century date and those who adopt a thirteenth-century date can get quite heated. At one point, for instance, Kitchen said that those who accepted an early date as the only option were "mentally lazy."[33] My own view is that those of us who think the exodus actually happened should cool down and realize that at least both schools of thought affirm a historical exodus of some sort. Whether traditional interpretation of archaeology or traditional interpretation of 1 Kings 6:1 needs to be revised (or a combination of the two) is not a matter of certainty. Thus, I personally don't feel it necessary to decide between the two.[34]

THE NEED TO READ EXODUS THROUGH JOSHUA CAREFULLY

Next, we must reckon with the possibility that a reason we don't have direct evidence outside the Bible for these events (and,

30. Hawkins, *How Israel Became a People*, 105–11.
31. At least as played by Yul Brynner in Cecil B. DeMille's still-famous 1956 movie, *The Ten Commandments*.
32. However, an argument can be made that this city had an earlier name in the fifteenth century BC and that the text simply updates its name for a later audience (as happens on occasion in the Pentateuch in passages traditionally labeled post-Mosaicas).
33. Kitchen, "Egyptians and Hebrews," 86. Also see the interchange between Wood ("Exodus-Conquest Theory") and Hoffmeier ("Biblical Date").
34. See Provan, Long, and Longman, *Biblical History of Israel*, 182–84.

according to some, even have contrary evidence) is that when we read the biblical text incorrectly, it leads to false expectations. When we read the stories in Exodus through Joshua outside their ancient Near Eastern context, we picture the exodus as the movement of millions of people out of Egyptian slavery, through the wilderness, and then as a massive invading force into Canaan, where the Israelites first encounter Jericho, a Canaanite city with huge impenetrable walls.

A closer reading allows us to see that the number of Israelites leaving Egypt may not have been anywhere near as large. As Colin Humphreys has pointed out, the fact that Numbers 3:46 says that there were "273 firstborn Israelites who exceed the number of Levites" and the fact that *'eleph* does not necessarily mean "thousand" in a passage like Numbers 1:46 allow for the possibility that the Israelites leaving Egypt numbered in the thousands and not the millions. This perhaps explains why there is no direct Egyptian evidence of Israel's presence in the land of Egypt or their departure through the wilderness.[35] Also, with Hoffmeier, we must remember that the Egyptians were not in the practice of memorializing those who defeated them, which explains why the Egyptians left no record of the Israelites' presence.[36]

When it comes to Jericho, and indeed all of Joshua 1–11, we should recognize the obvious hyperbole used in accounts of these battles. The emphasis in these chapters is on victory, celebrating the beginning of the fulfillment of the Abrahamic promise of land. Also, Lawson Younger has reminded us of the use of hyperbole in ancient Near Eastern conquest accounts. This helps resolve some of the difficulties with the archaeological evidence against

35. Humphreys, "Number of People." Criticisms may be found in Milgrom, "Decoding Very Large Numbers," and Heinzerling, "Census Lists." See Humphreys's response in "Numbers in the Exodus."

36. This is especially the case since most of what we know from the Egyptians comes from the walls of inner rooms in pyramids, obelisks, and the like, hardly places where a humiliating event like the exodus would be mentioned. See Hoffmeier, *Israel in Egypt.*

widespread destruction of Canaanite cities as well as the apparent conflict with Judges 1, which makes it quite clear that many Canaanites remained in the land even after the death of Joshua.[37]

In addition, Rick Hess has recently helped us arrive at a more nuanced reading of the Jericho account, indicating that the language may point to a sparsely populated military outpost whose main defensive structure was a wall of "'a single line of unbaked mudbricks' or better, a small circle of mud-brick houses that form a continuous wall around the center [of the city]."[38] Such a wall could have eroded away, not leaving traces for later archaeologists to discover.

But Why No Direct Evidence?

Before looking at the indirect evidence in favor of the exodus and conquest, we need to ask why the biblical text is the only direct evidence that we have of these events. We have already mentioned in response to Sparks above that the Egyptians were not in the habit of recording their defeats (in spite of his unpersuasive attempts to argue otherwise). But still, why aren't there some remnants of Israelite occupation in the area where they rebuilt the store cities, for instance? Kitchen, the eminent Egyptologist, explains that the Israelites were in the East Delta zone and that "this fact imposes further severe limitations upon all inquiry into the subject. The Delta is an alluvial fan of mud deposited through many millennia by the annual flooding of the Nile; it has no source of stone within it. Mud, mud and wattle, and mud-brick structures were of limited duration and use, and were repeatedly leveled and replaced, and very largely merged once more with the mud of the fields."[39] Thus, Kitchen explains that the lack of direct evidence for Israelites in Egypt is not evidence of there being no exodus.

37. Younger, *Ancient Conquest Accounts.*
38. Hess, "Jericho and Ai." See also the discussion on the archaeology of Jericho in Hawkins, *How Israel Became a People*, 91–105.
39. Kitchen, *Reliability of the Old Testament*, 246.

The Indirect Evidence in Favor of the Historicity of the Exodus and Conquest

Once we do this kind of careful reading of the text to see what the books of Exodus and Joshua actually say about the exodus and conquest, we can then marshal the considerable indirect evidence that would support the direct evidence (testimony) of the Bible for a historical exodus and conquest. A partial list of such indirect evidence would include the following.

THE MERNEPTAH/ISRAEL STELE

The Merneptah Stele, dated to the very end of the thirteenth century BC, contains the first extrabiblical mention of Israel, which is why it is sometimes called the Israel Stele. The name Merneptah Stele comes from the commemoration of a campaign into Canaan by the pharaoh of that name. Among his other victories in the region, he proudly (and hyperbolically) proclaimed that "Israel is laid waste, his seed is not."

A number of scholars, particularly the so-called minimalists, downplay or even dismiss this stele as evidence that Israel had entered the land by this stage. They say that this Israel should not be confused with the later Israel. Their strongest argument is from the manner in which the stele refers to Israel. Egyptian utilizes what are called determinatives to let the reader know how to read signs that follow them. They in essence announce that the next word is, for example, a god's name or a rock or a personal name. When it comes to the reference to Israel in the Merneptah Stele, the determinative that precedes it indicates a people group, not a nation-state.

In response, it is sufficient to point out that whether the exodus and conquest were early (fifteenth century) or late (thirteenth century), the time period of the Merneptah Stele would have been the biblical period of the judges, a time when there were still lots of Canaanites around and the Israelite tribes themselves are described as politically fragmented. So labeling Israel as a people group at this stage in their history isn't in conflict with the biblical account. Thus, it seems simply tendentious to dismiss the evidence provided by the Merneptah Stele.

The Amarna Tablets

Discovered at the end of the nineteenth century, the Amarna tablets are among the most important and most discussed cache of ancient texts discovered in the Near East. They are named the Amarna tablets because they were discovered in the ancient Egyptian capital of Amarna, but they were written in Canaan by the city kings from places like Jebus (Jerusalem), Gezer, Lachish, Ashkelon, Megiddo, and Shechem, who were vassals of Egypt. Thus, they are also called the Amarna letters, and we have over three hundred of them. How they relate to the biblical account of the conquest is much debated, but at a minimum they reflect the kind of social and political structure that we also glimpse in the biblical text. For instance, for the most part these city-states were independent of one another and even quarreled among themselves until they faced a common enemy, which caused them to ally with one another to present a unified front.

By the way, the preceding paragraph is true whether the exodus and conquest are fifteenth-century or thirteenth-century events, even though the letters themselves can be dated to the fourteenth century during the reigns of Amenhotep III and his son Amenhotep IV. After all, the cities from which these letters came were not among those taken and occupied by Israel during the time of the conquest.

More interesting, and more controversial, in terms of the connection between these tablets and the biblical conquest account is the role of the so-called *hapiru/habiru* (hereafter *habiru*). One reason these kings were writing the pharaoh was to call on Egypt's aid in the light of the threat provided by the *habiru*. One tablet says, "Let the king, my lord, learn that the chief of the 'Apiru [*habiru*] has risen (in arms) against the lands which the god of the king, my lord, gave me; but I have smitten him. Also let the king, my lord, know that all my brethren have abandoned me, and it is I and 'Abdu-Heba (who) fight against the chief of the 'Apiru."[40]

We can certainly understand why there was a connection made between the *habiru* and the Hebrews when these tablets first were translated, just based on the similarity of sound. Many thought that the letters were being written in response to the intrusion by the Hebrews led by Joshua in order to enlist the help of their overlord, the pharaoh. Of course, the Bible doesn't mention Egyptian involvement in Canaan in this period, but then again, that reflects the frustration that the city kings express because the pharaoh does not seem to heed their request and send any troops to help against the *habiru*.

The lack of Egyptian response may be explained by the fact that during this time the Egyptians had their own internal issues. Amenhotep IV is better known by his name Akhenaten, and he is the pharaoh who supported the worship of one god and one god only, namely the sun disk Aten (originally an aspect of the sun god Re). While modern readers occasionally marvel appreciatively at a non-Israelite who was a monotheist (or at least a henotheist), the ancient world found such a radical idea unsettling, and there was widespread unrest in Egypt.

In any case, over time it became clear that a simple equation between the *habiru* and the Hebrews was simply not tenable. The term *habiru* was found in other ancient sources at time periods when and also in regions where it could not possibly refer to the Israelites. Indeed, today it is well recognized that *habiru* is not an ethnic term like Hebrew but rather a sociological term designating people who live outside of cities and threaten their inhabitants. They might be bands of outlaws or people otherwise

40. This is a letter from Shuwardata, the head of the region around the city of Hebron, south of Jerusalem, to the king of Egypt. The translation is by W. F. Albright and is found in Pritchard, *Ancient Near Eastern Texts*, 487. 'Apiru is his rendition of *habiru*.

disenfranchised. Though it is probably too positive an analogy (and it has other weaknesses as well), I tell my students to think of Robin Hood and his band of Merry Men to get a picture of the *habiru*. They live in Sherwood Forest outside Nottingham and threaten civilization, represented by that city's sheriff. A more sinister analogy may be ISIS in the Middle East.

Thus, no one today would accept the reference to the *habiru* as direct evidence of the biblical conquest. However, I for one am open to the possibility that it provides indirect evidence supporting the general picture of Canaan that we find in the biblical text. I would also remind people that the Canaanites would have described Joshua and his people as *habiru* in the sociological sense.

EGYPTIAN INFLUENCE ON THE EXODUS AND WILDERNESS WANDERING GENERATION AND BEYOND

Further indirect evidence of the reliability of the exodus story in the Bible comes from the authentic Egyptian flavor of the narrative. Jim Hoffmeier and others have furthered the work of his professor R. J. Williams, who asserted that "the evidence is overwhelming that Israel drank deeply at the wells of Egypt. In a very real sense the Hebrews were 'a people come out of Egypt' (Num 22:5, 11)."[41]

Both Hoffmeier and Hess[42] build on the work of T. J. Meek, a scholar of a previous generation,[43] that shows that the names of many Levites bear an Egyptian imprint. Hoffmeier also concludes that "Egyptian terms among the priest's regalia and the word for 'censer' in Num 16 all point to the influences of Egyptian religion on the Hebrews."[44] Add to this Benjamin Noonan's study of Egyptian loanwords, in which he demonstrates that "the exodus and wilderness traditions contain significantly higher proportions of

41. Williams, "'A People Come Out of Egypt,'" quoted in Hoffmeier, "Egyptian Religious Influences," 3.
42. Hess, "Onomastics," 3.
43. Meek, *Hebrew Origins*, 31–32.
44. Hoffmeier, "Egyptian Religious Influences," 34.

Egyptian terminology than the rest of the Hebrew Bible," and Joshua Berman's demonstration of "strong affinities" between the Kadesh inscription of Ramesses II and the account and celebration of the crossing of the sea in Exodus 13:17–15:19 that can't be explained by "stock formulas," and we have recent and accumulating indirect evidence for the reliability of the account of the exodus in the Bible.[45]

EMERGENCE OF VILLAGES IN THE CENTRAL HILL COUNTRY

Archaeologists over the past two or three decades have uncovered some interesting evidence that may well bear on the emergence of Israel at the beginning of the Early Iron Age.[46] Of course, if this emergence is associated with the exodus, then that may well push us toward the later date, but the evidence is not so definitive that it confirms that date. Indeed, as we will see, the leading archaeologists who discuss these finds do not associate them with a foreign people coming into the land, but rather see them as an inner-Canaanite development.

The two archaeologists who have been at the forefront of this discussion are Israel Finkelstein and William Dever.[47] They describe the collapse of large Canaanite cities on the Mediterranean coast and the resulting appearance of about three hundred small villages in the central hill country. What is interesting is that these villages share a number of features, including the development of olive terracing and the use of plaster-lined cisterns for water collection. What is remarkable is the complete absence of pig bones at these sites. It is the lack of pig bones that constitutes evidence that these villages should be associated with later Israel, which prohibited the consumption of pigs as part of their food laws.

---

45. Noonan, "Egyptian Loanwords," and Berman, "Kadesh Inscriptions."
46. For a concise discussion of the archaeological evidence discussed in this section, see Hawkins, *How Israel Became a People*, 121–57.
47. See, for example, Finkelstein and Silberman, *Bible Unearthed*; Dever, *What Did the Biblical Writers Know*.

To be clear, Finkelstein and Dever agree that there is a connection between the collapse of these Canaanite cities and the emergence of these villages, though they vociferously disagree on why the collapse happened. Thus, they both assert, these new villages were populated by Canaanites who may well have been in transition to becoming what is later known as Israel. In other words, the emergence of Israel was an inner-Canaanite phenomenon. They believe that their thesis is supported by the idea that there does not seem to be a distinctive Israelite or Hebrew pottery type; rather, the typical Canaanite pottery continues.

I have two responses to their conclusion on this matter. First, the biblical description of the exodus does not preclude the idea that there was a Canaanite element to it, perhaps a sizable one. One way we distort the story of the exodus and the conquest is by describing it in purely ethnic terms, as if all the people coming up from Egypt were physical descendants of Abraham (notice that the description of the community that confirmed the covenant early in the conquest near Shechem included "foreigners" [Josh. 8:33, 35]) and only the occasional Canaanite (Rahab and those in her room with her) was permitted to escape the sword. From the number of later Israelites with foreign names (the most famous of which are Uriah the Hittite and Shamgar, but there are plenty of others), we should reconsider this perspective. Rahab's story and perhaps Ruth's (later) story are illustrative of the means by which Canaanites could escape the judgment God was bringing on that people.

Indeed, as we already suggested, the slaves who escaped from Egyptian bondage could have numbered in the thousands, not the millions. And when they came to Canaan, the underclasses may well have, like Rahab, come over to their side in droves and then ultimately identified with them. Indeed, those who study cultural memory suggest that the descendants of these Canaanites could have made the exodus story their own just as Americans who are not descendants of the Pilgrims and whose ancestors even came to America much, much later still rightly celebrate Thanksgiving every November and claim it as their story.[48]

Second, the intrusion of a foreign people (the Hebrews) into Canaan would not necessarily require a change in pottery making or other technologies. In a recent essay, Lawson Younger points out that we have a number of other examples of solid textual testimony to a change of peoples in a region but find no change in pottery technology or any other indication of a transition in the archaeological record. He cites, for example, the Aramaean incursions into Syria in the thirteenth and twelfth centuries BC and also the even earlier Amurrite incursion into Mesopotamia in the middle of the third millennium BC.[49] The same may be said, as Alan Millard pointed out years ago, for the Norman invasion of England, which took place as recently as the eleventh century AD.[50] Thus, including Israel's entry into Canaan, we have four examples of incursions of foreign peoples into a region where there is an abundance of literary evidence of the incursion (who doubts the Normans invaded England!) but no significant archaeological marker.

Indeed, according to the account of Joshua, there was little property damage in the Israelite invasion. Most of the fighting took place on the open battlefield and only three cities were said to be burned (Jericho, Ai, and Heshbon). Perhaps most significant in terms of this question is what we read in Deuteronomy 6:10–12:

> When the LORD your God has brought you into the land that he swore to your ancestors, to Abraham, to Isaac, and to Jacob, to give you—a land with fine, large cities that you did not build, houses filled with all sorts of goods that you did not fill, hewn cisterns that you did not hew, vineyards and olive groves you did not plant—and when you have eaten your fill, take care that you do not forget

48. Ansberry, "Exodus," 67–68.
49. Younger, "Origins of the Arameans."
50. Millard, "Amorites and Israelites."

the Lord, who brought you out of the land of Egypt, out of the house of slavery. (NRSV)

In the light of the biblical text itself, which implies that the Israelites took over the use of existing structures, it is no wonder there is little direct evidence of widespread destruction and reconstruction in the archaeological remains that have so far come to light. Again, we do have direct evidence, the testimony of the biblical text itself, and significant indirect evidence that supports the biblical picture. In addition, there is no insurmountable contrary evidence. It is reasonable to believe that the exodus and conquest accounts preserve authentic historical memory that is essential for the theological message of these narratives.

Conclusion

The purpose of this chapter is to enter into the controversy within evangelical Protestant circles concerning the reliability of the historical record found in the Bible. The debate is recent in these circles, though we acknowledge that outside these circles the Bible's historical reliability has long been questioned; but then again, evangelical Protestants have affirmed a different view of the nature of biblical revelation, believing that the Bible is true in all that it teaches.

We have noted the tendency among evangelicals to overhistoricize the Bible as well as to treat the Bible as if the description of historical events is devoid of figurative elements (like hyperbole). Even so, few would doubt that it was the *intention* of the biblical authors to reference historical events in connection to what we might call the history of redemption from creation (Gen. 1–2) through the postexilic period (Ezra-Nehemiah and Esther). Though we are interested in the whole of this redemptive history, we have focused on the exodus and conquest as examples, since they are often among the most questioned parts of that history.

Some authors (we have cited Sparks, Enns, and Moore and Kelle as examples) have recently suggested that there is little, if any, reliability to the history given in Exodus through Joshua, but even so they still attempt to preserve important theological teachings in these stories. They personally believe that the historicity of these events has no effect on their theological message.

They do affirm, by the way, the historical nature of the crucifixion and resurrection of Jesus and are thus not denying at all Paul's assertion that "if Christ has not been raised, our preaching is useless and so is your faith" (1 Cor. 15:14). I would wholeheartedly agree that the exodus and conquest stories do not hold the same critical importance to our faith as the events surrounding Christ's work do. Indeed, this insight led to George W. Ramsey's witty chapter title "If Jericho Was Not Razed, Is Our Faith in Vain?"[51] He answered no (and I would agree, though I think our confidence in Scripture would be damaged), but as the reader can see, I disagree with his conclusion that it didn't happen.

My point here is that there is a significant inconsistency in the affirmation of the historicity of the cross and especially the resurrection and the denial of the historicity of the exodus and the conquest. Why do some evangelical scholars doubt the historicity of the exodus and conquest? Because of a lack of direct evidence to support the Bible's testimony. But where is the direct evidence of the resurrection? There is none, and we wouldn't expect any.

I once asked one of my evangelical friends who holds the views I am pushing back against about the apparent inconsistency on this matter. I won't reveal his name because it was a private, spontaneous (and irenic) conversation. He responded by appealing to the tremendous and powerful influence on later generations. How can we explain the rapid growth of the church if this great event did not actually happen? How can we explain Christians willing to die for

51. First published in 1981, but now available as Ramsey, *Quest for the Historical Israel*.

their faith otherwise? I agree wholeheartedly, but I responded by saying that that is not at all different in principle from, say, the exodus, which, as we can tell from later Scripture, had such an impact on the faith and theological beliefs of later Israelites. Though I know I did not convince him, he did not have a good comeback to that point.

The question we have addressed in this section has to do with the relationship between history and theology in the history of Israel. We have approached this issue in the light of recent evangelical attempts to separate the two when it comes to events like the exodus and the conquest. Is the theological message of the exodus and conquest related to the history of these events? My answer—and this would be my answer to all questions related to the redemptive history of the Bible—is yes, it does matter. I agree with Paul when he tells the Corinthians about the exodus and wilderness wanderings, saying that "these things *happened* to them as examples and were written down as warnings for us, on whom the culmination of the ages has come" (1 Cor. 10:11; italics mine). True, our faith does not depend on our proving the historical reliability of these events beyond a shadow of a doubt (which is good, because we never will) any more than our proving that the resurrection is a historical event, particularly to those who do not share our worldview, which includes a belief in a supernatural universe.

The apologist Josh McDowell wrote a still-popular book (now in its fourth edition and coauthored with his son Sean) with the provocative title *Evidence That Demands a Verdict*.[52] It is a bold statement, but untrue. There is no evidence that demands a positive verdict from every reasonable person. This is not surprising, because our faith does not depend on our ability to prove it to ourselves or to others (we do not "understand in order to believe," but we "believe in order to understand"). Our faith is not proved by reason, but it is not contrary to reason either.

52. J. McDowell and S. McDowell, *Evidence That Demands a Verdict*. The first edition was published by Campus Crusade for Christ in 1972.

Levite Origins of the Exodus?

Just as I was wrapping up this book, Richard Elliott Friedman published a fascinating book on the exodus with interests similar to mine (as you can tell from his subtitle, *How It Happened and Why It Matters*) that is well worth mentioning along with brief interaction.[53]

He argues, similarly to me, that the exodus did indeed happen but that the escape from Egypt involved a much, much smaller group than is usually imagined. He wonders how else you could explain the exodus as the founding story of the nation if there were nothing behind it. He also agrees with the plausibility of the exodus based on what we are calling indirect evidence. I resonate with much of his argument.

His most distinctive idea has to do with the identity of the ones who escaped from Egypt. He points out that it has long been recognized that Levites tend to have Egyptian names. All eight people who have Egyptian names in the exodus account (Moses, Merari, Hophni, Hur, Mushi, Pashhur, Phinehas [times two]) are Levites. Thus, he argues that the Levites escaped from Egypt, encountered the Israelites in the land (the Levites could have come into the land after the Merneptah Stele mentions Israel), and introduced the worship of Yahweh. The Israelites were worshiping El at the time, and for a while both El and Yahweh may have been worshiped before Yahweh took sole place.

I don't accept the details of Friedman's thesis. We differ in our understanding of the date of the biblical source materials and other matters. Still, it is a fascinating thesis that shows that the exodus could very well have a historical connection and also demonstrates the importance of such for what I would call its theological significance.

---

53. Friedman, *Exodus*.

DISCUSSION QUESTIONS

1. How much of the Old Testament claims to speak about past events? Make a list of those books where you think the author claims to be talking about the past.

2. What is at stake in whether the biblical authors of the books you have listed reliably describe past events?

3. How would you describe the relationship between history and theology in the Bible?

4. Why do you think there isn't more direct evidence for the exodus and conquest outside the Bible?

5. What role can and should archaeology play in our study of the Old Testament?

6. Is it appropriate or inappropriate to use the biblical text to understand what we find through archaeological explorations? Why?

7. What are the issues surrounding the dating of the exodus? How crucial is it to settle the question of the date of the exodus?

8. What is the indirect evidence that supports the exodus and conquest accounts in the Bible? How convincing is it to you?

9. Why do Sparks, Enns, and Moore and Kelle question whether the exodus and conquest happened in the way the Bible describes them?

10. In the final analysis, do you believe that the theological teaching surrounding the exodus and conquest depends on their actually having happened?

3

Divine Violence

Does God Kill?

Starting early in my career, I was interested in what scholarship calls the divine-warrior theme, referring to those descriptions of God and reports of his activities that liken him to a soldier engaged in battle. Once sensitized to the image, I began to see just how pervasively it runs through the Old Testament, beginning with the Torah and continuing through the rest of Israel's history. God fought for Israel and against Israel. Many psalms utilize warfare language to describe God, and indeed, many were prayers sung before, during, and after a battle. In an early study, I identified forty-nine of the one hundred fifty psalms as having their original setting in the context of battle.[1] The prophets too speak of God as a warrior, warning that if Israel does not repent of its sins, the divine warrior will come and administer judgment against his people. I eventually realized that virtually every biblical book,

1. Longman, "Psalm 98."

with very few exceptions—namely, Ruth, Ecclesiastes, and Song of Songs—speaks of God as a warrior.

One of my first articles was on this theme,[2] and a little over ten years later I coauthored a book on the subject.[3] While I was working on this topic during this early phase of my career, no one seemed to have special interest in the subject except for Mennonite scholars who felt that they needed to address it, since, at least on the surface, it seemed to fly in the face of that denomination's stand on pacifism.[4]

This relative disinterest and lack of controversy associated with this theme completely disappeared as a result of a single day: September 11, 2001. After 9/11 Christians and non-Christians alike began to see the theme of God as a warrior who brought violent judgment against his human creatures as a problem to be solved or alleviated. After all, the actions of, say, Joshua and the Israelites at the time of the conquest sounded eerily like the actions of al-Qaeda and its leader Osama bin Laden.

Atheist thinkers began to use this theme to question the ethics of Christianity.[5] Was God a "moral monster"?[6] Christians also reacted by feeling embarrassed by this portrayal of God in the Old Testament, often asserting that it conflicted with the picture of a loving God found in the New Testament.

In this section, I will begin by carefully describing the picture of God as a warrior that troubles so many. I will then examine strategies utilized by some evangelical scholars to remove the offense of the images of violence associated with God. Finally, I will offer a positive presentation of the biblical picture of God as a warrior. While some believe that there is an incredible distance

2. Longman, "Divine Warrior," based on a lecture I had given the year before at the annual Evangelical Theological Society meeting.
3. Longman and Reid, *God Is a Warrior*.
4. Examples include Lind, *Yahweh Is a Warrior*, and Eller, *War and Peace*.
5. See Dawkins, *God Delusion*.
6. From the title of Copan's book *Is God a Moral Monster?*

between the wrathful God of the Old Testament and the loving Savior of the New, the central thesis of this chapter is that the two testaments present a coherent and unified picture of God, who fights and ultimately defeats evil in the world.

God's Violence

That the Old Testament depicts God as violent is not hard to establish. Anyone reading through the Bible understands this, and examples are many. Here are just a few highlights (or, as some would have it, lowlights).

The Flood (Genesis 6–9)

The flood is one of the most memorable stories in the Old Testament. While children's picture books illustrate a happy Noah on a boat filled with smiling animals, the book of Genesis emphasizes the death and destruction that come about when God sends a flood to "wipe from the face of the earth the human race [he has] created—and with them the animals, the birds and the creatures that move along the ground" (6:7).[7]

The Reed Sea Crossing (Exodus 14–15)

After a series of plagues (themselves quite violent, particularly the plague that causes the death of the firstborn of the Egyptians in Exod. 12), Pharaoh finally allows the enslaved Israelites to leave Egypt and return to the promised land. Surprisingly, even after Moses and the Israelites have passed by the sea, God instructs Moses "to turn back and encamp near Pi Hahiroth, between Migdol and the sea" (Exod. 14:2). God is setting Pharaoh and the Egyptians up for a trap. Pharaoh will think that Israel is helpless

---

7. For more on the flood story, see Longman and Walton, *Lost World of the Flood*.

since their backs are against a watery wall. They will be easy pickings for his elite chariot troops.

An embarrassed and angry Pharaoh then sets out in hot pursuit of the Israelites and attacks them at the sea. The story is well known. God opens up the sea so the Israelites can go through, but when the Egyptians follow, he closes the sea on them. Moses and the Israelites celebrates this divine act of violence in a song known today as the Song of the Sea:

> The LORD is my strength and my defense;
> > he has become my salvation.
> He is my God, and I will praise him,
> > my father's God, and I will exalt him.
> The LORD is a warrior;
> > the LORD is his name.
> Pharaoh's chariots and his army
> > he has hurled into the sea.
> The best of Pharaoh's officers
> > are drowned in the Red Sea.
> The deep waters have covered them;
> > they sank to the depths like a stone.
> Your right hand, LORD,
> > was majestic in power.
> Your right hand, LORD,
> > shattered the enemy. (Exod. 15:2–6)

This passage is the first time God is explicitly called a "warrior" in the Bible, though he has acted like one before this point (see Gen. 3:24; 14:19–20).

The Conquest

In the conquest, perhaps the most famous (or, in the minds of some, infamous) example of divine violence, we see God acting violently against Israel's enemies. Later, we will consider God's commands to Joshua and Israel that they engage in violence,[8] but here we will survey God's violent acts connected to the taking of the land from the Canaanites.

On the eve of the first battle against the walled city of Jericho, a figure "with a drawn sword in his hand" appears to Joshua. Joshua then asks him, "Are you for us or for our enemies?" (Josh. 5:13), to which the figure responds, "Neither, but as commander of the army of the LORD I have now come" (5:14). While at first glance this identification is unclear to the modern reader, it is anything but to Joshua, who immediately falls to the ground and, at the figure's command, takes off his sandals, "because the place where [he is] standing is holy" (5:15). This interchange clarifies the situation for the modern reader, since there is an intertextual allusion back to the burning bush in Exodus 3. This military figure is none other than God himself, the divine warrior.

Thus, when the walls of Jericho "come tumbling down" in the ensuing battle, we are in no doubt as to who caused this to happen. After all, for seven days the army has marched around the city with the ark of the covenant, the most potent symbol of God's presence. On the seventh day, after completing the seventh march around the city on that day, the priests sound the trumpets, which likely mimic the thunder that accompanies the appearance of the divine warrior.

A second example of divine violence during the conquest comes during Joshua's battle against a coalition of southern Canaanite kings. The kings have allied together and attacked the Gibeonites, who have just deceived Joshua into entering a treaty (Josh. 9). Joshua responds, and the "LORD threw them [the Canaanites] into confusion before Israel, so Joshua and the Israelites defeated them completely at Gibeon" (10:10). The Israelites then pursue the retreating Canaanites. God extends the day[9] so that the Israelites

8. See the section "After the Battle" later in this chapter.
9. According to Josh. 10:12–14 the "sun stopped" allowing the day to continue and the battle to be completed. Exactly what happened to extend the day is debated (literally stopping, light refraction, eclipse, celestial omen; see discussion in

might have an even more complete victory. God enters the battle himself by using a hailstorm to batter the enemy, so that the narrator tells the reader that "more of them died from the hail than were killed by the swords of the Israelites" (10:11). As the narrator sums up, "Surely the LORD was fighting for Israel!" (10:14).

The final major conflict of Joshua's conquest of the Canaanites comes against a coalition of northern Canaanite kings. Before the battle, God tells Joshua, "Do not be afraid of them, because by this time tomorrow I will hand all of them, slain, over to Israel" (Josh. 11:6). While the narrator does not give the details of God's involvement in this battle as he did in the previous battle against the southern alliance, he clearly states that "the LORD gave them [the northern coalition] into the hand of Israel" (11:8).

The Period of the Judges

The period of the judges was a time of spiritual confusion, moral depravity, and political fragmentation. The narrator in the appendix to the book (chaps. 17–21) describes the situation well: "Everyone did as they saw fit" (Judg. 17:6; 21:25). The main body of the book tells the story of Israel's judges. In response to Israel's cry to him for help, God raises up judges to save Israel from oppressors whom God had previously allowed to take land from Israel. Even in such a dark time, God the warrior fights on behalf of his repentant people.

For example, God rescues his people from Jabin, a Canaanite, when Israel is under the leadership of Deborah (Judg. 4). In the narrative of the battle, we learn that "on that day God subdued Jabin king of Canaan before the Israelites" (4:23), and we get some of the details from the song that Deborah sings along with the Israelites to celebrate God's victory (Judg. 5).

The song begins with a poetic depiction of God's appearance as warrior:

Hubbard, *Joshua*, 293–98), but the text takes this event as a sign that "the LORD was fighting for Israel" (10:14).

> When you, LORD, went out from Seir,
>> when you marched from the land of Edom,
> the earth shook, the heavens poured,
>> the clouds poured down water.
> The mountains quaked before the LORD, the One of Sinai,
>> before the LORD, the God of Israel. (5:4–5)

As she proceeds, Deborah points out how God fought on behalf of Israel using his very creation as his weapons:

> Kings came, they fought,
>> the kings of Canaan fought.
> At Taanach, by the waters of Megiddo,
>> they took no plunder of silver.
> From the heavens the stars fought,
>> from their courses they fought against Sisera.
> The river Kishon swept them away,
>> the age-old river, the river Kishon. (5:19–21)

In this powerful and ancient song, Deborah praises those among Israel who fought and berates those who failed to come, but she knows that the ultimate victory was the result of the intervention of God himself.

The Monarchy

God wages war during the monarchical period as well. When the king and Israel are faithful, God fights on their behalf. Two examples will have to suffice.

At the very beginning of his reign over a united Israel, David fights the Philistines in the Valley of Rephaim. He appropriately asks God whether he should go into battle, and God responds: "Do not go straight up, but circle around behind them and attack them in front of the poplar trees. As soon as you hear the sound of marching in the tops of the poplar trees, move quickly, because that will mean the LORD has gone out in front of you to strike the

Philistine army" (2 Sam. 5:23–24). God and his angelic army move in above and ahead of David and bring victory against the Philistines.

A second example comes later, in the ninth century BC, during the reign of Jehoshaphat. The book of Chronicles gives the account of that king's defensive battle against invaders from Moab and Ammon. After Jehoshaphat delivers a stirring prebattle speech ("Have faith in the LORD your God and you will be upheld; have faith in his prophets and you will be successful" [2 Chron. 20:20]), the army marches into battle singing hymns ("Give thanks to the LORD, for his love endures forever" [20:21]), with the ark at the front symbolizing God's presence. The result is victory: "As they began to sing and praise, the LORD set ambushes against the men of Ammon and Moab and Mount Seir who were invading Judah, and they were defeated" (20:22). Indeed, by the time the army reaches the enemy, the enemy troops are already dead or have fled because God has caused the different factions of the enemy army to turn against one another.

However, few kings of Israel and Judah were as faithful as David and Jehoshaphat. During the periods of royal apostasy, the divine warrior was not absent but was with the prophets. Here we will only look at a single example. In 2 Kings 6 we learn that the king of Aram is frustrated that Israel has anticipated his every military move against them. He suspects a mole within his administration but eventually learns that it is Elisha, the prophet, who is reporting his every move to the Israelite king. The Aramaean king mobilizes his army against Dothan, the city where Elisha and the prophets dwell. As this foreign army surrounds the city, one of the prophet's servants panics. Elisha calms him by informing him that "those who are with us are more than those who are with them" (6:16). He then prays that God would open the servant's eyes, and when he does, the servant sees "the hills full of horses and chariots of fire all around Elisha" (6:17). This is none other than God's heavenly army, there to protect the prophet and the city of Dothan.

The Prophets

The depiction of God who wars is not restricted to the historical books. The Prophets, too, talk about God threatening and waging war against his human creatures. Indeed, the theme of God as a warrior permeates the prophetic books. For our purposes, I have chosen three examples to illustrate three different prophetic uses of the divine-warrior theme: Jeremiah's announcement of judgment on Israel's king, Nahum's prophecy about God's warring activity against the Assyrians, and Daniel's vision of God coming as a warrior in the future to save his people from evil oppressors.

Jeremiah 1–25 is a collection of mostly judgment oracles and sign-acts that threaten or promise judgment on Judah for their egregious sins.[10] There is no clear-cut arrangement of these oracles, and only a few, like our present example, can be dated to a specific time in Jeremiah's life.

In Jeremiah 21 we learn that King Zedekiah (ruled 597–586 BC) sends two messengers, a man named Pashhur and a priest named Zephaniah, to the prophet with a request. Zedekiah has been resisting the message of Jeremiah for years, but now that the Babylonians are attacking Jerusalem (21:2, dating the following oracle to sometime between 588 and 586 BC), he wants Jeremiah to intercede on his behalf with the Lord.

Jeremiah, speaking on behalf of the Lord, refuses to intercede for Zedekiah and instead levels three intense oracles of judgment against the king. The first oracle illustrates the prophetic use of the divine-warrior theme to speak about God's judgment against his sinful people.

> But Jeremiah answered them, "Tell Zedekiah, 'This is what the
> LORD, the God of Israel, says: I am about to turn against you the

10. There are other types of literature in this section as well, including Jeremiah's famous laments (e.g., 20:7–18).

weapons of war that are in your hands, which you are using to fight the king of Babylon and the Babylonians who are outside the wall besieging you. And I will gather them inside this city. I myself will fight against you with an outstretched hand and a mighty arm in furious anger and in great wrath. I will strike down those who live in this city—both man and beast—and they will die of a terrible plague. After that, declares the LORD, I will give Zedekiah king of Judah, his officials and the people in this city who survive the plague, sword and famine, into the hands of Nebuchadnezzar king of Babylon and to their enemies who want to kill them. He will put them to the sword; he will show them no mercy or pity or compassion.'" (Jer. 21:3–7)

Here God tells Zedekiah that he himself is actually fighting against Judah "with an outstretched hand and a mighty arm." The language is from the exodus story where God fought against Egypt in order to deliver Israel (Exod. 6:6; Deut. 4:34; 5:15; 7:19; 9:29; 11:2; 26:8). God's exodus power is here being used against Judah because of their sin. He uses classic divine-warrior language when he announces, "I will give Zedekiah king of Judah into the hands of Nebuchadnezzar." Though on the surface it looks like the Babylonians through their own military power will defeat Judah, it is actually God himself who does it.

Our second example comes from the minor prophet Nahum. The book of Nahum is a war oracle against Assyria and its capital, Nineveh.[11] It was written sometime between the fall of Thebes (664–663 BC), alluded to in 3:8, and the anticipated fall of the Assyrian capital, which took place in 612 BC.

After the superscription, the book begins with a hymn to the divine warrior:

> The LORD is a jealous and avenging God;
> the LORD takes vengeance and is filled with wrath.

11. For details, see Longman, "Nahum," 786.

> The LORD takes vengeance on his foes
> > and vents his wrath against his enemies.
> The LORD is slow to anger but great in power;
> > the LORD will not leave the guilty unpunished.
> His way is in the whirlwind and the storm,
> > and clouds are the dust of his feet.
> He rebukes the sea and dries it up;
> > he makes the rivers run dry.
> Bashan and Carmel wither
> > and the blossoms of Lebanon fade.
> The mountains quake before him
> > and the hills melt away.
> The earth trembles at his presence,
> > the world and all who live in it.
> Who can withstand his indignation?
> > Who can endure his fierce anger?
> His wrath is poured out like fire;
> > the rocks are shattered before him. (Nah. 1:2–6)

An interesting feature of this hymn is that it plays with the acrostic form. An acrostic is a poem in which each successive unit of the poem begins with a successive letter of the Hebrew alphabet. This acrostic is complete in the first half of the alphabet for the most part, but then it begins to fall apart. A complete acrostic signals coherence and totality; a broken acrostic like the one in Nahum 1 signals the opposite. Thus, the literary style of this passage supports the message. When the divine warrior appears, the sea dries up, the vegetation withers, the mountains quake and melt, and acrostics break apart!

The rest of this relatively short book describes how God will destroy Nineveh. In 2:13 God announces:

> "I am against you,"
> > declares the LORD Almighty.

"I will burn up your chariots in smoke,
  and the sword will devour your young lions.
 I will leave you no prey on earth.
The voices of your messengers
  will no longer be heard."

As we know from the historical record, both the Bible and ex-trabiblical sources, the city of Nineveh fell to a Babylonian army under the leadership of Nabopolassar, who was allied with the Medes. But Nahum knows that behind this human military victory is the guiding hand of the Lord, who is judging the Assyrians for their cruel behavior.

Our last example comes from another future-oriented book. The book of Daniel is not technically a prophetic book but rather an apocalyptic one. While prophets spoke God's words to God's sinful people in order to elicit their repentance, Daniel receives visions that are interpreted by an angel, and their purpose is to comfort God's people with the knowledge that God will come and remove their oppressors.

We will briefly look at the first of the four visions that compose the last half of the book of Daniel. In chapter 7 Daniel has a visionary dream in which he sees four beasts emerging from a chaotic sea. The sea setting itself suggests disorder and chaos, and the beasts themselves are disturbing. The first is a hybrid like a lion with eagle's wings, but then it transforms into a human being. To an ancient Israelite reader hybrids were in most contexts repulsive and always fearsome, as we know from the Levitical laws against mixing seed in a field or wearing garments composed of more than one type of material or allowing two types of animals to mate (Lev. 19:19). The second beast is not a hybrid but a violent bear gnawing on three ribs. The third is a hybrid whose component parts, the body of a leopard with four heads and four wings like a bird, emphasize speed. The final beast is only described as having "iron teeth" (Dan. 7:7), "bronze claws" (7:19), and ten horns, emphasizing its power. The passage then focuses on one of these horns, which "had eyes like the eyes of a human being and a mouth that spoke boastfully" (7:8).

Over the centuries, pages and pages have been written about the meaning of these beasts and the horns. Fortunately, for our purpose in this book, all we need to know about these beasts is what the interpreting angel explicitly tells Daniel: "The four great beasts are four kings that will rise from the earth" (7:17).[12] These are kings of kingdoms that will oppress the people of God. No matter the identity of the kingdoms represented by the beasts, the second half of the vision depicts their demise, and here we see the divine warrior at work. In an amazing picture of the divine realm, we read of a figure that surely represents God, called the "Ancient of Days" (7:9). He is seated on a throne, and he is ready to render judgment. Into his presence comes "one like a son of man, coming with the clouds of heaven" (7:13). What is surprising about this figure is that he is riding a cloud. This comes from ancient Near Eastern storm-god imagery and is used of Yahweh in a number of places in Scripture (Deut. 33:26; 2 Sam. 22:10 = Ps. 18:9; Pss. 68:4; 104:3; Isa. 19:1; Nah. 1:3). In other words, we have a second figure in this vision who is also described in terms that strongly suggest divinity. No wonder the New Testament authors cited this passage in reference to Jesus (Matt. 24:30; Mark 13:26; Luke 21:27; Rev. 1:7).

The main message of this vision is that God will defeat the evil human kingdoms that oppress his people. In the present it looks like evil people are in control, but that perception is incorrect. God is in control, and he will have the final victory.

The Poets

Even the poets of the Old Testament speak of God as a warrior. We will look at two poetic collections: Psalms and Lamentations.

---

12. For those who want to see my understanding of a more specific identification, see Longman, *Daniel*, 174–98.

Divine violence permeates the book of Psalms in a way that most modern Christian readers don't recognize because of the propensity to spiritualize warfare language. As we will later discuss, it is not wrong for us to apply the conflict language to our lives in this way, but we should realize that in their original setting the psalms often refer to physical wars and conflicts of the people of God against their flesh-and-blood enemies. The forty-nine psalms situated in warfare include laments that call on God to help before a battle, psalms of confidence that express trust in God in the midst of battle, and hymns that celebrate victory. We might add another type of psalm, laments that bemoan defeat in battle. What unites all of these psalms is an affirmation that God is a warrior. We will look at an example of each type of psalm and then turn to Lamentations.

Psalm 7: A Lament before Battle

In Psalm 7, the composer, identified as King David in the title,[13] calls on God to help him against his enemies ("Save me and deliver me from all who pursue me, or they will tear me apart like a lion and rip me to pieces with no one to rescue me" [7:1b–2]). In a plea for help, the psalmist calls on God to "arise," a telltale sign of a prebattle lament (see also Pss. 3:7; 9:19; 10:12, etc.):

> Arise, Lord, in your anger;
>> rise up against the rage of my enemies.
> Awake, my God; decree justice. (7:6)

In the midst of his fear of violence from his enemy, the composer expresses his hope in the effective power of God, who is his

---

13. The reliability and canonical status of the titles are much debated. My own view is that they are canonical (what manuscript evidence do we have that they are not?) and reliable even though they are clearly added by an anonymous later editor. That said, my comments do not depend on their veracity, though if it is the king speaking in the first person, it makes it clearer that he is speaking on behalf of the nation. For more on titles, see Longman, *Psalms*, 23–31.

"shield" (7:10) and who he knows will respond to the threat with violence toward the enemy:

> God is a righteous judge,
>> a God who displays his wrath every day.
> If he does not relent,
>> he will sharpen his sword;
>> he will bend and string his bow.
> He has prepared his deadly weapons;
>> he makes ready his flaming arrows. (7:11–13)

Psalm 91: Confidence in the Midst of Battle

From its opening lines ("Whoever dwells in the shelter of the Most High will rest in the shadow of the Almighty" [91:1]), Psalm 91 exudes confidence in the midst of the most extreme trouble. The author uses military metaphors ("refuge" and "fortress" in v. 2) to describe the nature of God's protection, but it is in the description of the trouble itself that we recognize the situation's military nature:

> Surely he will save you
>> from the fowler's snare
>> and from the deadly pestilence.
> He will cover you with his feathers,
>> and under his wings you will find refuge;
>> his faithfulness will be your shield and rampart.
> You will not fear the terror of night,
>> nor the arrow that flies by day,
> nor the pestilence that stalks in the darkness,
>> nor the plague that destroys at midday.
> A thousand may fall at your side,
>> ten thousand at your right hand,
>> but it will not come near you.
> You will only observe with your eyes
>> and see the punishment of the wicked. (91:3–8)

137

Here the psalmist expresses his confidence that God will protect him in the midst of battle not only from the enemy's weapons but also from the plagues that so threatened ancient war camps.

PSALM 18: THANKSGIVING FOR VICTORY

It is not my intention to provide a full interpretation of this lengthy thanksgiving psalm but to use it as an example of warfare in the psalms, in this case after a victory, and of divine violence. The composer, identified as David in the title, proclaims that God "is worthy of praise" because he, the composer, has "been saved from [his] enemies" (18:3), a statement typical of a thanksgiving psalm. Then he describes God's appearance in response to his plea for help in the most dramatic terms:

> The earth trembled and quaked,
> > and the foundations of the mountains shook;
> > they trembled because he was angry.
> Smoke arose from his nostrils;
> > consuming fire came from his mouth,
> > burning coals blazed out of it.
> He parted the heavens and came down;
> > dark clouds were under his feet. (18:7–9)

I want to pause briefly here to point out that the reference to clouds under his feet indicates that God here is being pictured as riding a cloud into battle. This depiction has roots going back to ancient Near Eastern storm-god imagery and, as we earlier observed, appears in a number of places in the Old and New Testaments. This storm cloud is his war chariot, from which he attacks the psalmist's enemies:

> The LORD thundered from heaven;
> > the voice of the Most High resounded.
> He shot his arrows and scattered the enemy,
> > with great bolts of lightning he routed them.

138

> The valleys of the sea were exposed
>> and the foundations of the earth laid bare
> at your rebuke, LORD,
>> at the blast of breath from your nostrils. (18:13–15)

As the psalmist continues, it is clear that he himself does not simply step back and assume a passive stance. No, he fights with all his might (e.g., "I pursued my enemies and overtook them; I did not turn back till they were destroyed" [18:37]). But he knows that his success is the result of God training him and actively participating in the battle ("He is the God who avenges me, who subdues nations under me, who saves me from my enemies" [18:47–48a]). Thus the psalm ends:

> He gives his king great victories;
>> he shows unfailing love to his anointed,
>> to David and to his descendants forever. (18:50)

PSALM 89: A LAMENT IN DEFEAT

Whenever God fights for his people, the outcome is not in doubt. But God is not at Israel's beck and call, as Psalm 89 indicates. Again, we will focus on the psalm's depiction of God's activity in war. The bottom line of this prayer is that it is a lament questioning God's lack of involvement in battle, considering the promises that God made in his covenant with David (with allusions to 2 Sam. 7; see Ps. 89:3–4). Specifically, this psalm recalls God's promise to protect David and his descendants from their enemies ("I will crush his foes before him and strike down his adversaries" [89:23]).

All this established, the psalmist takes a radical turn in the final section of the psalm, because in the present circumstance God has not followed through on his promises and appears to "have renounced the covenant with [his] servant and have defiled his crown in the dust" (89:39). Indeed, rather than helping his people, God has aided their enemies ("You have exalted the right hand of his foes; you have made all his enemies rejoice" [89:42]). Thus, the psalm ends with an appeal that God remember his commitments to his people and change his attitude and protect them (89:46–51).

We have seen that many psalms find their original setting in warfare. Laments, hymns, thanksgivings, and psalms of confidence are addressed to God as warrior. To remove warfare language from the book of Psalms would totally change the character of this great hymnbook of the temple.

LAMENTATIONS

The book of Lamentations is set after the destruction of Jerusalem by the Babylonians in 586 BC,[14] though the precise setting is debated.[15] In my opinion, the raw emotions expressed in the book indicate that the five poems that constitute the book were written soon after the fall of the city.

Each chapter is composed of twenty-two or (in the case of chap. 3) sixty-six verses, and with the exception of chapter 5, the poems are acrostics; each successive unit begins with a successive letter of the Hebrew alphabet (which has twenty-two letters).[16]

Lamentations 2 is particularly relevant to our topic of divine violence. Though aware that a human, indeed a Babylonian, army

14. See the insightful essay by Thomas, "Neglected Witness."

15. Provan, *Lamentations*, argues that the book does not have its setting in the defeat of Jerusalem by the Babylonians, since they are not named in the book. Others (for instance, Gwaltney, "Lamentations") believe that the book was written not in the immediate aftermath of the destruction of Jerusalem but when the temple was being rebuilt. This view is based on analogy with Sumerian lamentations. Even if these views are correct, they do not affect the point I am making about divine violence in the book.

16. Though not an acrostic, chapter 5 has twenty-two verses. Since an acrostic communicates totality and completion, the poet likely uses a "broken acrostic" here to indicate that resolution between God and his people has not been achieved by the end of the book. See Longman, *Jeremiah, Lamentations*, 334–56.

destroyed the city, the poet understands that God is ultimately responsible. After all, the poem opens with the startling exclamation:

> How the Lord has covered Daughter Zion
>> with the cloud of his anger!
> He has hurled down the splendor of Israel
>> from heaven to earth;
> he has not remembered his footstool
>> in the day of his anger. (2:1)

Indeed, throughout the chapter God is said to act "like an enemy," as for instance in 2:4–5:

> Like an enemy he has strung his bow;
>> his right hand is ready.
> Like a foe he has slain
>> all who were pleasing to the eye;
> he has poured out his wrath like fire
>> on the tent of Daughter Zion.
>
> The Lord is like an enemy;
>> he has swallowed up Israel.
> He has swallowed up all her palaces
>> and destroyed her strongholds.
> He has multiplied mourning and lamentation
>> for Daughter Judah.

Thus, Lamentations too joins the chorus of books in the Old Testament that bear witness to God's warring activity.

Wisdom Literature

Many characterize Old Testament Wisdom literature[17] as universal in scope, grounded in creation theology, cosmopolitan, and

---

17. The category "Wisdom literature" has been challenged over the past few years (see Kynes, *Obituary for "Wisdom Literature"*). For a defense of the usefulness of the category, see Longman, *Fear of the Lord*, 276–82.

even secular. Elsewhere I have disputed this characterization,[18] but still one must acknowledge different, though not competing, interests and focuses from the redemptive-historical, legal, and prophetic traditions. And this applies to the topic of divine violence in that it does not appear quite as frequently in the Wisdom literature. However, the theme is detected even among these books. Both Proverbs and Job speak of divine violence.

In Proverbs, we hear mostly about the threat of violence in the announcement of consequences for foolish (wicked or godless) behavior and attitudes. In this way, proverbial wisdom describes consequences similar to the judgments that the covenant announces toward those who break the law.[19] While most of the consequences are announced in such a way that the punishments and rewards seem to be a natural outcome of the act itself ("If someone curses their father or mother, their lamp will be snuffed out in pitch darkness" [Prov. 20:20; see also 17:5; 19:9]), some specify that God himself will bring the painful consequences on those who follow the way of folly rather than of wisdom:

> The LORD works out everything to its proper end—
>   even the wicked for a day of disaster.
> The LORD detests all the proud of heart.
>   Be sure of this: They will not go unpunished.
>   (Prov. 16:4–5)

> Fear the LORD and the king, my son,
>   and do not join with rebellious officials,
> for those two will send sudden destruction on them,
>   and who knows what calamities they can bring?
>   (Prov. 24:21–22)

Then there is Job. Job himself thinks that he is the object of unjust divine violence:

18. Longman, *Fear of the Lord*, 109–76.
19. For the view that wisdom is a cousin of law, see Longman, *Fear of the Lord*, 163–76.

The arrows of the Almighty are in me,
  my spirit drinks in their poison;
    God's terrors are marshaled against me. (Job 6:4)

God assails me and tears me in his anger
  and gnashes his teeth at me;
. . . .
All was well with me, but he shattered me;
  he seized me by the neck and crushed me.
He has made me his target;
  his archers surround me.
Without pity, he pierces my kidneys
  and spills my gall on the ground.
Again and again he bursts upon me;
  he rushes at me like a warrior. (16:9, 12–14)

It turns out that Job is right and wrong. He is right that God has brought suffering and pain into his life. While the prologue to the book distances God from Job's affliction by allowing the "Adversary" to apply it to him (see Job 1–2), the distance is slight, since in the first place the Adversary could do nothing without God's permission and, secondly, the Adversary is a member of God's angelic council (he is one of the "sons of God").[20] However, Job is wrong to believe this violence is unjust, and God, while not telling him the reason for his suffering, does assert that Job's charge of injustice is wrong (40:8).

Conclusion

The purpose of this survey is to demonstrate the pervasiveness of the theme of divine violence in the Old Testament. With the exception of Ruth, Ecclesiastes, and Song of Songs,[21] every other

20. This view is widely held by biblical scholars. See Longman, *Job*, 91–92.
21. In Ecclesiastes, Qohelet seems more concerned about God's indifference toward his creation (5:1–7), though 5:7 warns care in case God does get upset "and destroy the work of your hands" (5:6). As for the Song of Songs, there are

biblical book, whether historical, legal, prophetic/apocalyptic, or poetic, speaks of divine violence in one form or another.

Modern readers can't ignore the theme. But, particularly in the church in the West, one can sense uneasiness and even embarrassment with the idea that God perpetrates violence toward humans and also commands his people to be violent toward others in the Old Testament. Therefore, in the next section we will examine several attempts to minimize or even eradicate a supposed problem.

Silencing a God of Judgment

Before presenting my view on God's violence, we need to examine some recent attempts to erase divine violence from the biblical text or at least explain it away. Before describing and challenging these rereadings of the biblical text, I do want to say that they are sincere and honest attempts to deal with a perceived problem, at least to a twenty-first-century Western audience.

Of course, divine violence has unsettled some Christian readers in the past, but over the years the church has pretty much rejected as misreadings such attempts to erase this theme, seeing them as committing the fundamental error of failing to affirm the Old and New Testament canons as authoritative for Christians.

The classic case of this in church history is that of Marcion (AD 85–160), a popular preacher and theologian in Rome. Marcion found the Old Testament substandard to a Christian ethic because of its violence, so he argued that it was no longer authoritative for the Christian. Christ was the standard of what God really was like, and the Old Testament God did not live up to that standard. After a while, it became clear to Marcion that even the Jesus of Revelation did not live up to the standard of Jesus in the Gospels, and so it too was effectively removed from his canon.

---

martial images of the love between the man and the woman (e.g., 6:4), but no hint of divine violence.

Indeed, Marcion found more and more of the New Testament to reflect Old Testament ideas and ejected those parts of it from the canon, so that at the end of the process very little was left.

In response, the church censured Marcion and his followers. In the next generation, the theologian Tertullian wrote a famous critique of Marcion's views. And over the centuries the church has essentially affirmed its early rejection of Marcion. After all, reading the Gospels, we can see that Jesus fully affirmed the Old Testament. He did not critique or reject the picture of God that we find there.

How do some recent attempts to deal with divine violence relate to Marcion's perspective? As mentioned, both outside and within the church there has been a vociferously negative reaction to the picture of God as a warrior. Atheists like Richard Dawkins have pointed to this theme to try to turn people away from the biblical God. The God of the Bible is a moral monster, according to Dawkins. Who would ever worship such a God (as though we get to define the God we would worship)?

I have to be honest. There is no way to satisfy the Dawkinses of the world. They begin with the premise that there is no God. They don't accept the Bible as divine revelation. All the attempts to mollify this type of criticism are bound to fail. I am not really interested in responding to Dawkins. Responding to Dawkins is a bit like Eve feeling it necessary to respond to the serpent in Eden rather than simply ignoring its attempts to undermine her and Adam's relationship with God.

I am interested in speaking to the church, those of us who are followers of God in Christ and who believe that God has revealed himself to us in the Bible. Our attitude should be to turn to the Bible as God's revelation and learn about the nature of God. Since the Bible is the revelation of God, we put ourselves under its authority. There is no ethical basis outside of the Bible by which we should evaluate the Bible.

So, what are we to make of this picture of God that so pervades the Old Testament (and, we will soon see, the New as well)? Christians have had varying reactions to this theme, and I want to examine two strategies for responding to it. The first is to deny that the picture of God as a warrior in the Old Testament is the actual God who exists. Variations of this argument have been put forward by Eric Seibert, Peter Enns, and Greg Boyd. The second strategy is not to deny the picture of God as a warrior but rather to try to alleviate it. Here I will look at the work of Paul Copan.

Before starting my interactions with these different scholars, let me begin by stating my appreciation and respect for their work. We are all grappling with an issue that has often been troubling to Christians, and our anxieties have only been intensified over the past couple of decades. We all love God and place our trust in Jesus. I have heard some who vilify the work of particularly the first group, but I know that those in this group have the best intentions and are also extremely bright and insightful. While I am largely unpersuaded by their strategy, I have learned from them and thank them for their work. I will say that I have been more persuaded by those who advocate the second strategy, but even here, in the end, I disagree with their approach.

The Real God versus the Depicted God (Seibert, Enns, and Boyd)

SEIBERT: NOT A MARCIONITE(?)

In his book *Disturbing Divine Behavior*,[22] Eric Seibert examines the biblical material that describes violent activity on the part of God. As a pacifist, he finds many of God's actions deeply disturbing, as his title indicates, since they involve the harm and death of many human beings. He begins by taking on the Old Testament to ask whether the God depicted there is the actual God,

22. In the following discussion, page references will be given in the text.

but eventually he turns his attention to the disturbing description of God and Jesus himself in the New Testament to ask whether we have understood Jesus's teaching, particularly about the eschatological judgment, correctly. I will briefly describe Seibert's approach and then offer some criticisms before clarifying my own views on the matter.

Seibert begins by reviewing some of the many texts that depict a violent God in the Old Testament. He restricts himself to narrative texts and examines, for example, the exodus from Egypt and the conquest, particularly the events at Jericho, the command to annihilate the Amalekites, and so on.

He asserts that these portrayals of God are inadequate. I say "he asserts" because, at least at this point in his book, he has not argued for this view but seems to assume that his readers will accept this judgment as self-evident. Indeed, some will, particularly in his pacifist community, but readers who do not find his moral stance to be self-evident will likely be frustrated by his approach. In other words, Seibert operates with an a priori understanding of what is ethical and what is not, what is virtuous and what is morally inadequate. And so it seems that right from the start he is using an extrabiblical ethical standard to evaluate the pictures of God we get in the Old Testament.

He might justify this approach, at least in part, by stating that the human nature of the Bible gives us permission to think that perhaps the God depicted in the Bible is not always the actual God but sometimes a flawed human conception of him (5). But at this point he simply asserts this view and does not take into account the possibility (and the long-held belief of the church) that the human origins of the Bible do not violate the divine origins of the Bible and introduce error any more than Jesus's humanity makes him a sinner, which he is not.

As we read on in Seibert, though, he does seem to present a rationale for his belief that many Old Testament portrayals of

147

God are not ethical. He holds up Jesus as the basis for his ethical standard, and of course there are good reasons to do so. After all, Jesus is the very presence of God and the fullest revelation of him ("Anyone who has seen me has seen the Father" [John 14:9]; "The Son is the radiance of God's glory and the exact representation of his being" [Heb. 1:3]). Seibert describes what he calls his "Christocentric hermeneutic" (185) later in the book, where he says that we must judge the rest of the Bible by the standard of Jesus. Indeed, Seibert may justify his assertion of a self-evident moral standard in this way, but I believe his justification falls short. Although he uses Jesus as an ethical standard, he is quite selective in his picture of Jesus, as we will discuss later.

How, then, does Seibert handle the obvious and pervasive pictures of God as violent in the Old Testament while maintaining his fervent belief that God is not violent? As noted above, Seibert says that as a general principle we must bear in mind that the God that the Old Testament depicts is not always the actual God. He says, "I discovered numerous texts in which God's behavior seemed highly problematic and seriously out of line with my beliefs about God's character" (2). The Old Testament presentation of God as a warrior particularly troubles Seibert. For example, though God is reportedly "merciful and gracious" (Exod. 34:6 NRSV), such qualities seem utterly lacking when it comes to the divine directive to kill Canaanites and to "show them no mercy" (Deut. 7:2). Seibert describes a contradictory and confusing presentation of God in the Old Testament and says that we can't have it both ways; either God is merciful or he is not (33).

Now let me pause here to say that, in principle, Seibert is correct. We do sometimes get what appear to be contradictory descriptions of God, and all of us will read certain biblical texts and say to ourselves, "God is not like that." Seibert helpfully gives us a couple of examples (172–73). The first is the description in Genesis 2–3 of God as limited in knowledge and even having a body. We know from other Scriptures that God is a spirit, so he does not literally breathe into the dust to form Adam or walk in the garden in the cool of the day. We know from other Scriptures that God is omniscient, but in Genesis 3 he does not appear to know where Adam is or who told him he was naked. The Bible also teaches that God does not change his mind (Num. 23:19; 1 Sam. 15:29), but in other places it says that he does change his mind (Jer. 18:8; Jon. 3:9). So we debate which of these depictions of God are really pointing to the actual God.

Seibert points to other factors to give us pause before accepting the Old Testament narrative presentation of God as a warrior. The first factor has to do with the historical reliability, or better yet unreliability, of the biblical narrative's descriptions of God's warring activity (chap. 5). Let us take, for instance, Jericho. Of course, Joshua's account of the fall of Jericho is jarring to Seibert. After all, God not only wins the victory over the city by causing the walls to fall; God also orders the death of every man, woman, and child. But Seibert says that this never happened. Here he rehearses the well-known issues concerning the historicity of the conquest story in general and the battle of Jericho in particular. Since the archaeological investigation of Tell es-Sultan (= Jericho) in the 1950s, there has been doubt about whether Jericho was inhabited at the time of the conquest. Seibert uses the historical skepticism of the day to conclude that, since the battle of Jericho never happened, we can be relieved that God never ordered the death of the men, women, and children of Canaan.[23]

But of course Seibert realizes that this does not solve the ethical question completely. To make a distinction between history and theology and say that the Bible is not true in the area of history but is true in its theology does not resolve the issue. The theology of the book of Joshua presents God as a warrior. Here Seibert explores the worldview of the Israelites (chap. 8). He concludes

23. For a full discussion of matters of historicity, see chap. 2 above.

that their worldview did not allow for secondary causes. God was behind everything, good and evil. He then asserts that we just don't believe that anymore. "And thus it did not bother OT writers that God was the author of evil actions. Well it does bother us today" (161). So at this point he appeals to our more enlightened understanding over against the biblical worldview. Of course, his comments here have important implications for his view of the Bible as God's Word, but we will comment on that in a moment.

In his argument that we should not easily adopt the biblical worldview as our worldview, he gives two examples, cosmology and polygamy, and says that it is pretty obvious that we should accept neither as part of our view of the world today. Let me comment on his two examples. As John Walton points out, the Bible does not intend to teach cosmology to its readers. Rather, it adopts the cosmology of its "cognitive environment" in order to shape our worldview by informing us that God created the cosmos and humanity.[24] Thus, to reject the Bible's cosmology is not to reject the worldview the Bible intends to impart to us.

Polygamy is a trickier subject. The appropriate question here is, What is the Bible's view on marriage? I would argue that the Bible's standard of marriage is monogamy, based on Genesis 2, but that polygamy is a concession in the law, perhaps to be explained on the basis of the hardness of their hearts (referring to Jesus's explanation of why God was more permissive of divorce in the Mosaic law [Matt. 19:1–10]).[25] While it is true that the New Testament does not reject polygamy, it indicates that polygamy is not the ideal by saying that elders and deacons must be monogamous (1 Tim. 3:2, 12; Titus 1:6).[26] While there are developments within

24. Walton, *Genesis 1 as Ancient Cosmology.*
25. See "The Theology and Politics of Same-Sex Marriage in the Church" in chap. 4 below.
26. NIV (2011) obscures this meaning by rendering the relevant phrase "faithful to his wife." The Greek says "the husband of one wife" (*mias gynaikos andra/ andres/anēr*).

the biblical material and even beyond, so that we would say that polygamy is wrong today, that does not mean it was immoral or wrong during the Old Testament period or even in the New Testament period. Indeed, I would agree with those today who say that if a polygamous person becomes a Christian, he or she should not initiate a divorce.

My point is that Seibert's comments about worldview are not relevant to his argument. As I read him, he argues that the issue of polygamy will be the same as divine violence. Our worldview today says polygamy is wrong; therefore, he argues, the biblical worldview is wrong. Following from that, if our worldview today finds divine violence disturbing, then the biblical picture of God as a warrior is wrong. But I would say that even though I agree that both polygamy and holy war are wrong today, they were not wrong during the Old Testament period. I will make my case for Yahweh war below.

But first, where does Seibert get his worldview? On what grounds does he critique the violence of the Old Testament? As mentioned above, he looks to Jesus and develops a Christocentric hermeneutic. He says we should attend to Jesus's actions and teachings and use those as a tool to evaluate whether other parts of Scripture give us actual or distorted pictures of God. He quotes Gareth Lloyd Jones, who says, "If a biblical concept corresponds to what we know of God in Christ, it is acceptable, if not, it is invalid" (183).[27] Of course, Jesus says to turn the other cheek (Matt. 5:39; Luke 6:29) and to love our enemies (Matt. 5:44; 6:27, 34), so this teaching clearly indicates to Seibert that the Old Testament pictures of God as warrior are inaccurate depictions.

Seibert's argument is considerably more complicated than I have just described, but still, the outline carries its core premises. His argument may lead us to think, "Wait a minute. Jesus utilized violence at least once in his ministry by using a whip to drive out

27. Quoting Jones, "Sacred Violence," 198.

the money changers (John 2:15). That is hardly turning the other cheek." Jesus also teaches during his earthly ministry about a future violent judgment (e.g., Matt. 8:11–12, 28; 18:9; 21:41–44; 24:37–39 // Luke 17:26–29).Or perhaps we might think of Jesus's role in eschatological judgment. For example, the book of Revelation depicts Jesus coming on a cloud chariot (Rev. 1:7; cf. Mark 13:26–27 and parallels) and riding a white horse with a sword coming out of his mouth and bringing judgment that results in a feast of corpses for the vultures (Rev. 19:11–21).

Seibert approaches these issues in much the same way that he approaches the Old Testament. He says, for instance, that the New Testament can also give us inaccurate depictions of God and Christ. He says that there are questions about the historicity of the New Testament, like the Old Testament, sometimes citing the Jesus Seminar's doubts about something Jesus said or did. He also pulls out a panoply of resources to question Jesus's teaching about hell, arguing in favor of conditional immortality (a position also known as "annihilationism").

Further, he questions the penal substitutionary model of the atonement, saying it inappropriately pits the Father against the Son. He quotes J. Denny Weaver, who says, "Jesus did suffer and die a violent death, but the violence was neither God's nor God directed. Suffering and dying were not the purpose or goal of Jesus' mission" (198).[28] Weaver and Seibert are right to criticize a crude popular understanding of substitutionary atonement,[29] but this is a view held by no serious theologian. Suffering and dying were not "the purpose or goal" of Jesus's ministry, but Jesus accomplished his goal through suffering and dying.

Finally, Seibert seeks to avoid the charge of Marcionism. His approach is very similar to one taken by C. S. Cowles in the book *Show Them No Mercy*, and he is aware that Cowles fell open to

28. Quoting Weaver, "Narrative Christus Victor," 25.
29. See Wright, *Day the Revolution Began*.

that charge.[30] Seibert and Cowles both develop a Christocentric hermeneutic, which they use to critique other biblical pictures of God. Seibert's main counter to this anticipated charge is that though these texts promote distorted and even dangerous pictures of God, they still have some other redeeming value, so we should not throw them out.

In a final appendix Seibert presents his doctrine of Scripture. He rejects the idea of plenary verbal inspiration as well as any view in which "God exercises a high degree of control over the process" (265). He argues instead for what he calls the "general inspiration" of the Bible (273–74). He initially defines this as the view that acknowledges God's involvement in the process but does not conclude that God was responsible for everything in the Bible (like plenary and, to a lesser degree, conceptual inspiration). In a word, he argues that God's involvement is indirect. He sees God as a foreman who directs a task without micromanagement. The Bible does not reflect God's absolute truth. Seibert believes that "while there is much that can be affirmed and embraced, there is also some that must be resisted and rejected" (274).

Seibert's approach is open to criticism on a number of points. First, let me address his assertion that it is self-evident that there are instances where the depiction of God is clearly at odds with what we understand to be the actual God. The depictions of God in Genesis 2–3 and God changing his mind are his primary examples. He is correct that Genesis 2–3 is at odds with other texts that assert God's omniscience and the idea that God is a spiritual being. He is also correct that God is depicted as both changing and not changing his mind. However, the issue of divine violence is not the same as these examples. There is no contradiction or even tension in the statements about God's violence in relation to Jesus's nonviolent statements in the light of progressive revelation

30. See Cowles's chapter and my critique in Cowles et al., *Show Them No Mercy*, 13–44, 57–60.

and the progress of redemption. Contrary to Seibert's view, the Bible's view of God as a warrior is perfectly coherent and consistent. It tells a single story of God's victory over evil (I will say more on this below).

Second, one can, indeed must, question Seibert's evaluation of the historical issue. In other words, we should not be willing to concede that the historical narrative concerning the conquest is simply wrong. In chapter 2 of this book I addressed this question directly, and I refer you also to the book I coauthored with Iain Provan and V. Philips Long, *A Biblical History of Israel*, for a vigorous defense of the essential historicity of the conquest.[31] So for those of us who are not persuaded that the conquest did not happen, Seibert's argument is not persuasive.

Third, I challenge Seibert's Christocentric hermeneutic, which ends up pitting Christ against the rest of the canon and producing a canon within a canon. Jesus himself never disowns the Old Testament, and Seibert's portrait of Jesus from the New Testament is selective (I will deal with this issue more fully below as I interact with Boyd).

Fourth, I find Seibert's view of Scripture problematic even on its own grounds. You will remember that he thinks that God is like a foreman, directing and guiding. But on Seibert's understanding, God would be a very incompetent foreman since so much of the Bible gives a distorted view of God. It would be like a foreman whose workers built a house that would crumble as soon as it was built.

Finally, I do not believe Seibert completely avoids the charge of Marcionism. He is not a Marcionite per se because he does not intend to decanonize the Old Testament. He salvages bits and pieces of it, but he still finds much of it misleading and unhelpful and even, in his mind, dangerous. And like Marcion, his critique extends beyond the Old Testament into the New Testament and even into the Gospels themselves.

31. See Provan, Long, and Longman, *Biblical History of Israel*, chap. 7.

PETER ENNS: THE ISRAELITES TELL THEIR OWN STORY

In his entertaining (at least I find Enns's style entertaining; his sarcastic humor strikes others in a negative way)[32] and often insightful book *The Bible Tells Me So*, Peter Enns tackles the question of divine violence in the Old Testament at some length.[33] This book is written for a broad audience, so there is not a careful presentation of the material or description of other views,[34] but there is a serious argument behind his bantering (I mean this in the best way).

He first describes the divine violence that we have in the Old Testament. He pulls no punches (nor should he) in terms of the graphic violence we find there. He suggests that "it's hard to appeal to the God of the Bible to condemn genocide today when the God of the Bible commanded genocide yesterday" (30). (I will dispute this point below.)

He then criticizes three common justifications for divine violence that are frequently presented as a group but often with some variation. In a section titled "If Jesus Sends Some People to Hell, What's So Bad About Killing Some Canaanites?" he says that hell "is a tricky subject"[35] and that the killing of Canaanites was a lot worse than going to hell. But to say that hell isn't to be pictured literally ("with demons, pitchforks, and eternal flaming agony" [42]) and that Revelation is not literal does not mean that hell is a pleasant place or that Revelation does not point to a horrific fate for some. Yes, we are dealing with metaphors here, but metaphors

32. He's like that in real life (remember from the introduction that he is a close friend of mine).

33. Enns, *Bible Tells Me So*, 29–70. In the following discussion, page references will be given in the text.

34. This is not to say he does not interact with other views (as we will see), but he does not give a nuanced description of them or associate them with specific scholars, though I recognize myself in his discussion (remember I was his professor, and I lectured on this topic). True, *The Bible Tells Me So* is not that type of book; it's written for a general audience.

35. I, and many others, would dispute that.

of pain and violence point to pain and violence whether we like it or not.

The most mystifying (to me) part of this chapter is when Enns says that people should not use Jesus's teaching to support the divine violence of the Old Testament because "Jesus was against" it (44). I'm not sure how Enns can say that, since I don't know anywhere that Jesus voiced a specific opinion about it and a fair reading of Jesus shows that he pretty much affirmed what we call the Old Testament. If anything, his silence should be taken as approval. That Jesus instituted a new phase of the battle against evil (as I argue below) does not mean that he disowns the battle that took place in the past or will happen in the future.

In the next section, "God's Nicer Side," Enns asserts that those who argue that God's mercy and grace outbalance and justify his violent side are wrong. I agree with him here, but I actually don't know anyone who argues that way (and he gives us no footnotes). It is true that in the debate over God's "dark side" people point out that the Old Testament also presents God in a more "positive" manner, but that is only to push back against those who perpetuate the stereotype that God is always angry in the Old Testament and always loving in the New. We will see below that God is angry and loving in both Testaments (and Enns knows this, because he has to remind us a couple times not to take hell or Revelation "literally").

The third chapter, devoted to rebuffing views different from his own, is titled "Worst. Sinners. Ever." (He actually talks like that in real life.) Here he considers those who justify the divine violence against the Canaanites by saying that the Canaanites were especially sinful and therefore deserved this judgment more than anyone else. He says that "some defenders of this view go so far as to say that wiping out the Canaanites is a sneak preview of the end of the world and a warning to us all" (51). Since this is a line I have used for decades in my lectures (and Enns heard those lectures way back), I take this as a personal (but loving) swipe at his old professor (though I am not really that much older than he is; I started young). But even so, I agree with him that "giving Canaanites first prize in the 'worst sinner ever' contest is a caricature, and a bit of propaganda" (50), and there are those who do so.[36] The basic idea of a sneak preview of the final judgment (or an intrusion of end-time ethics into the period of common grace) is not dependent on the Canaanites being the worst sinners ever but is dependent only on them being sinners. I will make the case below.

After considering these justifications and finding them wanting, Enns goes on to tell us (in the section "Digging for Answers") that in any case the conquest as described in Joshua did not happen. After rightly expressing his reservations about the pronouncements of archaeologists, he expresses his agreement with the consensus that there never was a violent invasion by Israel in the first place. It never happened. (I looked at this issue in chap. 2.) And Enns, to his credit, realizes that his conclusion does not do away with the problem totally. He has to deal with the fact that the Bible describes Israel's entry into the land as an act of divine violence. Even if the conquest didn't happen, the Israelites seem comfortable with the idea of a violent God. So how does he deal with that? In a variation of Seibert's view, he argues that God allows his children the Israelites to describe him and his ways in their own language. They are, after all, an ancient tribe, and "they saw the world and their God in tribal ways" (61).

I agree with Enns in principle that the Bible was written in an ancient "cognitive environment"[37] and that we always need to read it in that context and not impose modern expectations on it. But that is a far cry from agreeing that the Bible gives us misleading impressions of God and our relationship with him. And as I will demonstrate, there is no difference between the Old and New

36. Merrill, "Case for Moderate Discontinuity"; Sprinkle, *Fight*, 76–77.
37. The phrase is from Walton, *Genesis 1 as Ancient Cosmology*.

Testaments on this subject. The Bible gives us one coherent picture of who God is, including in the matter of his battle against evil. Thus, I don't find Enns's approach satisfying.

The Cruciform Hermeneutic of Gregory Boyd

The Crucifixion of the Warrior God by Gregory Boyd is the most recent (2017) and certainly the lengthiest sustained argument to reinterpret the violent passages of the Old Testament in a way that removes what the author considers to be an inappropriate and embarrassing portrait of God.[38] Boyd's argument, as I will point out, is very similar to that of Seibert and Enns. That said, because of his detailed argumentation, extensive interaction with previous studies, and irenic style, his case is the most (superficially) attractive of the trio. In spite of this, in the final analysis, I for one remain unpersuaded. Even so, let me begin by highlighting a few key areas of agreement.

First, I agree with Boyd's basic understanding of what we might call the location of the meaning of the text. He does well to honor the intention of the original authors of the biblical books. He avoids a disregard for authorial intent that would allow an interpreter to attribute all kinds of arbitrary meanings to a passage (as some allegorical readings in the early church illustrate). But he also does not restrict the meaning of a text to the human author's conscious intention as some do, but rather acknowledges that there can be a "surplus of meaning" (534) that carries the meaning beyond (but not in contradiction to) the original human intention.

38. In the following discussion, page references will be given in the text. Boyd wrote a shorter book, titled *Cross Vision*, that came out after I read the longer book. I assume that this shorter version was written because he or the publisher recognizes that few will read 1,400-plus pages. I've already done that, so I am going to assume that the shorter version presents the same basic argument, since it came out just a couple months after the long version (I wish it had come out a few months before that!). A very similar argument is put forth by Fleisher, *Old Testament Case for Nonviolence*.

He thus rightly advocates a double reading of Old Testament texts, as do Brevard Childs and others.[39]

Second, Boyd correctly recognizes that the New Testament authors read the Old Testament in the light of the work (he would specify the crucifixion) of Christ, which allowed them to see this surplus of meaning.[40] Such a Christocentric understanding of the Bible takes Jesus's comments on the Scriptures in Luke 24:25–27, 44–45 seriously.[41]

Third, and this point is extremely important, I agree with Boyd that the Bible's teaching on Jesus and violence instructs the church to adopt a position of nonviolence in regard to the church's mission. The citations of divinely authorized violence in the Old Testament or in the apocalyptic portions of the New Testament do not give direction or permission to the church to ever use violence to support or further its mission. However, the sad fact that these texts have been misused in support of religious wars (whether the Crusades[42] or the atrocities committed by the Europeans/Americans against the natives who occupied the Americas when they first arrived here) or, more recently, the shooting of abortion doctors should not lead us to find ways, as Boyd does, to dismiss the divine violence of these portions of Scripture.

Fourth, I appreciate Boyd's affirmation of the historical character of the biblical events that depict God's violence. He differs in this respect from Seibert and Enns, who find some type of solace

39. See Longman, *Reading the Bible*; Childs, *Biblical Theology*, 76.

40. There remains the question of whether the New Testament authors are bringing out a Christocentric reading of the Old Testament that should have been available to Old Testament readers (thus Beale, "Cognitive Peripheral Vision," who advocates a kind of christological reading) or that could only be seen in the light of the cross (thus Enns, *Inspiration and Incarnation*; R. B. Hays, *Reading Backwards*; and Boyd, who all advocate what some call a Christotelic reading). I affirm both views; see Longman, "'What Was Said.'"

41. That said, I will fundamentally disagree with some of the conclusions he draws from this insight.

42. Earl ("Joshua and the Crusades"), however, has made the argument that the book of Joshua played virtually no role in the theology of the Crusades.

in the supposed nonhistoricity of, say, Joshua's depiction of the conquest.[43]

Fifth, I even agree with him that there are places in the Bible where the depicted God is not the same as the actual one. This is particularly true in what scholars today call "anthropomorphisms," the description of God as having human characteristics that are at odds with other descriptions of God. Genesis 2 and 3 famously provide examples. Genesis 2 depicts God as blowing on dust (as if God has lungs) in order to create the first human. In Genesis 3 we read that God was taking a stroll in the garden "in the cool of the day" (v. 8) and was unaware of where Adam was hiding. Elsewhere we learn that God is a spirit and that he is omniscient.

While agreeing with Boyd that the actual God does not always align with the depicted God, I believe he wrongly applies this idea to the issue of divine violence. The difference begins with the fact that it is unlikely in the extreme that the original author of Genesis 3 believed that God actually walked or lacked the knowledge of Adam's location. In this figurative depiction of an actual historical event,[44] the author utilized anthropomorphic language to tell the story. Boyd himself states that the biblical authors actually thought that God acted in violent ways. In other words, the biblical author in Genesis 3 knew that the actual God was not like the God depicted, whereas the biblical author in Joshua believed that the actual God actually caused hailstones to fall from the sky to kill fleeing Canaanites.

Indeed, we can only really discern a difference between the actual and the depicted God if there is a conflict between the way God is depicted in different parts of Scripture (in this case God

43. But both of them recognize that the mere fact of the description of a violent God ordering the death of men, women, and children still presents a problem to twenty-first-century Western readers of the biblical text.

44. See the extensive treatment of the genre of Gen. 1–3 in "Genre: Theological History" in chap. 1.

as spirit and God as embodied, or God as limited in knowledge and God as omniscient). When it comes to divine violence, my contention is that there is no such conflict. The biblical picture is coherent as we move from Genesis to Revelation and follow God's fight against evil, human and spiritual, that starts at the beginning of Genesis and ends only with Jesus's second coming.

But this, of course, is where I differ the most from Boyd. He believes that there is such a conflict between the God of the Old Testament and the crucified Christ. And here he is most like Seibert, though not identical. He puts forward the argument that it is in Christ, and in particular in Christ on the cross, that we have the fullest revelation of who God actually is. He then utilizes this standard to judge whether a description of God, in the Old Testament in particular but also in the New, is an accurate depiction of God or whether it is the result of the fallen and depraved perception of God's people.

One of the main problems of this approach in my mind is that it creates a canon within the canon. By using the crucified Christ as a standard by which to judge other parts of the Bible, Boyd in effect neutralizes the teaching of vast swathes of the biblical text, though he does his best to recover some lesson from even those texts. To accomplish this, Boyd and others like him must place themselves in judgment over the canon rather than submitting to the canon that was given to us. Granted, all of us must engage in interpretation of texts, which involves our own human judgments. But that is considerably different from saying that a passage teaches x, but x is not from God but rather is the result of the sinful human author's perception of God.

A second problem is that Boyd's standard is too restricted. This problem affects not only Boyd but also Seibert and Enns. Boyd tries to get around this problem with his focus on Christ on the cross, which is narrower than Seibert and Enns. Thus, his standard is not simply the biblical presentation of Jesus as the fullest revelation of God but specifically Christ on the cross. But if Christ is the fullest revelation of God (as I believe he is, as well; see Heb. 1:3), then it is Christ on the cross, as well as the resurrection, as well as his teaching, as well as his return that should be that standard. And when we look at the Old Testament God in the light of the full revelation of Christ in the New Testament, we see that there is no conflict between Jesus and the God of the Old Testament. We will demonstrate this below when we look at the full biblical teaching on God as a warrior.

Now the main problem with using Christ as the standard to judge the Old Testament is not only that the Gospels give strong witness to the fact that Jesus himself fully embraced the Old Testament without qualification but also that the New Testament presents Jesus speaking of his violent return to bring judgment against all human and spiritual enemies (Matt. 23; Mark 13; Luke 21). The book of Revelation is, of course, the most problematic of all for Boyd's view.

To his credit, Boyd does not dismiss Revelation as noncanonical (unless it speaks of divine violence directly, at which point it too is part of the fallen and culturally conditioned perspective of its human author); nor does he reject the idea of a final judgment (which he believes results not in God bringing pain or suffering on an individual but rather in his withdrawing his presence from those people). Instead, he uses Christ on the cross as a hermeneutical principle to interpret the book of Revelation in a way that distances Christ from violence.

But this involves some pretty tenuous interpretive decisions.[45] Space does not allow a detailed critique, so let me point out one of the more bizarre readings that he presents. In Revelation 6, as Jesus the Lamb opens the seals, the living creatures, who encircle the throne of Jesus the Lamb (Rev. 5:6), call out four times, "Come!"

45. For a careful interpretation of Revelation in relation to the divine warrior theme, see Bandy, "Vengeance, Wrath, and Warfare."

Then four horsemen come forth to wreak havoc on the earth. It certainly appears that these are agents of God's judgment, but according to Boyd they are demonic forces that are being restrained by God. He also asserts that the angels who later bring judgment are not God's holy servants but rather demons (607–10).

I agree with Boyd that "we should resist any temptation we might have to interpret any of the graphic word-pictures in Revelation in a literal way" (599). However, as we saw above in our discussion of Enns, the metaphors and similes of the book are carefully chosen to communicate a message that is consonant with their nature. As Susan Hylen puts it, "The violent content of Revelation's metaphors is not magically transmuted into something nonviolent."[46] In other words, violent metaphors, though not giving us a literal picture, are telling us about a violent judgment.

Perhaps the most unpersuasive move Boyd makes comes with his interpretation of Revelation 19:11–20, which he tackles at some length because he recognizes that this passage, at least on the surface, is the most violent depiction of judgment that the book, perhaps even the whole Bible, has to offer. He adopts the extreme minority view, and one that is overly subtle, that the blood on Jesus's robe is his own blood rather than the blood of the enemy (as it is in the Isaiah passage [63:3], which is clearly the background). He acknowledges that the sword comes out of Jesus's mouth to kill his enemies, as the passage itself says ("The rest were killed with the sword coming out of the mouth of the rider on the horse, and all the birds gorged themselves on their flesh" [19:21]), but he takes the sword as a reference to speech and not to physical violence. In that case, however, these are words that kill, and so this interpretation doesn't solve his problem.

Perhaps the greatest stumbling block for me and other traditional Protestant evangelicals is Boyd's view of Scripture. One doesn't have to be an advocate of inerrancy to feel troubled by

---

46. Hylen, "Metaphor Matters," 778; see discussion in Miller, *Dragon*, 277.

his view that large swathes of the Old Testament and even some parts of the New Testament are the result of the "fallen and culturally conditioned" perspective of the human authors. Anything that conflicts with the standard he derives from his narrow view of Christ on the cross (and this includes all accounts of divine violence) is considered an offensive and sinful depiction of God that is not to be believed. He accuses even Moses, that venerable servant of God who is so honored in the Old and New Testaments and by Jesus himself, of being sinful when he states that God commanded the death of Canaanites. And Joshua never should have believed him, because Moses was falsely claiming God gave him the command. Boyd says that even though "God had given the Israelites overwhelming proof that Moses was indeed his spokesperson," there are no "epistemic conditions" that "should suffice to convince rational people that another person instructs them to murder others" (925–26).

Let me reiterate that even though I find Boyd's argument ultimately unpersuasive, I appreciate and understand his difficulties with the biblical material. It is very hard for me as a twenty-first-century Westerner to come to grips with God bringing or ordering violence against anyone, particularly, as Boyd constantly emphasizes, "innocents" and babies. But here is the rub. The concept of innocents is a very nonbiblical category; at the very least Boyd needs to do better than to simply appeal to our emotions or our gut feelings when he so labels the victims of divine violence.

Let me be clear. Boyd and the others are not Marcionites, at least on a theological level. They are not completely abandoning the Old Testament and the apocalyptic portions of the New Testament, as Marcion and his followers advocated. They find significance even in the passages that describe divine violence. But they are rejecting the main message of what even they believe the passages are teaching, and in that way they are what we might call "practical Marcionites."

Boyd, for reasons that many of us living in the twenty-first century can appreciate, has trouble thinking that God would directly inflict violence on any human being. He interprets the biblical text in a way that denies that the actual God acts in such a way against evil human beings. He even has a problem with divine violence directed toward spiritual powers and authorities, the devil and his minions. There is a consistency here, since after all they are sentient beings that God created "good."

Even so, Boyd does admit that there are evil human beings and evil spiritual powers and that they are judged, and judged violently. He is not a universalist; he just doesn't think that God ever, whether in the conquest or the judgment at the end of time, punishes people directly. God does not wield violence himself, but he does withdraw his presence and allow human beings to bring his judgment against others. Boyd labels his understanding of how God judges a form of "divine Aikido," from the Japanese term that means "the way of peace" or "the way of the harmonious spirit" (767). He goes on to say that "Aikido is a martial arts technique that trains 'warriors' to engage in nonresistant combat, turning the force of aggressors back on themselves in order to neutralize their opponent and hopefully to enlighten them regarding the evil in their heart that fueled their aggression" (767–77).

I agree with him that God often, though not always, judges by using human or angelic agents. But if God withdraws his protective presence and allows others to bring his judgment, does this really alleviate the issue? I don't think so.

Take the book of Job for instance. Now even if (as I believe) Job is not a historical book, it does present a picture that illustrates what Boyd has in mind. God does not directly bring violence on Job, but he does give his permission and allows "the accuser," one of his angels, to harm Job's family and property and eventually Job himself (Job 1–2). Is God really any less responsible for

Job's suffering? And for a similar example from a prose historical account, consider the two versions of David taking the census. In 2 Samuel 24:1 we read that "the anger of the LORD burned against Israel, and he [God] incited David against them, saying, 'Go and take a census of Israel and Judah.'" This census that God incited David to take leads to a severe judgment in the form of a plague that "the LORD sent" (2 Sam. 24:15). The version found in 1 Chronicles has a small but significant variation when the story begins: "Satan rose up against Israel and incited David to take a census of Israel" (21:1). Again, as in Job, scholars recognize that this is not the devil but rather God's emissary (and angel). The text can describe it either way because even when God uses an agent to carry out his will, it is as if God himself has done it.[47]

In conclusion, one gets the impression from reading Boyd that he approaches the topic of divine violence as a problem to be solved. He reads the biblical text to solve the problem and not to exposit the text as it stands before him. The problem, according to Boyd, is that the Bible, from Genesis to Revelation, presents God as involved in violence toward human and spiritual evil. But his belief is that God cannot be directly involved in violence, so how does one read the Bible to find a nonviolent God? One must begin by saying that the actual God is not coterminous with the God depicted in the Bible.

But then how does one discern the difference between the actual God and the depicted God? The process begins by choosing Jesus as the standard by which to judge the rest of the Scriptures. If a picture of God does not conform to the standard provided

47. For this reason Boyd takes the marginalized view that in Job "Satan" is the devil (see Longman, *Job*, 91–92), but this seems more like a matter of convenience for his argument. And, we have to remember, he always has the trump card that this perspective is the result of the depraved and culturally conditioned viewpoint of the biblical author (an opinion that those who hold to a traditional view of Scripture will find unpersuasive).

by Jesus, then it is not the actual God. However, one still has a problem, first because Jesus himself does not disown the Old Testament, but even more because the picture of Jesus is not entirely nonviolent either, particularly in the apocalyptic portions of the New Testament. How does one handle this? First, Boyd asserts that the standard is not just Jesus Christ but Jesus Christ on the cross. One then evaluates other portions of Scripture by (and provides interpretations of particular passages that conform to) the picture of Jesus on the cross. One must read Scripture with what he occasionally calls a "magic eye" (xxxiv–xxxv).[48]

Another strategy is to read biblical texts in such a way that what looks like divine violence and judgment is really a matter of divine withdrawal, so that even though sinners and evil powers are being harmed by humans and by evil powers, and this is God's judgment, God at least is not directly involved in bringing harm on others. Most people would say that if God withdraws while knowing that harm will come, or even giving permission for harm, God is involved in the violence.[49] That is particularly the case if the agents of judgment are angelic powers, which is why Boyd opts for the view held by very few scholars today that "the Satan" in Job is the devil and not one of God's divine assembly and, even less likely, that the angels of the book of Revelation who bring judgment are actually demons.

But when all else fails (and to his credit he does his best to avoid this conclusion, though he always has it handy), if there is a picture of God that shows him directly involved in violence, then this, Boyd says, is not the actual God but rather the creation

---

48. I find this a particularly unfortunate term that reveals that you have to read with a certain mind-set in order to see a message that one would otherwise miss seeing, a message behind the surface of the text. Such an approach, though not as crass, bears a kind of similarity to recent attempts to uncover "Bible codes." While Boyd recognizes that this term may evoke the idea of treating the Bible like a cryptogram, I don't think he completely escapes this criticism.

49. His attempt to mitigate this critical perspective is anemic; see Boyd, *Crucifixion*, 902–4.

of the corrupt, morally flawed, culturally conditioned human author.[50]

Softening the Blow: Paul Copan, David Lamb, and Preston Sprinkle

While finding the Seibert-Enns-Boyd approach deeply flawed,[51] I have greater appreciation for the approach of Paul Copan, David Lamb, and Preston Sprinkle.[52] Since Copan offers perhaps the most detailed presentation of the approach and the others present similar arguments, I will use Copan (including the book he coauthored with Matthew Flannagan) as the main representative of this second contemporary strategy for grappling with divine violence in the Old Testament. Even though I find this approach often helpful and illuminating, in the final analysis, I believe there is a problem with his views as well. Copan does not reinterpret or reject the biblical depiction of God as a warrior, but he works overtime to diminish the level of violence presented in Scripture. As will be seen, I often agree with Copan's basic insights, but I think he overplays them in order to minimize the role of divine violence.

For instance, I agree with him that the battle reports of the conquest, including that of Jericho, are rife with hyperbole in keeping with the battle reports of the day.[53] I also agree that the popular imagination has magnified the size of cities like Jericho and that it is possible that Jericho could have been mainly a military outpost with few noncombatants at that time. But there were

---

50. For an even more detailed and devastating critique of Boyd's book, see P. Copan's review, "Greg Boyd's Misunderstandings of the 'Warrior God,'" The Gospel Coalition, January 26, 2018, www.thegospelcoalition.org/reviews/cruci fixion-warrior-god-greg-boyd/.

51. I would also add Cowles ("Case for Radical Discontinuity"), but he provides an earlier form of the arguments critiqued here. For my specific interaction with him, see my response in Cowles et al., *Show Them No Mercy*, 57–60.

52. Copan, *Is God a Moral Monster?*, and Copan and Flannagan, *Genocide*; Lamb, *God Behaving Badly*; and Sprinkle, *Fight*.

53. See Younger, *Ancient Conquest Accounts*.

noncombatants there (as he well knows) like Rahab and her family. Granted, Rahab was the type of woman (a prostitute) who would accompany soldiers to the front line, but she was still a noncombatant, and so was, we can safely presume, at least part of her family. It is doubtful that she was the only woman present.

And what are we to make of the statement that after the walls came down and the city came into Israelite hands, "they devoted [from *haram*] the city to the LORD and destroyed with the sword every living thing in it—men and women, young and old, cattle, sheep and donkeys" (Josh. 6:21)? Copan's response is that this language is merely stereotypical and doesn't actually mean that there were women and children present, or if there were, they would not be subject to *herem* (that is, the requirement that all captured people be executed).[54] He claims the same is true of the command in Deuteronomy that this act seems to put into effect ("However, in the cities of the nations the LORD your God is giving you as an inheritance, do not leave alive anything that breathes. Completely destroy them [from *haram*]—the Hittites, Amorites, Canaanites, Perizzites, Hivites and Jebusites—as the LORD your God has commanded you" [Deut. 20:16–17]). Copan wants to believe that this language too is stereotypical, but if so, then that makes no sense of the contrast with waging war with people outside the land (where *herem* is not applied). In this type of warfare, only the men are executed; the women and children are not (Deut. 20:10–15). As much as we might want to believe that God did not command the death of women and children, such a view finds no support in the relevant texts. The reason given in Deuteronomy 20 for this command is to prevent the spread of the Canaanites' idolatrous religion (something that would be spread by noncombatants, including women [see Jer. 44:15–19]).

54. "The use of 'women' and 'young and old' was merely stock ancient Near Eastern language that could be used even if women and young and old weren't living there." Copan, *Is God a Moral Monster?*, 126.

Further, Copan is surely correct to say that Canaanites had the option of coming over to the Israelite side. Rightly resisting the idea that we are dealing here with genocide or ethnic cleansing, as critics often inappropriately charge, Copan says that in the *herem* command "God was concerned with *sin*, not *ethnicity*."[55] Indeed, we have already considered the exodus and conquest from a historical perspective, so we have already commented on the very real possibility that Canaanite inclusion into Israel was significant indeed (see "The Need to Read Exodus through Joshua Carefully" in chap. 2).

But even here Copan stretches the biblical depiction in order to minimize what he and many others see as the offense of the biblical text. He has no real basis, for example, to suggest that "as with Gibeon (despite being sneaky treaty makers), a straightforward peace pact could have been available to any Canaanite city."[56] We have absolutely no indication that this is the case. Why, after all, were the Gibeonites sneaky? Because they somehow knew that there was a difference in the way that Israel was to treat those inside and outside the land. I do imagine that it would be possible for a group of Canaanites to corporately accept Yahweh as their God, reject their idolatrous worship, and thus become part of Israel, giving up their distinctive identity, but this does not seem to be what the Gibeonites or Copan have in mind.

That said, I do agree with Copan that it was never the mission to hunt down every last Canaanite. He strongly emphasizes the biblical teaching that they were to "drive out" the people of the land.[57] If Canaanites chose to flee outside the land, we know of no instance of Israel pursuing them (thus Copan rightly points to Exod. 23:27–30). But he is wrong to suggest that the presence of Canaanites in the land after Joshua or their reduction to forced

55. Copan, *Is God a Moral Monster?*, 163.
56. Copan, *Is God a Moral Monster?*, 180.
57. Copan and Flannagan, *Genocide*, 76–83.

labor is an indication that the *herem* was not to be applied. Passages like Judges 1:27–36; 1 Kings 9:20–21; Joshua 15:13; 16:10; 17:12–13 (cf. Ps. 106:34–35)[58] describe Israel's failure to execute God's command, with dire consequences for them. Psalm 106:34–39 puts it succinctly:

> They did not destroy the peoples
>> as the Lord had commanded them,
> but they mingled with the nations
>> and adopted their customs.
> They worshiped their idols,
>> which became a snare to them.
> They sacrificed their sons
>> and their daughters to false gods.
> They shed innocent blood,
>> the blood of their sons and daughters,
> whom they sacrificed to the idols of Canaan,
>> and the land was desecrated by their blood.
> They defiled themselves by what they did;
>> by their deeds they prostituted themselves.

For these reasons I have difficulty completely accepting Copan's (or Lamb's or Sprinkle's) account of the biblical material, though I deeply appreciate and have learned from his efforts. Indeed, there is much with which I agree, at least in principle. Yes, there is exaggeration in the battle accounts, and probably many of the Canaanites came over to the Israelite side and many others were driven out of the land and not killed. And yes, what we see in Canaan was not the normal way in which Israel was to wage war but was limited in scope and time. But even if Copan is correct about these things, he does not remove (and he acknowledges this) the "ethical problem." Minimizing, even as much as he does, does not remove the offense to many modern people. If

---

58. The list he gives us in *Is God a Moral Monster?*, 184.

even one noncombatant or one child dies,[59] then the criticisms and controversy do not go away.

Thus, rather than answering the criticisms, perhaps we ought to challenge the criticisms. In the first part of this section, I intended to do just that by describing what we actually see in the biblical text without trying to explain it away.

EXCURSUS

The Walton Thesis: Conquest as an Imposition of Order out of Disorder

Just before I finished this book, John and Harvey Walton published *The Lost World of the Israelite Conquest*, in which they deal with the issue of divine violence as it relates to Israel's entry into the land.[60] The Waltons' approach does not fit into the categories that we treated above. In other words, they are not interested in resolving people's qualms about the conquest by reinterpreting it in the vein of Seibert, Boyd, and Enns, nor are they interested in doing "damage control" by giving the most nonviolent reading possible in the manner of Copan, Lamb, and Sprinkle. Indeed, if anything, their view might raise the moral outrage that some feel toward the conquest. What they do want to accomplish (or so it seems to me) is to provide what they think is the correct understanding of the conquest in the context of the culture of the day. If they do have another purpose, it is to show that the type of behavior manifested in the book of Joshua has no place among God's people today.

Let me say at the outset that the Waltons' approach deserves a hearing and a more detailed critique than I am able to give here. That said, I find myself unpersuaded that they have given us a

---

59. His assertion that if any Canaanite children get killed they go into the presence of God and thus have a better life (Copan, *Is God a Moral Monster?*, 189) is, in my opinion, impossible to maintain in the light of the biblical material; Copan asserts this point and does not seem to make the attempt to justify it, at least in this book.

60. In the following discussion, page references will be given in the text.

correct reading of the biblical material. As for their second goal, I agree that the type of behavior that we see described in Joshua 1–12 is not normative or even allowable for Christians today, but my reasons are different, as I explain below.

Before launching into a critique, let me emphasize just how much I respect the Waltons' scholarship and their passion to read the Bible with integrity. This book is Harvey's first, but John has written excellent books for the past three-plus decades. Our careers overlap, and he is a close friend (some people even think we look a lot alike). As a matter of fact, we have recently coauthored two books together. That said, we do have some differences in our approach to the biblical material.

Those who are not biblical scholars may not realize just how eccentric some of the Waltons' ideas are in relation to views held commonly by other biblical scholars and through the history of interpretation. Granted, fresh readings can clear away the cobwebs of interpretations that are passed down from generation to generation and can lead to new insights into the text, but here there are so many new ideas that build on one another that the bar for acceptance is high. I don't think it is fair to say that the old view is fueled simply by a lack of awareness of the cultural background, since many of us who support more traditional readings also have competence in ancient Near Eastern studies.

The first of what I am calling the Waltons' "eccentricities" is that they move away from the categories of morality (goodness, sin, judgment, mercy/grace) and prefer to speak of order and disorder. This movement is particularly pronounced when it comes to non-Israelites who do not live in covenant relationship with God. The conquest of the Canaanites is not an act of judgment against their sin (they can't sin, since they are not in covenant with God). Rather, the Canaanites are "invincible barbarians" whom God deigns to be "removed from human use" (more on this below) because they represent disorder.

I agree that order and disorder are important categories in the ancient Near East and in the Bible, and that disorder does not always imply sin or evil. God's creative acts involve God taking disorder and putting it into an order that allows proper functioning. But after the fall, anything that causes disorder (thus working against God's intended order) is rebellion and thus morally culpable.

I disagree with the Waltons that the Canaanites can't be held morally culpable because they are not in covenant with God. My own view of the covenant with Noah is that all humanity is in covenant with God (see Gen. 9:1–17). Also, contrary to the Waltons' belief that gentiles are not sinners who are judged, passages like Amos 1–2 clearly show that non-Israelites can be and are judged for serious moral infractions. Even if, as they argue, there is no formal indictment against the Canaanites, the text is clear that their removal is primarily the result of their idolatry and the consequent sinful behavior that results from that (Gen. 15:16; discussed below). To me, the fact that this sin is couched in the language of their idolatry affecting the Israelites (Deut. 20:18; Ps. 106:34–39) does not undermine the fact that they engage in behaviors that offend God's sense of right and wrong.

And this leads us to the next eccentric interpretation, which has to do with the Waltons' understanding of Genesis 15:16. A traditional rendering understands that God is telling Abraham that the time is not yet ripe for judgment ("In the fourth generation your descendants will come back here, for the sin of the Amorites has not yet reached its full measure"), but the Waltons deny that this verse refers to a future retribution against the Canaanites carried out by Israelites. They give a tentative translation: "It won't be until after your lifetime is over that your family will return here because the destiny of destruction that has been decreed for your friends and allies has been and will continue to be deferred" (62). Here their argumentation becomes very technical. I won't give a full response, but it is noteworthy how often words and phrases like "cannot be determined with certainty," "we have to guess," "the best tentative interpretation," and so forth appear in their discussion. Strikingly, their concluding paragraph says: "This tentative interpretation [the one they offer in their book] has nothing to do with rationalizing the conquest. . . . While we cannot identify the precise nuance of this verse because of the ambiguity of *lōʾ šālēm*, we will also note that it is poor methodology to base a theological position—in this case the retributive purpose of the conquest—on a verse of which we cannot be sure of the meaning" (62–63). At this point I get the impression of hard work or overthinking in order to get a desired result. The bottom line is that I don't share their doubt about the traditional interpretation, even after they muddy the waters. The traditional reading is defended in the vast majority of commentaries.[61]

I am a bit more positively disposed toward their understanding of the word *herem* and its verbal form, or at least I don't object to it, partly because it is really not that far removed from a traditional understanding of what goes on at the conquest. Rather than "to completely annihilate" or the like, they offer the following rendering: "to remove from human use" (170). They don't offer this new reading to deny that the Israelites killed Canaanites during the conquest (after all, that is one way to remove from use), but they point out that this goal can be achieved by conversion (see Rahab) or by expulsion (see the frequent use of the term *grsh* in the text). How such means lead to exclusion from human use, however, is a question that only they can answer.

In conclusion, I am unpersuaded by the Waltons' overall approach to the conquest and divine violence in the Old Testament. As I mentioned, it is not their intention to answer the critics, but

61. E.g., Wenham, *Genesis 1–15*, 335; Hamilton, *Book of Genesis*, 435, 436; Matthews, *Genesis 11:27–50:26*, 174–75.

if it were, their approach would only magnify the ethical issue. If the Canaanites do not deserve the punishment because of their rebellion against God but rather are "being treated as chaos monsters (by means of the trope of 'invincible barbarians')" (166), that seems to me to present a cold, calculating God who wipes out people who do not deserve it, which does not fit well with the consistent picture of God we get through the Bible.

God's Strategy for Defeating Human and Spiritual Evil

Thus far we have observed the pervasiveness of the theme of divine violence in the Old Testament and have sampled and critiqued some recent attempts to address modern Western anxieties about the depiction of a warrior God. I personally cannot get away from the idea (because my analysis of the text leads me in this direction) that these well-intentioned and sincere attempts are trying to make the Bible say something different from what it intends to say, with the first group of thinkers veering toward a practical Marcionite approach that in essence says that the Old Testament is not really authoritative to the modern Christian.

But how are we to understand these texts? How does the Old Testament God compare to Jesus in the New Testament? How are Christians supposed to appropriate teaching about divine violence into our lives and our theology? These are the questions that will occupy us in the remainder of the chapter. We begin by considering a biblical theology of divine violence from the Old Testament into the New Testament. We will see that, far from being in contrast to each other, the two Testaments present one coherent picture of God's warfare against evil. This biblical theology may be presented in five phases.

Phase One: God Fights the Flesh and Blood Enemies of Israel

As you can tell from the survey of biblical texts above, there are many accounts of God fighting Israel's physical enemies, what I am calling "phase one": the crossing of the Reed Sea, the defeat of Jericho, the other battles of the conquest, David's battles against the Philistines at Rephidim, and on and on. From the warfare legislation in the book of Deuteronomy (chaps. 7 and 20) and the accounts of actual battles, we can paint the following picture of phase-one warfare. No one battle illustrates all of these elements, to be sure, but together they paint a picture of warfare as worship and God as active in victory.

BEFORE THE BATTLE

Inquiry. In the first place, God communicates to the war leader that it is his will to go to battle. This decision is not left to the human participants.

God sometimes makes his presence known in a direct way, as he does to Joshua at the beginning of the conquest (Josh. 5:13–16).[62] On other occasions, God communicates his will to engage in battle through an oracular device such as the sacred lots.

First Samuel 23:1–6 is such a moment. David has heard that the Philistines have attacked the Judean city of Keilah. David has already been anointed as the future king of Judah, but he is currently hiding from Saul, who sees him as a rival. Even so, David has an army and thus inquires of God whether he should "go and attack these Philistines" (1 Sam. 23:2). God responds affirmatively, but David's men are worried, so he inquires a second time and receives the same positive answer. He and his men then set out and rescue Keilah from the Philistines.

In what looks to be a parenthetical comment at the end of this story, we learn how David makes his inquiry. "Now Abiathar

---

62. See description in "The Conquest" above.

son of Ahimelek had brought the ephod down with him when he fled to David at Keilah" (1 Sam. 23:6). Whether the ephod contains the oracular devices known as the Urim and Thummim (Exod. 28:29–30) or whether the ephod itself is an oracular device is unclear, but what is clear is that the comments inform the reader that David has the ability to ask God his will in matters of warfare.

In these and other cases, God is the one who makes the decision to go to war. The biblical text is clear on this point, and it will be an important consideration as we talk about the ethics of warfare.

God's Presence and Spiritual Preparation. When God has directed his people to go into battle, he accompanies them and fights on their behalf. His presence is often symbolized by the presence of the ark of the covenant, which is carried by the priests into battle.

The ark was constructed in the wilderness, and it accompanied the Israelites during their long wandering toward the promised land. The ark was placed in the back third of the tabernacle, the most holy part, since it was where God made his presence known most tangibly. Indeed, the ark was thought to be the footstool of God's throne. The images of cherubim placed on the cover of the ark had their heads down because of God's intense glory that was imagined to be above them. This ark, the most potent symbol of God's presence at this time, goes along with the army into battle to represent his presence as warrior with them.

As a matter of fact, the march in the wilderness is described in military terms in the book of Numbers. Numbers 1 provides a military registration counting only "men twenty years old or more who were able to serve in the army" (1:20, 22, 24, etc.). The description of the wilderness camp also matches that of an ancient Near Eastern war camp, with the war leader's tent (God's tabernacle) in the middle, his personal bodyguards (the Levites) camped around the tent, and the rest of the army camped to the north, south, west, and east of his tent (Num. 2). To confirm the idea that Israel in the wilderness is presented as an army on the march, we note that whenever Moses breaks camp, he announces, "Rise up, LORD! May your enemies be scattered; may your foes flee before you" (Num. 10:35).[63]

God's presence with the army renders the battlefield holy space, and thus the army has to be as spiritually prepared to go to war as they would be to enter the tabernacle or, later, the temple. No wonder, then, that the Israelites are circumcised and observe Passover before they fight against Jericho (Josh. 5:2–12). Circumcision, of course, is a dangerous procedure when done in the vicinity of an enemy, since it puts a warrior in a weakened and vulnerable physical state.[64] However, the Israelites realize that it would be more dangerous to go into battle uncircumcised than to risk attack in the aftermath of the procedure.

Even Uriah the Hittite recognizes the need to be in a pristine spiritual state to go into the presence of God on the battlefield. While David is breaking the major commandments (adultery and eventually murder), Uriah will not sleep with his wife, because he realizes that an emission of semen would render him unclean ("How could I go to my house to eat and drink and make love to my wife? As surely as you live, I will not do such a thing!" [2 Sam. 11:11; see Lev. 15:16–18]).

From what we learn from 1 Samuel 13, it appears that it was also important to offer sacrifices before battle. Saul is ready to attack the Philistines, but Samuel the priest has not arrived to offer the requisite sacrifices and Saul's troops are beginning to grow afraid and desert. Saul panics and offers the sacrifices himself, bringing the ire of Samuel when he does show up at the camp.

63. In our survey above, we also saw that Jehoshaphat's march into battle against a coalition of nation-states to the east of Judah was like a religious procession.

64. As we learn from Gen. 34 when Levi and Simeon deceive the men of Shechem into getting circumcised and then slaughter them.

During the Battle

At first glance we might have sympathy for Saul, who offers the sacrifices only because of Samuel's tardiness.[65] But we need to remember that victory is achieved not by superior armies and weapons but rather by God's power. Indeed, the law of warfare in Deuteronomy specifically mentions that soldiers who are afraid should be encouraged to go home ("Is anyone afraid or faint-hearted? Let him go home so that his fellow soldiers will not become disheartened too" [Deut. 20:8]). Numbers don't matter, because God fights for Israel. They need to engage the enemy, but they are directed to do so in a way that makes it clear that it is God who wins the battle.

The story of Gideon is the classic example of this feature of divine warfare. Because of the sin of the Israelites, God allows the Midianites to make incursions into the land. But eventually the Israelites cry out to God, which is best taken as an acknowledgment that they need God and thus as an act of repentance. In response, as we see with previous episodes in the book of Judges (Othniel, Ehud, Deborah), God raises up a leader to free them from their oppressor.

An angel of the Lord, clearly to be understood as the Lord himself, comes and tells Gideon he will be with him to "strike down the Midianites" (Judg. 6:16). Gideon, however, is extremely reluctant and needs repeated assurances; he keeps asking God to respond to tests that he presents to him ("putting out the fleece"). Finally, after much convincing, Gideon gathers an army. The response is incredible, and thirty-two thousand men come to fight with Gideon. God, though, knows that if Gideon were to use an army of that size, the Israelites would claim, "My own strength has saved me" (Judg. 7:2), so God tells Gideon to send home those troops that are afraid (again referencing Deut. 20:8). But there are still too many—ten thousand!

65. As some commentators suggest, see Gunn, *Fate of King Saul*.

God then instructs Gideon to take the remaining troops down to the Wadi Harod and have them drink water from the brook. Some kneel down and drink, while three hundred get down and lap the water like dogs. God tells Gideon to go into battle with the three hundred men who lapped (Judg. 7:4–6). While some past commentators have sought to detect some quality in the dog-lappers that made them better soldiers, the point is that God is paring down the army to a size that will make it clear that if they win the battle with such a vastly undersized army—which, of course, they do—it would show God's hand in the victory.

Of the other examples I could provide, I will briefly mention a unique battle, a battle of champions, between David and Goliath. While Goliath is a well-armored and well-armed soldier of incredible size and great experience (1 Sam. 17:4–8), David at this point in the narrative is an inexperienced youth who is not even in the army but is in the camp to bring supplies to his older brothers. David articulates the heart of what we might call "holy-war theology"[66] just before he casts the stone from his sling and then cuts off Goliath's head:

> You come against me with sword and spear and javelin, but I come against you in the name of the LORD Almighty, the God of the armies of Israel, whom you have defied. This day the LORD will deliver you into my hands, and I'll strike you down and cut off your head. This very day I will give the carcasses of the Philistine army to the birds and the wild animals, and the whole world will know that there is a God in Israel. All those gathered here will know that it is not by sword or spear that the LORD saves; for the battle is the LORD's, and he will give all of you into our hands. (1 Sam. 17:45–47)

66. Many object to the use of "holy war," since it is never found in the Bible, preferring to speak of *herem* warfare or Yahweh war (see Chapman's excellent study "Martial Memory, Peaceable Vision"). However, since God's presence renders the battlefield holy space, I think the term is appropriate.

Before leaving the topic of the size of the army and the quality of the weapons, we should make two important observations. First, as we have seen, Israel does not need a superior force to win the battle, because God fights on their behalf. Second, God requires Israel to fight or at least to engage. I make this second point explicit because God doesn't really need Israel to win the battle. For example, God could have killed Goliath with a lightning bolt or by opening up the earth under his feet. Even so, God calls on his people to engage. Thus, these Old Testament battles are wonderful displays of the interaction between divine sovereignty and human responsibility.

AFTER THE BATTLE

If the battle is one in which Yahweh fights, then there is no doubt about the outcome, and the first reaction to victory is praise. In our survey we noted many examples of hymns of praise in the aftermath of victory, including the Song of the Sea (Exod. 15), the song celebrating Deborah's victory over the Midianites (Judg. 5), or the many psalms that praise God for victory (e.g., Pss. 24; 98). But it is the final act of war, at least when it comes to war within the promised land, that is the most disturbing. In Deuteronomy 20:16–18 we read: "However, in the cities of the nations the LORD your God is giving you as an inheritance, do not leave alive anything that breathes. Completely destroy them—the Hittites, Amorites, Canaanites, Perizzites, Hivites and Jebusites—as the LORD your God has commanded you. Otherwise, they will teach you to follow all the detestable things they do in worshiping their gods, and you will sin against the LORD your God." The verb translated "completely destroy" is a form of *haram*, from which we get the noun *herem*, variously translated as "annihilation," "complete destruction," or "the ban." This feature of warfare within the land is so distinctive that sometimes this type of warfare is identified by scholars as *herem* warfare.

No matter what you call it, and no matter that it does not seem to be consistently applied, modern audiences are often struck by the apparent brutality of episodes like the aftermath of the battle of Jericho, where we read, "They *devoted* the city *to the* LORD [from the verb *haram*] and destroyed with the sword every living thing in it—men and women, young and old, cattle, sheep and donkeys" (Josh. 6:21; italics mine). It is in particular the *herem* that will be the focus of our attention in our later ethical reflections.

Phase Two: God Fights Israel

In our survey, we observed that God fought not only foreign enemies on behalf of Israel (phase one) but also Israel itself when they disobeyed God. Here we look at three examples where God as divine warrior judged Israel.

After the dramatic victory over Jericho, Joshua sends troops to defeat a small town in the central hill country of Judah (Josh. 7–8). This town's name is Ai, which in Hebrew means "Ruin," giving us the impression that it's not much of a place, especially when contrasted with Jericho, whose walls have just fallen to Israel. Even so, when the troops go to Ai, they are soundly defeated and thirty-six Israelite soldiers are killed. When the report comes to Joshua, he is beside himself with grief and confusion. God then informs Joshua that "Israel has sinned; they have violated my covenant" (Josh. 7:11). As it turns out, an Israelite named Achan has broken the rules of *herem* warfare by stealing some of the plunder. When his crime is exposed, he is executed. Here we have an example of an Israelite acting like a Canaanite and thus being treated like one. His treatment contrasts with that of Rahab (Josh. 2), who is a Canaanite but acts like an Israelite and thus is treated like one. Once Achan dies, God allows the Israelites to take the city of Ai.

A second example of God allowing the enemies of the Israelites to defeat them comes in the early chapters of 1 Samuel during the time that Eli is judge and his two wicked sons, Hophni and

Phinehas, are leading the army against the Philistines (1 Sam. 4). In the first engagement, the Philistines soundly defeat the Israelites. On reflection, Hophni and Phinehas realize that they neglected to bring the ark of the covenant into the battle. The narrative clearly implies that these two reprehensible leaders are thinking of the ark as a magical box of some type. Thus, even though the ark accompanies the army the next day, the Philistines defeat Israel, kill Hophni and Phinehas, and cart off the ark to one of their main cities, Ashdod, placing it beside the statue of their chief god, Dagon. The next day, however, the statue has fallen on its face. The Philistines lift the statue back up, but the same thing happens again, only this time Dagon's "head and hands had been broken off and were lying on the threshold; only his body remained" (1 Sam. 5:4). Needless to say, this episode makes it clear that the Israelite battlefield loss is not the result of Yahweh's inability but his unwillingness to win the battle for faithless Israel.

The most terrifying example of God the warrior fighting against his people comes at the time of the Babylonian destruction of Jerusalem. Shockingly, God uses the pagan nation as the tool of his judgment against Judah. But it wasn't as if they weren't warned. God had sent his prophets to warn them that if they did not repent of their long-standing and pervasive idolatry and rebellion against God, the covenant curses would go into effect and God would allow them to be defeated by a foreign power. From Jeremiah's "temple sermon" (Jer. 7), it appears that the people of Judah put their trust not in God himself but in God's self-interest, since his temple is in the city. They reason that as long as the temple is there, God will protect it and they will not be touched, so they can sin as much as they want. Thus, according to Jeremiah, they are simply repeating the mantra "This is the temple of the LORD, the temple of the LORD, the temple of the LORD!" (Jer. 7:4) to reassure themselves that the hard work of repentance is not needed to keep them safe.

Perhaps they were conveniently misappropriating what today we call "Zion theology," expressed, among other places, in the book of Psalms:

> God is our refuge and strength,
>   an ever-present help in trouble.
> Therefore we will not fear, though the earth give way
>   and the mountains fall into the heart of the sea,
> though its waters roar and foam
>   and the mountains quake with their surging.
>
> There is a river whose streams make glad the city of God,
>   the holy place where the Most High dwells.
> God is within her, she will not fall;
>   God will help her at break of day.
> Nations are in uproar, kingdoms fall;
>   he lifts his voice, the earth melts. (46:1–6)
>
> Great is the LORD, and most worthy of praise,
>   in the city of our God, his holy mountain.
>
> Beautiful in its loftiness,
>   the joy of the whole earth,
> like the heights of Zaphon is Mount Zion,
>   the city of the Great King.
> God is in her citadels;
>   he has shown himself to be her fortress.
> . . . .
> As we have heard,
>   so we have seen
> in the city of the LORD Almighty,
>   in the city of our God:
> God makes her secure
>   forever. (48:1–3, 8)

These Zion-theology passages in the Old Testament presuppose a faithful Israel. God does not fight for Israel "right or wrong" but will fight against them to punish them when they turn against him. Thus, Ezekiel reports that, contrary to the people's expectation, God abandons the temple in anticipation of the fall of Jerusalem. We can chart the progress of the glory of God as he moves from his throne in the holy of holies to the threshold of the temple (9:3), progresses to the courtyard where he meets the cherubim and mounts his divine war chariot (10:18), stops momentarily at the east gate of the temple (10:19), and is last seen heading east (toward Babylon?) above the Mount of Olives (11:23).

The next time we see God is at the head of the Babylonian army, which he uses as a tool of his anger. We have already cited Jeremiah 21:5, where God announces, "I myself will fight against you with an outstretched hand and a mighty arm in furious anger and in great wrath." But the Babylonians were his agents. Later Jeremiah quotes God as reflecting back on the destruction of Jerusalem and addressing the Babylonians:

> You were my mace,
> a weapon of war.
> With you I crushed nations,
> struck kingdoms down,
> with you crushed horse and rider,
> with you crushed chariot and charioteer,
> with you crushed man and woman,
> with you crushed old man and young,
> with you crushed young man and girl,
>
> with you crushed shepherd and flock,
> with you crushed ploughman and team,
> with you crushed governors and magistrates. (Jer. 51:20–23 NJB)[67]

67. Translators differ over the English tense used to render this section. Some translate present tense and believe the reference is to the nation that God will use to punish Babylon. I agree with the NJB, which takes it as a reference back to God's use of Babylon to destroy Jerusalem (Longman, *Jeremiah, Lamentations*, 312–13).

The passages that inform our understanding of phase two are an important reminder that God's actions as warrior are strictly intertwined with his judgment on sin, no matter who the sinner is. Even so, we see that God's judgment on his sinful people is not the note on which the Old Testament ends. Thus, we turn to what we call "phase three" to complete our picture of the warfare theme in anticipation of the New Testament.

Phase Three: God Will Come and Fight Israel's Oppressors

As we surveyed the Prophets and the apocalyptic books of the Old Testament, particularly those written during the exilic and postexilic period, we observed that they were announcing the good news that God would come again as warrior. During this period, Israel was under the oppressive hand of a foreign ruler. They were incorporated in turn by the Babylonians, the Persians, and, beyond the time of the Old Testament, the Greeks and the Romans. Daniel, Zechariah, and Malachi spoke to this difficult period by encouraging God's people that the divine warrior would come in the future to rescue them.

In our earlier survey of the theme of God's violence in the Prophets, we looked at Daniel 7, which fits into our developing biblical theology of warfare at this point. To briefly recap, Daniel has a vision of four beasts emerging from a chaotic sea. These, we learn from the angelic interpretation in the second half of the chapter, represent evil human kingdoms that are oppressing the people of God. The second half of the vision describes how the divine warrior (the one like a son of man riding the clouds of heaven) will come in the future to deliver his people from the hands of their oppressors. Since we looked at this in more detail earlier, we will turn our attention to Zechariah and Malachi.

Zechariah

The prophet Zechariah was an important figure in the early postexilic period. His most urgent purpose was to encourage or even prod the returning exiles to get on with the reconstruction of the temple. After all, Cyrus the king of Persia had told the Jews that they could rebuild their temple in 539 BC (2 Chron. 36:23; Ezra 1:2–4), but when they returned, they encountered a number of problems that delayed their work (Ezra 3:8–4:5, 24; 5:1–6:22; Hag. 1:5–11; 2:15–19; Zech. 8:9–13). Zechariah's (and Haggai's) message was to get back to work (Ezra 5:1–20).

This present concern occupies Zechariah 1–8, but in the final chapters (chaps. 9–14) the prophet's attention turns to a distant future, and the text includes eschatological and apocalyptic imagery. Zechariah 14 speaks of a future "day of the LORD" (14:1). When we examine the use of this phrase throughout the Prophets (Isa. 13:6, 9; Joel 1:15; 2:1, 11; Amos 5:8–20; Zeph. 1:7–8), it appears that it always refers to a future day of divine battle.[68]

The prophet then draws a picture of Jerusalem under siege from "all the nations" (14:2). But just when it looks like the battle is lost, "the LORD will go out and fight against those nations, as he fights on the day of battle" (14:3). In that future day there will be cosmic disruptions (earthquakes, loss of the distinction between day and night, water flowing from Jerusalem), disease, and destruction. But God, leading his "holy ones" (his angelic army; see 14:5), will prevail, and as a result "the LORD will be king over the whole earth. On that day there will be one LORD, and his name the only name" (14:9).

MALACHI

In the English canon (based on the Septuagint), the book of Malachi is the last book of the Old Testament. As we will see, this position highlights a connection with the beginning of the gospel story that is relevant to our present topic.

We know very little about the man Malachi, so little that some scholars believe Malachi is not a personal name and should be

68. As argued early on by von Rad, "Day of Yahweh."

translated "my messenger."[69] Be that as it may, the only thing of which we are certain is that Malachi is a postexilic prophet, since not only has the temple been rebuilt but a sense of disillusionment has come over the community. It is possible that Malachi is the last prophetic voice heard during the Old Testament time period, an idea supported by the book's position as the last of the twelve Minor Prophets.

In the bulk of the book, Malachi confronts the community with their sin. In these prophetic oracles, Malachi presents five challenges to God's people. These challenges take the form of disputations, where God describes his character, points out the sins of his rebellious people, and then announces his judgment. Walter Kaiser lists five ethical principles violated by the Jewish people at the time that call for God's judgment: mixed marriages (Mal. 2:11–15), failure to tithe (3:8–10), failure to keep the Sabbath (2:8–9), priests who are corrupt (1:6–2:9), and various social problems (3:5).[70]

The end of the book, however, turns to a vision of a time to come (notice how 4:1 begins: "Surely the day is coming") that is hopeful for those who turn to God. Indeed, God will intervene and, while bringing judgment on the rebellious, will usher in a glorious future:

"Surely the day is coming; it will burn like a furnace. All the arrogant and every evildoer will be stubble, and the day that is coming will set them on fire," says the LORD Almighty. "Not a root or a branch will be left to them. But for you who revere my name, the sun of righteousness will rise with healing in its rays. And you will go out and frolic like well-fed calves. Then you will trample on the wicked; they will be ashes under the soles of your feet on the day when I act," says the LORD Almighty.

"Remember the law of my servant Moses, the decrees and laws I gave him at Horeb for all Israel.

69. Torrey, "Prophecy of Malachi," 1.
70. Kaiser, *Malachi*, 16.

"See, I will send the prophet Elijah to you before that great and dreadful day of the LORD comes. He will turn the hearts of the parents to their children, and the hearts of the children to their parents; or else I will come and strike the land with total destruction." (4:1–6)

Thus, the tone with which the Old Testament ends is one of expectation, an expectation of divine intervention in the midst of the continued oppression of the people of God. In one sense the exile ended in 539 BC with Cyrus's decree that the Jewish exiles could return to their homeland (2 Chron. 36:22–23; Ezra 1:2–4), but in another sense, as the angel Gabriel told Daniel, the exile continued well beyond this time (this is the gist of the prophecy of the "seventy 'sevens'" in Dan. 9:20–27) and into the New Testament times. Israel continued to live under the thumb of foreign oppressors as the Persians took the Babylonians' place; eventually the Greeks would take their place, and then the Romans.

Nevertheless, the hope expressed by Daniel, Zechariah, Malachi, and others burned on in the minds and hearts of the faithful. The "great and dreadful day of the LORD" would indeed come one day, a day of which the arrival of the prophet Elijah would be a harbinger (Mal. 4:5).

Phase Four: Jesus Fights Spiritual Powers and Authorities

As we turn our attention from the Old Testament to the New Testament, we should first be reminded that God's people living under the oppression of foreign powers yearned for a better day. The literature of the so-called intertestamental period expresses this desire as it continues the message of the Old Testament prophets who spoke of a future warring king.

It's against the background of this biblical and intertestamental expectation that we should read the words of John the Baptist, one of the first voices that we hear in the New Testament and the one that Jesus will later identify as "the Elijah who was to come" (Matt. 11:15; anticipated in Mal. 4:5). John is baptizing out in the wilderness and expecting one who will come after him "who is more powerful than I, whose sandals I am not worthy to carry" (Matt. 3:11). This one, John continues, "will baptize you with the Holy Spirit and fire. His winnowing fork is in his hand, and he will clear his threshing floor, gathering his wheat into the barn and burning up the chaff with unquenchable fire" (3:11–12). In short, his expectation of a Messiah who battles his enemies aligns with the Old Testament prophets.

Jesus comes out to the Jordan, and John baptizes him as the one for whom he was looking. John then is arrested and placed in jail, while Jesus begins his ministry. John hears reports about Jesus, who is healing the sick, exorcising demons, and preaching the good news. In jail John worries that he may have baptized the wrong person, so he sends his disciples to ask Jesus, "Are you the one who is to come, or should we expect someone else?" (Matt. 11:3). Jesus replies, "Go back and report to John what you hear and see: The blind receive sight, the lame walk, those who have leprosy are cleansed, the deaf hear, the dead are raised, and good news is proclaimed to the poor" (11:4–5).

What is Jesus saying to John? His later actions indicate that he is in essence saying, "John, I am the divine warrior. But I have heightened and intensified the war so that it is now directed not toward flesh and blood but toward the spiritual powers and authorities. This enemy will be defeated not by killing but by dying." As Timothy Gombis puts it, "God defeats the powers through the death and resurrection of Jesus Christ, which is a radically subversive way of doing things. The cross turns everything on its head—God wins by losing; the powers lose by winning. The powers' triumph over Christ on the cross was their own defeat, and Christ's defeat won him victory."[71]

71. Gombis, "Rhetoric of Divine Warfare," 93.

Indeed, when Jesus is arrested, Peter tries to defend him with a sword, cutting off the ear of the high priest's servant. Jesus rebukes him: "Put your sword back in its place, for all who draw the sword will die by the sword. Do you think I cannot call on my Father, and he will at once put at my disposal more than twelve legions of angels? But how then would the Scriptures be fulfilled that say it must happen in this way?" (Matt. 26:52–54).

As we read on, Scripture is fulfilled on the cross, where Jesus defeats Satan through his death and resurrection. Notice how Paul looks back on these redemptive events using military language in Colossians 2:13–15: "When you were dead in your sins and in the uncircumcision of your flesh, God made you alive with Christ. He forgave us all our sins, having canceled the charge of our legal indebtedness, which stood against us and condemned us; he has taken it away, nailing it to the cross. And having disarmed the powers and authorities, he made a public spectacle of them, triumphing over them by the cross." Or again, in reference to the ascension, Paul cites an Old Testament war psalm (Ps. 68):

This is why it says:

> "When he ascended on high,
>   he took many captives
>   and gave gifts to his people." (Eph. 4:8, quoting
>   Ps. 68:18)

Other examples could be given that use military language in reference to these great redemptive acts. God defeated Satan and the spiritual powers on the cross, but we soon come to understand that this great victory is an "already / not yet" rescue. More is to come.

Phase Five: Jesus Wins the Final Battle

Was John the Baptist wrong? When we left that story, we observed that while John announces a violent Messiah and points the finger at Jesus as the expected one, he is disoriented by the agenda of Jesus's earthly ministry.

But of course John, a bona fide prophet of God, was not wrong; he simply spoke better than he knew (see 1 Pet. 1:10–12). After all, "no prophecy of Scripture came about by the prophet's own interpretation of things. For the prophecy never had its origin in the human will, but prophets, though human, spoke from God as they were carried along by the Holy Spirit" (2 Pet. 1:20–21). John was simply not aware that his prophecy would be fulfilled in two stages. Christ would return again, and later Scripture describes this return as a violent judgment against evil people and evil powers. We are given just a glimpse of these future events, which are described in highly figurative language in the apocalyptic portions of the New Testament, particularly the "little apocalypses" of the Gospels (Matt. 24; Mark 13; Luke 21:5–38) and, most pointedly, the book of Revelation.

The Gospel apocalypses picture Jesus returning on a cloud, an obvious allusion to Daniel 7:13–14, a passage from what I have called "phase three" that looks forward to a victorious deliverer for God's people from their oppressive enemies: "At that time people will see the Son of Man coming in clouds with great power and glory. And he will send his angels and gather his elect from the four winds, from the ends of the earth to the ends of the heavens" (Mark 13:26–27). This picture derives from the Old Testament where God rides a cloud into battle (Pss. 68:4; 104:3–4; Isa. 19:1; Nah. 1:3) and ultimately from ancient storm-god imagery. In other words, this is not a white fluffy cloud but a storm cloud, God's war chariot.

This highly figurative depiction of Christ's return is complemented by a different image in Revelation 19:11–21. This passage begins with a description of Jesus riding a white horse, a depiction filled with miniquotations from and allusions to passages in Deuteronomy, Psalms, and Isaiah that refer to Yahweh the warrior:

I saw heaven standing open and there before me was a white horse, whose rider is called Faithful and True. With justice he judges and wages war. His eyes are like blazing fire, and on his head are many crowns. He has a name written on him that no one knows but he himself. He is dressed in a robe dipped in blood, and his name is the Word of God. The armies of heaven were following him, riding on white horses and dressed in fine linen, white and clean. Coming out of his mouth is a sharp sword with which to strike down the nations. "He will rule them with an iron scepter." He treads the winepress of the fury of the wrath of God Almighty. On his robe and on his thigh he has this name written:

KING OF KINGS AND LORD OF LORDS. (19:11–16)

This introduction to the appearance of Christ as a warrior is followed by an announcement and a description of the demise of the enemies of Jesus that makes the violent scenes of the Old Testament pale by comparison:

And I saw an angel standing in the sun, who cried in a loud voice to all the birds flying in midair, "Come, gather together for the great supper of God, so that you may eat the flesh of kings, generals, and the mighty, of horses and their riders, and the flesh of all people, free and slave, great and small."

Then I saw the beast and the kings of the earth and their armies gathered together to wage war against the rider on the horse and his army. But the beast was captured, and with it the false prophet who had performed the signs on its behalf. With these signs he had deluded those who had received the mark of the beast and worshiped its image. The two of them were thrown alive into the fiery lake of burning sulfur. The rest were killed with the sword coming out of the mouth of the rider on the horse, and all the birds gorged themselves on their flesh. (19:17–21)

Thus, the Bible ends with the celebratory note of God's victory in Christ over all evil. While the description is obviously figurative, metaphors point to a reality that is in keeping with their nature. These are images of a Jesus who is violent toward evil people and powers; he has come to judge them for their wicked actions.

Concluding Reflections

I have done my best to present the biblical material as I see it and to interact with some contrary viewpoints. Again, I appreciate and respect the various voices that grapple with this difficult issue, but in the end I find them unpersuasive for the reasons I have suggested (with a few more to come). But before leaving the vexed question of divine violence and moving on to our next controversial issue, I want to end with some final reflections on the theme of divine violence in Scripture as well as its continuing importance and relevance for us today.

The Coherence of the Biblical Account

When it comes to divine violence (as well as other topics), many people, scholars included, wrongly believe that the New Testament presents a different picture of God than the Old Testament does. God is angry and violent in the Old Testament, but Jesus is loving and peaceful in the New. It's almost as if God had a lobotomy, or at least anger counseling, in the intertestamental period. This disjunction lies behind the thinking of many of those with whom I have interacted above, and they then assert that we must evaluate the depiction of God in the Old Testament by the standard of Jesus in the New.

But there is no contrast between the Old and New Testaments. While we learn more about God and our relationship with him as we move to the New Testament, the development can be described by words like *progress*, *growth*, and *deepening* but not *correction*. We do not go off in a different direction, but rather we go further in the same direction.

If we want to follow Jesus and use him as a standard of our understanding of God, then let's begin with the fact that the Jesus we meet in the Gospels does not disown the Old Testament and its "violent" God but fully embraces the witness of the Old Testament. He does not retreat or distance himself from the Old Testament but cites it authoritatively in his debates with Jewish leaders who disagree with him. He does not believe that he has come to reveal and make present a different God than we encounter in the pages of the Old Testament, but believes rather that the Old Testament anticipates his coming. Indeed, he presents himself as the fulfillment of the Old Testament expectation of a violent Messiah, first of all bringing his warfare against spiritual powers and authorities and then, by his own testimony within the Gospel record, judging all evil as he speaks of his return on the divine war chariot (Matt. 24, etc.). To claim that the Old Testament picture of God is not the actual God goes against Jesus's own views of the matter as presented in the Gospels.

And then we must also insist that Jesus, the standard by which Seibert, Enns, and Boyd evaluate the rest of Scripture, is more than the Jesus of the Gospels. Conveniently for their purposes, they bracket or discount the Jesus of the apocalyptic portions of the New Testament. Jesus will return to render judgment, violent judgment, against all who resist him, spiritual powers as well as human sinners.

The five phases of God's warfare against evil show a coherence that is not recognized by those who want to divide the witness of the Old Testament from the New. There is not a dramatic shift between the Old and New Testaments but rather a progress of the fight against evil that heightens and intensifies and finally climaxes at the end of history.

Not Genocide or Ethnic Cleansing

While it certainly doesn't resolve all our ethical concerns, it is important to describe the biblical picture accurately. To label the *herem* warfare of the Old Testament as a matter of genocide or ethnic cleansing is not accurate and is simply a rhetorical flourish utilized by those who wish to paint the biblical picture as darkly as possible. The intention is to get an immediate and visceral emotional rise from the reader in order to discount the Bible or the Christian faith.

Earlier we quoted Paul Copan's insightful comment that this warfare is not a matter of ethnicity but rather a matter of sin. The connection between *herem* warfare and God's judgment will be developed below, but for now it is important to see that this battle is not between those who descended biologically from Abraham and those who did not but between those who follow Yahweh and those who do not. Granted, this distinction will not appease New Atheists like Richard Dawkins, but then this book, as I have mentioned, is not written for people like Dawkins.

By the time that Israel left Egypt, they were described as a mixed multitude in the sense that there were "foreigners" among them as well as "native-born" (Josh. 8:30–35). But even more importantly, as we consider the conquest, we also need to keep in mind that Canaanites weren't doomed simply by being Canaanites and Israelites weren't safe from judgment simply by being Israelites. I don't think we should underestimate the importance of the treatments of Rahab and her family on the one hand and Achan and his family on the other. We observed above that the Canaanite Rahab was spared because of her actions that showed her allegiance to Yahweh, and that the Israelite Achan died because his actions showed his betrayal of Yahweh.

We are not to think that Rahab is the only Canaanite to come over to Yahweh's side. While it is speculative and perhaps a bit of wishful thinking to imagine large parts of Canaanite society coming over to the Israelite side, there are a number of non-Israelite names in later Israelite history that may indicate that their numbers were not small. Among the most obvious are Caleb (the

Kenizzite), the judge Shamgar ben Anat (Anat being a Canaanite goddess), Uriah the Hittite, and perhaps even the people of the Canaanite city of Shechem as a whole,[72] and there may be many more whose names or identifiers do not make their Canaanite background obvious.

What about Us Today?

What are the implications of the biblical teaching, presented as five phases of warfare, for our lives today?

First, we need to always remember that we live in the period between the first and second comings of Christ (phase four), the period of spiritual warfare. Christians should never use physical violence to further the gospel or in the name of Christ.[73] In the light of biblical teaching, the Crusades were sinful. Shooting an abortion doctor is murder. The Bible proscribes such acts and any like them. In this I agree with Boyd and also push back on Enns's assumption that if it was all right during the Old Testament time period, then it is hard to say it's not all right now. For the Christian today, Paul tells us that our battle is against spiritual powers and the only weapons we can use are spiritual weapons: "Finally, be strong in the Lord and in his mighty power. Put on the full armor of God, so that you can take your stand against the devil's schemes. For our struggle is not against flesh and blood, but against the rulers, against the authorities, against the powers of this dark world and against the spiritual forces of evil in the heavenly realms" (Eph. 6:10–12; see also 6:13–20; 2 Cor. 10:1–6).

What this battle looks like on the ground is beyond the scope of this chapter, but we can be suggestive here. In one sense, life is a battle. The forces of evil manifest themselves in the actions of people, to be sure, but again we know that we don't fight with

72. Copan and Flannagan, *Genocide*, 72–74.
73. The issue of "just war" and whether a Christian can use violence in policing or the national military is a separate issue not addressed in this book.

physical weapons. However, we stand up against injustice, like when the powerful exploit the vulnerable. In addition, the New Testament describes evangelism in words that allude to battle (when a person becomes a Christian, the old person dies and the new person rises up to new life [Col. 2:11–12]). When a person becomes a Christian, they move from the realm of darkness to the realm of light, a victory against the spiritual powers and authorities. We must also remember that our battle is not just "out there" against others, fighting against injustice, but we also battle against sin that remains in our own hearts (Rom. 7:7–25).[74] But then how do we understand the continuing significance of the violence of the past (phases one and two) and of the future (phase five)?

Preview and Warning of the Final Judgment

We can see the connection between the two Testaments particularly in the way that the judgment at the end of history (phase five) relates to the physical warfare of the Old Testament (phases one and two). The wars of the Old Testament and the end-time judgment are acts of divine judgment against evil. Indeed, we are to think that Joshua's battles are a preview and a warning of the final judgment.

Let's take the conquest of Canaan as an example. According to the Bible, these wars are not intended to simply make room for Israel to live. They are considered an act of God's judgment against sin. According to the biblical testimony, God uses the Israelites as a tool of his judgment because of the extensive and long-standing sin of the Canaanites. We should remember the words God speaks to Abraham concerning the promised land. He says that Abraham's descendants will eventually live in the land, but not now or in the near future; rather they will do so when "the sin of the Amorites . . . [reaches] its full measure" (Gen. 15:16). That the author of Hebrews understood the conquest as judgment for disobedience/

74. For more on this, see Allender and Longman, *Bold Love*, chap. 5, "Our Divine Warrior: Hope for Triumph in Battle."

unbelief is clear in the statement "By faith the prostitute Rahab, because she welcomed the spies, was not killed with those who were disobedient" (11:31).

In terms of phase two we have seen that the Israelites did not receive carte blanche but themselves became the objects of God's violent judgment when they rebelled against God. This too demonstrates that there is a connection between God's acts of violence toward people and his judgment on their sin.

To understand the relationship between the Old and the New Testaments, and particularly the acts of divine violence in the Old Testament and in the New Testament description of the final judgment, Meredith Kline introduced the concept of intrusion.[75] Using the language of traditional systematic theology, he argued that events like the conquest and the Babylonian destruction of Jerusalem were intrusions of end-time ethics into the period of common grace. The period of common grace is the normal condition of the historical period between the fall and the consummation. During this time there is no strict delineation between God's people and those who rebel against him. Sometimes wicked people prosper and righteous people suffer. But at the end of history, after the return of Christ, a new situation arises. In biblical metaphorical language the wheat is separated from the chaff or, to use another metaphor, the sheep are separated from the goats (Matt. 25:31–33; Luke 3:17). Kline's point is that the conquest and other acts of God's judgment during the historical period are instances when God, for his good purposes, introduces conditions that anticipate the end times. They serve as a preview and thus as a warning to others.

Serving the Interests of Justice

Social justice is a big issue in the church today, especially among our youth, as I have seen in the college students I have taught over

75. Kline, "The Intrusion and the Decalogue."

the past few decades. Such passion is certainly appropriate and in keeping with the Bible, particularly as we hear the prophets call for just treatment of the vulnerable and the oppressed.

I imagine most (though not all) of my readers are native English speakers living in North America, England, New Zealand, or Australia. I also imagine that most of my readers, like me, do not live in the type of oppressive environment that the people of God lived in during the biblical period. I don't raise this issue because we lack issues of justice in our societies. But I hazard to say that most of my readers, and again I include myself, do not live under daily threat of torture, extreme mistreatment, and death, as did many of the people to whom the biblical text was first addressed.

I wonder whether our generally comfortable setting obscures our appreciation for the picture of God who comes in and "sets things right" for his oppressed people—not just helping them but bringing justice on the heads of the perpetrators who have so exploited them. I imagine that those who are deeply troubled by the God depicted in Scripture live lives fairly distant from the type of incredible mistreatment faced not only by the ancient biblical people of God but also by Christians today who, for instance, live in ISIS-dominated territories in the Middle East. This point is well made by Craig Koester in his writing on the book of Revelation: "Some modern readers are bothered by the martyrs' cry for justice, arguing that it does not measure up to the standard of turning the other cheek and loving one's enemies, as Jesus taught; but the plea for justice cannot be easily dismissed. The martyrs suffered not because they were sinners but because they were faithful. One rightly asks: Does God care? Does genuine love turn a blind eye while the wicked shed the blood of the innocent? Or is mercy another name for indifference?"[76]

But it's not just the book of Revelation or the apocalyptic portions of the Gospels. This passion for justice may be heard in Paul's

76. Koester, *Revelation*, 87.

encouragement to the suffering Christians who lived in Thessa-
lonica. After he tells them that they are suffering for the kingdom
of God, he reminds them,

> God is just: He will pay back trouble to those who trouble you
> and give relief to you who are troubled, and to us as well. This
> will happen when the Lord Jesus is revealed from heaven in blaz-
> ing fire with his powerful angels. He will punish those who do not
> know God and do not obey the gospel of our Lord Jesus. They
> will be punished with everlasting destruction and shut out from
> the presence of the Lord and from the glory of his might on the
> day he comes to be glorified in his holy people and to be marveled
> at among all those who have believed. This includes you, because
> you believed our testimony to you. (2 Thess. 1:6–10)

Robert Miller well argues that the frequent pictures of God
slaying a dragon figure in the Bible (one manifestation of the
divine-warrior theme) demonstrate that evil is a formidable force
against which God brings violent judgment. He speaks of how
"apocalyptic cosmic imagery is a deep engagement with human
suffering" at the hands of evil. He goes on to say that this is "why
the Bible does not reduce Leviathan (a dragon figure) to a guppy."[77]
Evil is powerful; its effects are catastrophic. Indeed, the dragon
slayer often experiences an initial defeat. But the final outcome is
always the same, and it is very reassuring to suffering people—the
dragon slayer will have the ultimate victory.

I conclude this section with a lengthy but important quota-
tion from Miroslav Volf, a theologian at Yale Divinity School,
who powerfully reflects on divine violence in the light of his own
experience in his native Croatia:

> I used to think that wrath was unworthy of God. Isn't God love?
> Shouldn't divine love be beyond wrath? God is love, and God
> loves every person and every creature. That's exactly why God

77. Miller, *Dragon*, 293.

is wrathful against some of them. My last resistance to the idea
of God's wrath was a casualty of the war in the former Yugosla-
via, the region from which I come. According to some estimates,
200,000 people were killed and over 3,000,000 were displaced. My
villages and cities were destroyed, my people shelled day in and
day out, some of them brutalized beyond imagination, and I could
not imagine God not being angry. Or think of Rwanda in the last
decade of the past century, where 800,000 people were hacked to
death in one hundred days! How did God react to the carnage? By
doting on the perpetrators in a grandfatherly fashion? By refusing
to condemn the bloodbath but instead affirming the perpetrators'
basic goodness? Wasn't God fiercely angry with them? Though I
used to complain about the indecency of the idea of God's wrath, I
came to think that I would have to rebel against a God who wasn't
wrathful at the sight of the world's evil. God isn't wrathful in spite
of being love. God is wrathful because God is love.[78]

The Death of "Innocents"

Let me continue with a confession. I don't want to give the impression that I have everything worked out in my own thinking and
heart. I still have a sense of unease when I think about the death
of children in the conquest. And I ask myself questions like, Why
does the entire family of Achan suffer the consequences of Achan's
sin? Were they complicit? Perhaps they were. They certainly must
have known that the illicit plunder was buried under their tent. But
can we be sure? And we can raise other questions as well.

I guess I too am a twenty-first-century Westerner. But my unease does not lead me to disown the Old Testament and its pervasive and consistent testimony of God's judgments. Nor does it
lead me to disown the picture in the book of Revelation of God's
future judgment. In the final analysis, like Job in the face of his
own suffering, we have to bow in silence before the wisdom and

78. Volf, *Free of Charge*, 138–39, cited in Copan, *Is God a Moral Monster?*,
192, who also cites Volf, *Exclusion and Embrace*.

power of the Creator, who gives life and takes it away. Job never learns why he suffered, and if he did, the answer probably would not have comforted him. God's response to Job's questions and his accusation that God was unjust was not to answer him but to assert his wisdom and power.

Of course, such a response is not very appealing to modern and postmodern audiences, and I am sure it wasn't to Job either. However, we have a choice when we can't have all our questions answered: reject God or at least try to remake him in the image of our own preferences, or bow before the mystery of God's ways.

A Final and Personal Word

As I read Boyd, Seibert, and Enns, I have the impression that they are concerned to make the Bible and its message more acceptable to a twenty-first-century Western audience. They believe that the Bible's depiction of divine violence is an obstacle to people who might be attracted to a more positive message. Of course, this attitude can be observed in the recent treatment of many other theological topics as well. Some, for example, question the traditional teaching on hell, opting for a view that denies conscious pain to nonbelievers (conditional immortality or annihilationism) or even the view that everyone gets to heaven eventually.[79]

I, though, question whether such rereadings of traditional interpretations, which I believe are wrong, are helpful in this way. Indeed, my own experience belies such a view. As I was growing up, my family attended a church that, to put it mildly, did not take the Bible seriously.[80] It was more like a community country club. Not very challenging. God was pretty much a friendly, benign person. Thus, at this point I didn't take the Bible or my faith very

79. Bell, *Love Wins*.
80. See the beginning of chap. 2 for the story of my becoming a member of this church.

seriously, and there was really no significant difference between my view of the world and my behavior and those of anyone else.

Then a friend gave me a book that was breaking sales records in the late 1960s and early '70s, *The Late Great Planet Earth*, by Hal Lindsey. Now today I would not endorse the interpretation provided by this book. It treats the highly metaphoric language of the apocalyptic portions of the Bible in a quasi-literal way. The author was reading the contemporary political situation into the polyvalent imagery to make it look like the Bible predicted that Jesus would come again in the next few years. Time has certainly revealed that his interpretation (like all such mistaken attempts to read the Bible as giving a timetable for Christ's second coming) was in error.[81] That said, Lindsey certainly got the main message right. The Bible, especially apocalyptic books like Revelation, teaches that Jesus is coming again and that he is coming to rescue his people and to judge those who resist him. That certainly came across in Lindsey's book, and as I read the book, I knew I was on the wrong side of that divide. In other words, the Bible's message of divine judgment was the catalyst that God used to bring me into a relationship with him.

The point I am making with this personal anecdote is simply that attempts to soften the Bible's message on judgment do nothing to promote the Bible's message to people today. We don't get to make God in our image; we must understand God in the way he reveals himself to us in his Word.

DISCUSSION QUESTIONS

1. Where do you see God acting violently in the Old Testament? In the New Testament?

81. For help in interpreting biblical apocalyptic, see Longman, *Reading the Bible*, 213–26.

2. Who is the object of God's violence in the Old Testament? In the New Testament?

3. Are you surprised by how frequently references to God's violence occur in the Old Testament?

4. A number of scholars want to make a distinction between how God is depicted in the Bible and the actual God. Do you think that is a helpful distinction? Under what circumstances?

5. Marcion was a second-century thinker who believed that the Old Testament and the violent parts of the New Testament should not be part of the canon for Christians. His views were condemned by the orthodox church. Is it fair to make a comparison between Marcion and those scholars who find the Old Testament picture of God's violence unacceptable? Why or why not?

6. The hardest part to understand about divine violence in the Old Testament concerns the death of women and children. What do you think about that?

7. According to the discussion in this chapter, we are involved in a spiritual battle. Does life seem like a battle to you? In what way? How do you fight that battle?

8. In this chapter, I developed the idea that the conquest was an "intrusion" of end-time ethics into the period of common grace. What does that mean to you? How do you imagine the second coming of Christ and the final judgment?

9. Can there be justice if evil people are not judged?

10. When it comes to divine violence, does it help to imagine your own struggle with sin as a battle that God wages alongside you?

4

Sexuality

Is Homosexual Practice Affirmed?

We come now to the final and by far the most difficult controversial issue of all—sexuality, particularly homosexuality. What
makes this topic difficult is not arriving at a clear understanding
of what the Bible teaches (as I hope to demonstrate). In spite of
efforts to obscure the issue (with which we will interact later), the
biblical teaching is quite clear. How else can we explain the virtual
consensus of the church universal for the past two millennia—at
least until about twenty or thirty years ago?[1] For that matter, how
else can we explain the continued broad-based agreement in the
church today?

The clarity with which the Bible prohibits homosexual activity
is often lost on many modern Western Christians, particularly

1. David Gushee acknowledges this even as he argues for a nontraditional
view: "Yes, it is true that until very recently the Christian church in all of its
major branches included as part of its two-thousand-year-old sexual morality
a rejection of the moral legitimacy of sexual acts between persons of the same
sex" (*Changing Our Mind*, 9).

those outside evangelical Protestant and Catholic circles where the traditional teaching continues with some exceptions. In mainstream Protestant denominations it seems like the "affirming" view (to be explained below) has definitively won the day. Although this is the case in the West, the same is not true in the global church, particularly in the Global South, as illustrated by the tensions between various members of the Anglican Communion. While churches in the West and some others, like Brazil, show openness and affirm membership for sexually active gay men and women or even same-sex civil relationships or marriage among clergy, the large Anglican churches in places like Africa strongly object to these changes to the traditional understanding of marriage.[2] In 2016 the American Episcopal Church was even suspended by the Anglican Communion for its views on sexuality.

It is not the biblical material that makes this a difficult topic. What makes it difficult is that we all have friends and relatives and others who are same-sex attracted, and we, or at least I, wish we could tell them that acting on their desires to have an intimate relationship with someone of their own gender is OK. And it is particularly difficult for someone like me who does not share their affection and desire for the same sex to write about this topic. I am happily married to someone I deeply love (with all its ups and downs), and it seems almost cruel for me to say to someone else that they can't have the same experience of marriage with someone of the same gender. For this reason, I think the most powerful writings on this topic come from Christians who are same-sex attracted but who have decided to live according to what they (in my opinion, rightly) perceive to be the celibate life that God calls them to, no matter how difficult. As the reader will see, I have been deeply influenced by the works of Wesley Hill, Rosaria Butterfield, Sam Allberry, and Ed Shaw.[3]

2. Jenkins, *Next Christendom*, 198–202.
3. Hill, *Washed and Waiting*; Butterfield, *Openness Unhindered*; Allberry, *Is God Anti-Gay?*; Shaw, *Same-Sex Attraction*.

There have been many times that I have considered not including this chapter in the book, partly—to be honest—for self-preservation. I know that what I say in this chapter will lead some to think I am a bigot. No matter the strength of the presentation of the biblical material, the charge will be that I hate gays. Nothing could be further from the truth. I do think that the church needs to repent of its attitude toward the LGBTQ community, and those of us who are heterosexual Christians need to think about how we can love our Christian brothers and sisters who are same-sex attracted.

The difficulty of the deep divisions surrounding this issue is probably due more to the church's attitudes than to anything else. Many have singled out and stigmatized homosexual sin and even desire. Christian parents sin against their gay children by kicking them out of the house, and Christian congregations abdicate their mission when they ostracize gay people who come to their church. While I do believe that our media, for all the great coverage, has a tendency to focus on the worst of us (think Westboro Baptist Church), we all bear the blame for the present situation. And a large part of that is our refusal to acknowledge that we are all in the same boat. Even if I don't share the same struggle with same-sex attraction, I certainly experience sexual brokenness in my own life. Indeed, that is something that we can say is true of 100 percent of us. All of us experience struggles, loneliness, and unfulfilled desires. That is what it means to be sinful people.

Todd Wilson points out that there are "alarmingly high rates of premarital sex, increasing cohabitation, adultery, divorce, out-of-wedlock births, dysfunctional sexual relations between spouses, the hook-up culture on college campuses, sexual abuse, and of course pornography."[4] At the time I am writing this, every day brings new names of powerful men in government, entertainment, news media, and, sadly, the church who have harassed or assaulted women in the workplace.

4. Wilson, *Mere Sexuality*, 32.

Even though I often considered avoiding this question (and may still come to regret addressing it), I ultimately came to the conclusion that that would be the height of cowardice. This book is about controversial subjects in the Old Testament, and in particular those controversial subjects where there has been a tendency in recent days to move away from a traditional understanding of biblical texts even among people who identify as evangelicals. Some in the evangelical community, scholars and thought leaders among them, think the time has come to reconsider the church's long-standing position on homosexual practice. This seems obvious to most—particularly those who are under thirty years old. Other Christian scholars and thought leaders have changed their minds on this topic.[5] As I suggested in the chapter on creation/evolution, there may at times be good reasons to overthrow traditional understandings. But that is not always the case, and I don't think it is the case here.

Even though the brunt of the controversy has to do with homosexuality, we must place this specific topic within the context of the topic of sexuality in the Bible. Thus, we turn now to a brief presentation of the biblical theology of sexuality.

The Biblical Theology of Sexuality

Gender and sex are major issues in the biblical story, just as they are a major part of the human experience. It is therefore no surprise that the topic reverberates throughout Scripture, beginning with creation and continuing through the rest of the biblical text.

Creation

In chapter 1 we gave specific attention to Genesis 1–3, noting that it is theological history, in which real events are depicted in

5. Gushee (*Changing Our Mind*) is an example, though he has recently announced that he no longer considers himself an evangelical.

largely figurative language. The story is told in such a way as to shape our worldview and provide a foundation to the rest of the biblical story.

The two creation accounts (Gen. 1:1–2:4a; 2:4b–25) tell us that God created the world and how he intended things to be. In this section, we will focus on what we learn about gender and sexual relationships among human beings. In the next section, we will consider the message of Genesis 3, which describes not how God intended the world to be but how it actually is. We will see that our present experience resonates with the message of Genesis 3 and that Genesis 1–2 describes the world as we can only imagine it and hope it to be (and as we will one day see).

As we have already insisted,[6] we must read Genesis 1–2 in its original "cognitive environment"—that is, in its ancient Near Eastern setting. When we do, we notice something that is unique: God himself is neither gendered nor sexually active. A modern Christian reader might not feel the impact of this revelation of the nature of God, but we must realize that Yahweh, the God of Israel, was the only deity so understood in the ancient Near East. All the other numerous gods and goddesses were either male or female and were often sexually involved. To put it pointedly, from the Bible's perspective, gender and sex are part of the creation, not the Creator.

That God is not sexually active is obvious from the text, but that he is neither male nor female needs some explanation. Our primary indication of this point is Genesis 1:27:

> So God created mankind in his own image,
>   in the image of God he created them;
>   male and female he created them.

The best understanding of what it means to be created in the image of God is that humans represent God (like an image/statue

6. See "It's More Complicated Than That" in chap. 1.

of a king or even, as recently suggested, a statue of a god)[7] and reflect who he is in the creation.[8] And here we learn in very clear language that this status (along with the mandate "Be fruitful . . . ; fill the earth and subdue it. Rule over . . ." [Gen. 1:28]) belongs to both men and women. Both men and women reflect who God is, and therefore male (king, warrior, husband, etc.) and female (mother, woman, teacher [Woman Wisdom], etc.) metaphors are used throughout Scripture to reveal the nature of God.

Thus, when we speak of gender and sexual activity, we speak of God's intention for his creation. The first emphasis we must highlight is the persistent teaching that men and women are equal to each other. According to the first creation story, both are created in the image of God, and in the second we learn that the woman was created from Adam's side/rib, thus emphasizing equality. Yes, she is his "helper" (Gen. 2:20, 'ezer), but since God is frequently said to be Israel's "helper" (Pss. 33:20; 89:18–19; see also Deut. 33:29), this term does not denote subordination.

That Genesis 2 also introduces us to marriage is also critical to our present topic. God created the woman to answer the problem of the man's loneliness (2:18). While this fact should not lead us to the conclusion that only a spouse can provide a solution to loneliness (and in any case we need to take into account Genesis 3 when we speak about the present experience of loneliness), it is clear that the creation of the woman and then the union of the man and the woman are the divine response to human loneliness in the garden.

This union, rightly taken as the biblical conception of marriage, is defined as follows: "A man leaves his father and mother and is united to his wife, and they become one flesh" (Gen. 2:24). The psychologist Dan Allender and I have developed the significance

7. C. L. McDowell, *"Image of God" in Eden.*
8. See "Humans in Genesis 1–3" in chap. 1.

of this threefold definition of marriage elsewhere,[9] but, briefly, we see that it involves a leaving of one's parents to form a new primary loyalty with one's spouse, a growing together of the two persons (perhaps through common experience and conversation), and sexual intimacy.

The final verse of Genesis 2 is pivotal to our understanding of God's intention for male-female marital relationships in creation. "Adam and his wife were both naked, and they felt no shame" (2:25). This statement indicates more than their willingness to be physically open and vulnerable to each other; it implies an emotional, psychological, and spiritual union that is untroubled.

Fall

The harmony created by God at creation and depicted in Genesis 1 and especially 2 falls rapidly apart in Genesis 3. In Genesis 2 the man is commanded to "work" the garden and "take care" of it. As many recognize, the verb *shamar*, translated "take care," is more naturally translated "guard." Perhaps the reason the translators don't opt for that obvious rendering is that in Genesis 2 there is nothing or nobody against whom the garden would need guarding. But then in 3:1 we hear about the walking "serpent," an ancient Near Eastern symbol for evil. We don't get the backstory on this figure, but we now realize that there is a reason to guard the garden and see that Adam and Eve fail miserably at this task.

We also learn in Genesis 2 that there is one command that humanity needs to observe, the prohibition of eating the fruit from the tree of the knowledge of good and evil (2:16–17). What is at stake with the prohibition? Certainly eating from the tree would not give them access to new knowledge in the sense of intellectual comprehension. They already know what is good and evil. It is wrong to eat of the tree. The significance of the tree and therefore

9. Allender and Longman, *Intimate Allies*, and Allender and Longman, *Intimate Mystery of Marriage*.

the act of eating is that it would lead to the experience (the doing) of evil. And Eve, after a futile attempt to defend God from ridicule as if he had commanded them not to eat from any tree, and Adam, who does not even say anything before eating, commit evil by disregarding God's prerogative to define what is good and evil and instead arrogate that right to themselves. The results are disastrous.

Most fundamentally, the rebellion of humanity destroys the harmony between God and his human creatures. This rupture has significance for the relationships between humans and also between humans and creation. For our purposes, we will look more closely at the implications of sin for our sexual relationships.

The fact that sin does trouble the relationship between the genders and sexuality is signaled in two obvious ways. The first is that Adam and Eve hide from each other and cover their bodies. At the end of chapter 2 they are naked and unashamed; now they can no longer endure such open vulnerability—not just physical but also emotional, psychological, and spiritual vulnerability. Second, the implications of sin for sexual relationships come through in the announcement of punishment on the woman, and in particular in the second part, where God announces, "Your desire will be for your husband, and he will rule over you" (Gen. 3:16). Even with this translation we can see how what was a harmonious relationship will become tumultuous. But this verse, as translated by the NIV, could lead to the mistaken impression that while the woman reaches out to the man with romantic desire, he responds to these overtures with force and domination. Such a picture does not conform to human experience and is not the correct understanding of the verse.

The word *desire* (*teshuqah*) is a rare one and occurs only two other times in the Old Testament (Gen. 4:7; Song 7:10). The most helpful occurrence is in Genesis 4, where God tells Cain that sin is crouching at his door and desires to have him. Now obviously personified sin is not waiting for the opportunity for healthy intimacy with Cain but rather desires to dominate him. Thus, the

NLT gets Genesis 3:16 right: "And you will desire to control your husband, but he will rule over you."

Therefore, we learn from Genesis 3 that the troubles we experience in the area of gender and sexuality are the result of sin. Let me be clear here; our particular sexual dysfunction, whatever it is (and we are all sexually dysfunctional at some level), is not necessarily the result of our own personal sin (though it can be if we act on our sinful sexual impulses, and we all do at some point). But it is the result of the fact that human sin disrupts the way God made us.

Fortunately, the story does not end with Genesis 3. God does not give up on his human creatures even though they have rebelled against him. The rest of the Bible is the story of God's passionate pursuit of reconciliation. But how does our sexuality fit into the story of redemption?

The Already / Not Yet Redemption of Our Sexual Lives

At the end of Genesis 2, the man and the woman are in the garden naked but unashamed. They are living in harmony in every aspect of their being—emotional, spiritual, psychological, and physical. However, in Genesis 3, in the aftermath of their rebellion and resultant guilt, they hide from each other. Their alienation is partially ameliorated by covering themselves. God shows his continued interest in relationship with them by providing them with clothing.

Sin results in struggle in every area of life. The message is that all God's human creatures will now live broken lives, including in their sexual experiences. No person can point at another in derision or pity because of their disturbed sexual desires and, like a Pharisee, say, "Thank God I am not like that!"[10]

That said, a picture of the restoration, at least the "already / not yet" restoration, of our sexuality comes from a surprising

10. The allusion is to Luke 18:11–12.

place—the Song of Songs. Many people wonder what in the world the Song is doing in the canon, but such a reaction can only come about by what I would call a hangover from the Neoplatonic influence of the Middle Ages—specifically, the idea that a human being is an embodied soul and that God only cares about our souls and not our bodies. This perspective gave rise to a celibate priesthood, monasticism, and the idea that angels as spiritual beings are asexual (more on this below).

But the Song of Songs, an anthology of love poems,[11] is first and foremost a celebration of sexuality.[12] A man and a woman are again in garden settings and enjoying physical intimacy. Reading this book in the context of the canon, we cannot help but take our minds back to the garden of Eden and be reminded of a better time, when harmony existed between the first inhabitants. However, the Song of Songs is not a naive book claiming that Edenic harmony is at hand to sinful humanity. A number of poems remind the reader that such intimacy is rarely achieved, and then only through struggle.[13]

The poem found in 5:2–6:3 begins with the man approaching the woman, desiring intimacy. The woman describes his approach:

> I slept but my heart was awake.
>> Listen! My beloved is knocking:
> "Open to me, my sister, my darling,
>> my dove, my flawless one.
> My head is drenched with dew,
>> my hair with the dampness of the night." (5:2)

But rather than opening the door to him (an obvious poetic sexual euphemism), she rebuffs him:

11. See Longman, *Song of Songs*, 48–49.
12. I was first introduced to this idea through the insightful writings of Phyllis Trible; see *God and the Rhetoric of Sexuality*.
13. Here the work of Schwab (*Cautionary Message*) is most helpful.

> I have taken off my robe—
>> must I put it on again?
> I have washed my feet—
>> must I soil them again? (5:3)

The man makes another attempt to approach her, and she ultimately responds:

> My beloved thrust his hand through the latch-opening;
>> my heart began to pound for him.
> I arose to open for my beloved,
>> and my hands dripped with myrrh,
> my fingers with flowing myrrh,
>> on the handles of the bolt. (5:4–5)

But now that she is ready to move toward him for intimacy, he has gone away:

> I opened for my beloved,
>> but my beloved had left; he was gone.
> My heart sank at his departure.
> I looked for him but did not find him.
>> I called him but he did not answer. (5:6)

The rest of the poem describes her search for him. She is beset by obstacles (represented by the "watchmen" of the city), but her desire for her beloved propels her beyond them. She enlists the "daughters of Jerusalem," and the poem anticipates ultimate union, but not without incredible struggle.

The poems of the Song, both those that celebrate sexuality and those that poetically describe struggles, indicate that glimpses of sexual joy are possible but that our sexuality will be tinged with brokenness and struggle.[14]

14. For an extended reflection on the Song's message relating to our sexual lives, see Allender and Longman, *God Loves Sex*. For a remarkably candid testimony to the brokenness of sexuality in the period of the "already / not yet" redemption of sexuality, see Willits, "Bent Sexuality."

Sexual Redemption Accomplished?

The language of "already / not yet" redemption often describes our reconciliation with God. Through Christ, we can experience a relationship with God that overcomes the alienation that resulted from our rebellion against God. But the fullness of that reconciliation will take place only at the consummation of time, when Jesus will return and once and for all defeat evil. Jesus defeated sin and death on the cross, but that victory will not be secured until his return. Oscar Cullmann made a helpful analogy between this reality and two key landmarks in the European theater of World War II: he compared the cross with D-Day, the battle that broke the back of the Nazi power, and the final victory at Jesus's return with V-Day, when Berlin fell to the Allied forces. After D-Day there was no doubt about the fall of the Nazis, though there was plenty of fighting and dying yet to happen.[15]

But what can we say about our sexuality? What do we have to hope for in the consummation?[16] Many believe that the consummation will bring an end to human sexuality. Such a view may be motivated in part by the fact that sex often brings so much pain into our lives that we think that the bliss of heaven means that that dimension of our lives will be done away with. Perhaps this opinion is connected to that Neoplatonic idea that we are really just souls temporarily encased in flesh and that in the future we will be something like disembodied souls.

Such mistaken views also lead us to misunderstand what Jesus says to some Sadducees as he responds to their mockery of his belief in the afterlife (Luke 20:27–40). They ask what happens when a woman has had multiple husbands who all have died: "At the resurrection whose wife will she be, since the seven were married to her?" (v. 33). Jesus responds: "The people of this age marry and are given in marriage. But those who are considered worthy

15. Cullmann, *Christ and Time*, 3.
16. My thinking in this section has been stimulated by Smedes, *Sex for Christians*.

of taking part in the age to come and in the resurrection from the dead will neither marry nor be given in marriage, and they can no longer die; for they are like the angels. They are God's children, since they are children of the resurrection" (vv. 34–36). Jesus goes on to affirm the afterlife, but this part of Jesus's response is what is important for our discussion.

Jesus clearly says that marriage is a matter of "this age" and not the "age to come." That seems to seal it: nothing like sex in heaven. But notice that this is not what Jesus says; he says there is no marriage in heaven, not that there is no sex. Then he says the resurrected dead are "like the angels," and we all know these powerful spiritual beings are not sexual. But is that right? Again, one must wonder whether the idea of sexless angels comes more from the medieval period than from the Bible. After all, it is clear that Jews from around the time of Jesus thought that angels were at least potentially sexual beings, since there is ample evidence from the intertestamental period (see 1 Enoch 1–36 [The Book of the Watchers]) and from the New Testament itself (Jude 6) that the "sons of God" who cohabited with the "daughters of men" and produced prodigious offspring known as the Nephilim (Gen. 6:1–6) were thought to be angels. In a word, angels were sexual beings, so to say we will be like angels in heaven means that something like sex is possible in the afterlife.

Does this mean, to put it rather crudely, that we are to think of heaven as some kind of orgy? No, but perhaps an orgasm, in which two people can lose themselves in each other, provides a glimpse of the type of intimate harmony that will exist between those who live in a harmonious relationship with God in the afterlife.[17]

Homosexuality and the Bible

Now that we have surveyed the Bible's theology of sexuality, we turn to the issue of homosexuality in the Bible. Why has the church

---

17. For more on this, see Allender and Longman, *God Loves Sex*, 152–54.

through its long history held that God prohibits the practice of homosexual sex? For that matter, why do the vast majority of Christians worldwide continue to affirm this historical perspective even in the light of many recent attempts to reconsider the matter?

To answer these questions, we will look at the key biblical texts that have led to the conclusion that the Bible holds a negative and nonaffirming view on homosexual behavior. After stepping back to look at how to interpret the Mosaic law, I will simply describe the traditional understanding of each passage; then I will describe and analyze more-recent attempts to interpret the text in a different, more affirming, direction.

Interpreting the Mosaic Law

Before looking at the laws that specifically address homosexual practice, we must first examine the place of the law in the Old Testament time period. According to Exodus 19–24, God gave the law, most famously the Ten Commandments, to Moses on Mount Sinai. The formalization of the law at Mount Sinai was a function of the transition of the people of God from being an extended family to having the status of a nation. After the exodus from Egypt, Israel became a nation chosen by God ("You will be for me a kingdom of priests and a holy nation" [Exod. 19:6]), and the law functioned as their national law with the intention of keeping them set apart as a nation.

The Ten Commandments are the bedrock of the law, announcing how the Israelites were to love God (commandments 1–4) and love their neighbors as themselves (commandments 5–10). The content of these commandments should not have surprised anyone when they were first given. For instance, murder was prohibited before the sixth commandment was written on the stone tablet.

These commandments state general ethical principles that beg for interpretation in specific situations, and that is the function of

220

the so-called case law that follows the Ten Commandments both in the book of Exodus (the Ten Commandments in 20:2–17 are followed by case law in 20:22–23:19) and in the book of Deuteronomy (the Ten Commandments in 5:6–21 are followed by case law in chaps. 6–26). Case law can also be found in the books of Leviticus and Numbers. The function of the case law is to apply the general ethical principles of the Ten Commandments to specific situations according to the sociological status and redemptive-historical position of the people of God at the time (Israel). Let me illustrate with a couple of examples.

At the end of Exodus 21 (vv. 28–36), there is a law concerning a goring ox. This law talks about what happens if an ox gores a person to death. Without going into detail, the first incident requires the death of the ox, but the owner will not be held responsible. However, if the ox is not killed and is not penned up and then kills another person, the results are much more serious. The owner is put to death unless the victim's family (perhaps with the agreement of a judge) agrees to a fine instead. While this passage has a number of interesting and debatable issues, the point here is that the law of the goring ox is an application of the sixth commandment, the general ethical principle "You shall not murder" (Exod. 20:13), in the case when a person's animal kills another person.

A second example that also applies the sixth commandment to a specific situation, roof construction, clearly illustrates that the case law takes into account the sociological situation of the people of God at the time. Deuteronomy 22:8 mandates that a fence be built around a roof. Now such a law strikes many of us living in the twenty-first-century West as odd. Why a fence around a roof? The answer comes when we realize that in ancient Israel the roof was living space. People routinely spent time on the roof, and if there were no safeguards, they could easily fall off and possibly die. Thus, this law applies "You shall not murder" to Israelite architecture.

A third example, killing in war, also applies the sixth commandment. This example illustrates that the case law takes into account the redemptive-historical moment that the ancient Israelites found themselves in. When a soldier kills someone in a God-approved war, does that constitute murder (the illegitimate taking of life)? According to Deuteronomy 7 and 20 (warfare legislation), the answer is that this is not a violation of the sixth commandment.

Thus, in these examples we can see that the case law applies the general ethical principles of the Ten Commandments to the specific sociological and redemptive-historical moment of the people of God at the time. Later we will consider how this affects the relevance of the case law in our time—namely, the post-Christ era. But first we want to turn our attention to the case laws that speak about homosexual practice.

Leviticus 18 and 20

THE TRADITIONAL INTERPRETATION

Leviticus 18 and 20 describe a whole series of prohibited sexual relationships. In chapter 18, many of the laws deal with incest. Leviticus 18:6 states, "No one is to approach any close relative to have sexual relations. I am the LORD." The verses that follow then specify those relationships that are considered close. There is also the prohibition on sleeping with your "neighbor's wife" (18:20) or with an animal (18:23) or with a woman who is having her period (18:19; we will come back to this one in a bit). The law that draws our attention in the present discussion is in verse 22: "Do not have sexual relations with a man as one does with a woman; that is detestable." Chapter 20 has many of the same laws that we have seen in chapter 18, including prohibitions on incest, adultery, bestiality, having sex with a woman during her period, and homosexual practice: "If a man has sexual relations with a man as one does with a woman, both of them have done what is detestable. They are to be put to death; their blood will be on their own heads" (20:13).

To understand the laws in Leviticus 18 and 20, we must remember the relationship that we have observed between the Ten Commandments and the case law. These case laws apply the seventh commandment ("You shall not commit adultery" [Exod. 20:14; Deut. 5:18]) to Israel's specific sociological and redemptive-historical situation. In the Old Testament, homosexual acts were considered a violation of the seventh commandment. But what about after the coming of Christ? Do we have any reason to think that matters have changed now that we are in a different sociological and redemptive-historical situation?

"Who Cares about Case Laws?"

One of the most common recent counterarguments to the statements about homosexual practice in the book of Leviticus is to simply identify them as case laws and suggest that the case laws as a whole are not relevant for Christian life today. And it is true that many are not. We don't care whether we are wearing clothing composed of more than one fabric (contra Lev. 19:19). When we plant our gardens or farmers sow their lands, we don't avoid sowing different types of seed in a single field (also contra Lev. 19:19). Christians have no qualms about sitting down to a dinner that might include bacon, pork chops, or lobster (contra Lev. 11). And we could go on.

However, dismissing the case law completely reveals an extremely superficial understanding of the laws of the Old Testament and their connection to our present behavior. We have already pointed out that the case laws are applications of the general ethical principles of the Ten Commandments according to the sociological and redemptive-historical status of the people of God at the time. Thus, we are not surprised that there are changes today at a different sociological and dramatically different redemptive-historical moment, after the coming of Jesus Christ. To properly understand how the case law applies to us, we have to pay attention to the context.

Let's begin with what Jesus says near the beginning of the Sermon on the Mount:

> Do not think that I have come to abolish the Law or the Prophets; I have not come to abolish them but to fulfill them. For truly I tell you, until heaven and earth disappear, not the smallest letter, not the least stroke of a pen, will by any means disappear from the Law until everything is accomplished. Therefore anyone who sets aside one of the least of these commands and teaches others accordingly will be called least in the kingdom of heaven, but whoever practices and teaches these commands will be called great in the kingdom of heaven. For I tell you that unless your righteousness surpasses that of the Pharisees and the teachers of the law, you will certainly not enter the kingdom of heaven. (Matt. 5:17–20)

Jesus says here that the law continues to remain relevant (and will until heaven and earth disappear) unless the purpose of the law is already accomplished. And we see this in the manner in which the rest of the New Testament appropriates the Mosaic law. Thus, we observe continuity and discontinuity between the Old Testament and the New Testament when it comes to the law.

Some of the laws supported God's will for Israel as a holy nation to stay separate from gentiles. Laws of separation (seed, fabric) illustrate this divine intent. The function of food laws was to keep Israelites from eating with gentiles. As we move to the New Testament, God's people no longer are called to be separate from the rest of the world. Indeed, the command is now to "go and make disciples of all nations" (Matt. 28:19). And Jews and gentiles who turn to God are no longer separate but one people, because Jesus "is our peace, who has made the two groups one and has destroyed the barrier, the dividing wall of hostility, by setting aside the law with its commands and regulations. His purpose was to create in himself one new humanity out of two, thus making peace, and in one body to reconcile both of them to God through the cross, by which he put to death their hostility" (Eph. 2:14–16). No wonder Christians no longer observe food laws (Acts 10:1–11:18)!

Indeed, a few years ago I was on a panel on the theology of sexuality at the Society of Biblical Literature when one of my fellow panelists, an advocate of queer interpretation,[18] said with a tone of exasperation, "We don't pay any attention to the food laws. Why do we care about the sexual laws?" My response at the time was, "Actually, if you look at the New Testament, while Jesus, Peter, and Paul clearly say that Christians are under no obligation to keep the food laws, the laws concerning sexuality are actually tightened up" (see comments in the next section on polygamy and divorce). He basically ignored my comment, not offering a response beyond "You care about the New Testament more than I do," which is true since he is Jewish (but teaching at a historically Christian seminary). But those of us who do care about the message of the New Testament can't simply dismiss the case law as irrelevant without argument.

Many of the case laws continue as guides to how God wants us to live according to his intention for our flourishing. For instance, the law of the goring ox and the law about building a fence around a roof are still helpful to us. The first guides us as to moral culpability when animals under our care and control harm someone (indeed American law has picked this up in what lawyers tell me they call "the law of the second bite," referring in this case to increased responsibility and liability when a dog bites someone a second time). The second makes us alert to protecting life (and thus observing the sixth commandment) in our own architecture

18. *Queer interpretation* is a label utilized by interpreters, many of whom are themselves gay.

(e.g., fences around swimming pools and infant plugs in electrical sockets).

Moving into the realm of sexuality, some draw attention to Leviticus 18:19 ("Do not approach a woman to have sexual relations during the uncleanness of her monthly period") and 20:18 ("If a man has sexual relations with a woman during her monthly period, he has exposed the source of her flow, and she has also uncovered it. Both of them are to be cut off from their people"). These two laws sit in the midst of other sexual laws that include the laws against homosexual practice, and the counterargument typically runs, "We don't observe this law today. So why should we bother about the laws concerning homosexual practice?" But if this is the case, why then don't we suggest that these also nullify the prohibitions about incest, since those laws also appear in this context?

More substantially, this law itself is a ceremonial law that is unique to Israel and is no longer relevant to the church. During the Old Testament time period, a woman was ceremonially unclean for a period of seven days, and anyone who touched her was unclean for a short period (till evening; Lev. 15:19). The comparable law for the Israelite male was that if he had an emission of semen (whether a so-called nocturnal emission [Deut. 23:9–10] or during marital relations, which also rendered the woman unclean [Lev. 15:16–18]), then he was ritually unclean until evening and then had to go through ritual washing.

The reason for these laws is nowhere explicitly stated, which is fairly typical for the Levitical ritual laws. The fact that both fluids (the woman's blood and the man's semen) are related to the reproductive system suggests that their special status has to do with the potential for offspring. In other words, these fluids are related to life and are therefore treated as holy. According to Old Testament ritual thinking, one way to enter a state of uncleanness is to come into contact with something holy. The Old Testament operates with an understanding that there are three realms: the unclean, the ordinary, and the holy. Holiness is connected to God and those things associated with him. Though it is unnecessary for our purposes to delve into all the difficult permutations of the ritual thinking of ancient Israel, the bottom line is that when Christ comes, he renders everything holy (Col. 2:16–23). Most obviously, there are no longer any separate and special holy times, holy places, holy people, or holy actions.[19]

Christian ethics are not concerned about whether a man has sex with his wife during her period or, for that matter, whether a man goes through a period of ritual uncleanness after having sex with his wife. But this does not abrogate the other laws in Leviticus 18 and 20 any more than the fact that we don't offer animal sacrifices does not nullify other laws, such as those concerning adultery or theft.

Theologians often speak of three categories of laws in the Old Testament. Ceremonial laws are those laws observed in the ritual of ancient Israel (sacrifices, food laws, laws of ritual purity, etc.), and they are not observed by Christians because their purpose has been accomplished now that Jesus has come. Civil laws have to do with Israel as a nation-state set apart for a special purpose (for instance, the law of kingship in Deut. 17:14–20 and the laws of *herem* warfare in Deut. 7 and 20), and now that Christ has come, the people of God are no longer a nation-state but a church composed of people from all the nations of the world. Finally, moral laws are those laws that apply the general ethical principles of the Ten Commandments that stay relevant into the New Testament time period.[20] The seventh commandment prohibiting sex outside of marriage and the related case laws fall into this category and must be observed by Christians today.

19. See Longman, *Immanuel in Our Place*.
20. The fourth commandment (Sabbath) is a ceremonial law, and its relevance is debated today. See Longman, *Immanuel in Our Place*, 163–84.

The bottom line is that it is not sufficient to argue simply that we don't observe case law *x*, so we don't need to observe case law *y*. Such an argument shows a lack of awareness about the nature of the case laws and the relationship between the Old Testament and the New Testament when it comes to the law.

Death Penalties in the Case Law

Christians reading the Old Testament case law typically find it harsh, since a surface reading leads many to believe that the death penalty is demanded even for transgressions that we find quite minor. For instance, cursing one's parents or hitting them could land a child the death penalty. And for our topic, Leviticus 20:13 states that both men involved in a same-sex act "are to be put to death; their blood will be on their own heads." For some the question is, If one accepts that this law is still valid, what about the penalty?

There is no way to completely soften Leviticus 20:13 for a modern audience. We cannot deny that it allows for the death penalty. But it should be pointed out that when the case law stipulates the death penalty, it is not tying a judge's hands. In the light of Numbers 35:31 and other passages, it is more likely that the death penalty was a maximum penalty probably reserved for egregious and repetitive cases. There we read, "Do not accept a ransom for the life of a murderer, who deserves to die. They are to be put to death." This statement that no exception should be made to the death penalty in the case of murder implies that exceptions would be allowed in other cases. This suggests that the only infraction that requires the death penalty is murder. In this light, Proverbs 6:34–35 ("For jealousy arouses a husband's fury, and he will show no mercy when he takes revenge. He will not accept any compensation; he will refuse a bribe, however great it is") suggests that a husband will press for the ultimate penalty if a man sleeps with his wife. That the offender might hope that the husband might not ask for the death penalty means that the death penalty was not required.

In any case, as we read the New Testament, the penalties of the Old Testament don't apply any longer. Adultery can lead to divorce, not death (John 7:53–8:11). Incest leads to excommunication, not death (1 Cor. 5). The penalties of the law in the Old Testament are best understood as connected to Israel's status as a nation that must remain holy; in the New Testament, as we discussed above, the people of God are a spiritual entity, the church, that does not take recourse to physical punishments.[21]

"What about Polygamy (and Slavery)?"

Another common strategy to question the continuing relevance of the Old Testament laws on sexuality, and in particular homosexuality, is to point to the tolerance for polygamy and slavery in the Old Testament. Unlike the previous section, here we are dealing not with ceremonial or civil law but with moral law. These are moral laws related to the general ethical principles of the Ten Commandments, in particular the law prohibiting adultery (polygamy) and the law prohibiting stealing (slavery). Though the principles of these laws remain in force, their application changes as we move into the New Testament and even beyond. In what follows I am reflecting the insights of William Webb, who shows how there is a redemptive-ethical trajectory from the Old Testament into the New Testament and beyond that takes the people where they are and moves them toward the intention God had for them at creation, what we will call God's "Edenic ideal."[22]

It is important to acknowledge that the case law does not mandate what we might call the "Edenic ideal," a shorthand phrase to describe the way God created the world and its inhabitants and

---

21. For a full treatment of the penalties of the Old Testament law in relation to the New Testament, see Longman, "God's Law."
22. Webb, *Slaves, Women and Homosexuals*.

intended them to live. The case law takes the people where they are and moves them toward the Edenic ideal. The clearest indication of this comes from Jesus's comments on divorce in Matthew 19. When some Pharisees ask him his opinion about divorce, he responds by citing Genesis 1 and 2 and pronounces, "What God has joined together, let no one separate" (19:6). They counter by citing the Old Testament case law that says a man can "give his wife a certificate of divorce and send her away" (19:7, referring to Deut. 24:1–5). To which Jesus responds by saying, "Moses permitted you to divorce your wives because your hearts were hard. But it was not this way from the beginning. I tell you that anyone who divorces his wife, except for sexual immorality, and marries another woman commits adultery" (19:8).

It appears that God in his wisdom does not mandate the Edenic ideal on marriage in the case law, because the people are not ready for it; rather, the case law takes the people where they are and moves them in the right direction. Webb points out that, even so, if one evaluates biblical law over against that of its ancient Near Eastern neighbors, the Bible puts in place protections for the vulnerable that are not there in the broader ancient Near East.

This seems to be the case with both polygamy and slavery. Exodus 21:2–11 deals with both of these topics:

> If you buy a Hebrew servant, he is to serve you for six years. But in the seventh year, he shall go free, without paying anything. If he comes alone, he is to go free alone; but if he has a wife when he comes, she is to go with him. If his master gives him a wife and she bears him sons or daughters, the woman and her children shall belong to her master, and only the man shall go free.
>
> But if the servant declares, "I love my master and my wife and children and do not want to go free," then his master must take him before the judges. He shall take him to the door or the doorpost and pierce his ear with an awl. Then he will be his servant for life.
>
> If a man sells his daughter as a servant, she is not to go free as male servants do. If she does not please the master who has

selected her for himself, he must let her be redeemed. He has no right to sell her to foreigners, because he has broken faith with her. If he selects her for his son, he must grant her the rights of a daughter. If he marries another woman, he must not deprive the first one of her food, clothing and marital rights. If he does not provide her with these three things, she is to go free, without any payment of money.

When we study the creation account, particularly Genesis 2, we note an emphasis on equality between the man and the woman (as discussed above).[23] Thus, this law in Exodus (and other related laws in the Torah) does not mandate the Edenic ideal (where marriage is clearly monogamous). But this law does provide some measure of protection for wives when their husbands do take a second wife. The tendency of some husbands would be to ignore an old wife over against a new one. And this law does provide protections for slaves, as compared to the cultures around them.

Once Jesus comes, the expectation for God's followers with regard to polygamy, like with divorce, moves even further toward the Edenic ideal, though we have to admit that even here, while there is progress, it is not yet at that ideal. We see the movement not in the complete abrogation of polygamous relationships in the church (there is no indication that a polygamous man would be excluded from fellowship) but in the requirement that an officer of the church be the husband of one wife (1 Tim. 3:2, 12; Titus 1:6)[24] and therefore reflect the Edenic ideal.

The same is true about slavery. Slavery is not abolished in the Old Testament, but it is regulated, including a mandatory release in the seventh year. The book of Deuteronomy even requires the slave owner to provide compensation for the departing slave (or

---

23. See also Longman, *Genesis*, 53–54.

24. NIV (2011) obscures this meaning by rendering the relevant phrase "faithful to his wife." The Greek says "the husband of one wife" (*mias gynaikos andra/andres/anēr*).

is *servant* a better term?), since otherwise they might quickly fall back into slavery without the wherewithal to support themselves (Deut. 15:12–18).

When we turn to the New Testament, we don't see an immediate return to Edenic ideals, where everyone is equal and no one oppresses another. Slavery continues, though seeds are sown that will eventually lead to its abolition. The principles that will lead to the undermining of slavery are found in texts like Galatians 3:28: "There is neither Jew nor Gentile, neither slave nor free, nor is there male and female, for you are all one in Christ Jesus." Further, in the short letter to Philemon, Paul sends Onesimus back to Philemon, his owner, but he tells Philemon that he sends his slave back to him as "a dear brother" (v. 16) and instructs him to "welcome him as you would welcome me" (v. 17). As a matter of fact, Paul includes "slave traders" in the list of those who are "contrary to sound doctrine" (1 Tim. 1:8–11; see v. 10).

While we see what Webb calls a "redemptive-movement herme-neutic"[25] (the Old Testament takes people where they are and moves them toward the Edenic ideal, and the New Testament brings them further and establishes principles that will lead to even post–New Testament developments) when it comes to polygamy, patriarchy, and slavery, the same cannot be said about homosexuality. The Old Testament is actually more negative about homosexual practice than the writings of its ancient Near Eastern neighbors. Further, as we saw above, the New Testament is not more permissive than the Old Testament but rather reaffirms the Old Testament's negative construal of homosexual relationships. In addition, the New Testament does not plant principles that will lead to further future development like we saw concerning women and slavery in Galatians 3:28.

We see that the New Testament and, even more, contemporary Christian ethics have moved beyond the Old Testament when it

25. Webb, *Slaves, Women and Homosexuals*, 31.

comes to women and slaves, but there is no such movement in regard to homosexuality. Thus, the argument that we are not obligated to hold to the Old Testament's perspective on homosexuality since we don't practice its views on the relationship of men and women or on slavery holds little water and should not be accepted.

"There Are Only Two Laws about Homosexuality"

One of the more banal objections to the traditional approach is simply that there are only two laws that explicitly address homosexual acts (Lev. 18:22 and 20:13). A second and related objection is that these laws speak only about men with men, not about women with women.

In terms of the first objection, for those of us who see the Bible as the Word of God, one verse is more than enough. I can only find two verses in the Old Testament that prohibit having sex with one's mother (Lev. 18:7 and 20:11), for instance. In addition, the New Testament reaffirms the Old Testament teaching about homosexual practice (see the discussion of homosexuality and 1 Cor. 6 below). Again, these laws and the others in Leviticus 18 and 20 are explicating the seventh commandment, so at heart homosexual practice violates not simply the case laws of Leviticus 18 and 20 but the commandment not to commit adultery.

It is true that the Old Testament laws only explicitly prohibit male same-sex acts, but then the law is explicitly addressed to men and would apply to women, *mutatis mutandis*.[26] It is true, too, that there is a heightened concern about semen and where it is placed, since semen is the potential of life that the biblical text surrounds with taboos because of its holy status. In any case, Paul addresses women having sex with women in Romans 1, which at least Christian readers must take seriously.

26. For a treatment of the patriarchy of the Old Testament and how it affects our reading of wisdom (with implications for how we should read the law), see Longman, *Fear of the Lord*, 199–213.

"Does Leviticus Really Prohibit All Same-Sex Sexual Acts?"

Saul Olyan, a brilliant and well-respected interpreter of the Hebrew Bible, has argued that Leviticus specifically sanctions the insertive partner in an act of anal intercourse, not the receptive partner. He argues further that the act that is in mind is a ritual copulation with male temple prostitutes who play the female role.[27] George Hollenback has recently challenged this view, arguing that it is the receptive partner who is in view and that "the passages reflect a common taboo in antiquity against a male's assuming a female function."[28] In any case, the argument that there is a ritual prohibition here is not supported by the context, and that both partners are faulted and suffer the consequences is clear from Leviticus 20:13.[29]

Another issue people raise in regard to Leviticus 20:13 is the identification of the prohibited act as "detestable" (the Hebrew word, to'ebah, can also be translated as "abomination"). Since it is true that this word often is connected to pagan rituals, this becomes an argument to say that this law prohibits not same-sex intercourse in general but specifically temple prostitution.[30] But besides the fact that the evidence for temple prostitution is contested, the word is not so restricted in its meaning, since Deuteronomy 25:16 announces that using deceptive weights in an economic transaction is to'ebah. As Michael Grisanti summarizes the meaning of the word, to'ebah "denotes the persons, things, or practices that offend one's ritual or moral order."[31]

---

27. Olyan, "'You Shall Not Lie.'"

28. Hollenback, "Who Is Doing What," 537. Hollenback is supporting an earlier study by Walsh, "Leviticus 18:22 and 20:13."

29. Hollenback's only comment here is that "the culpability of the insertive partner was probably a later development" ("Who Is Doing What," 537). But this is irrelevant to our concern, which focuses on the canonical text, not a speculative earlier version.

30. This view was made popular by Bird, "Christian Ethical Deliberation." See also Vines, God and the Gay Christian, 84–86.

31. Grisanti, "תעב," 314. See also Himbaza, Schenker, and Edart, Question of Homosexuality, 46–47.

EXCURSUS

Sodom and Gomorrah (Genesis 18:16–19:29) and the Levite and His Concubine (Judges 19)[32]

Before moving on to the New Testament, let's pause for a moment to consider the story of Sodom and Gomorrah, which over the years has often been cited as a text relevant to the issue of homosexuality. God tells Abraham that the sin of these cities is "so grievous" that he "will go down and see if what they have done is as bad as the outcry that has reached me" (Gen. 18:20–21). Abraham famously negotiates with God so that if there are as few as ten righteous people in the city of Sodom, God will save it.

In the next scene God's two angels enter the city and find that only Abraham's nephew Lot is willing to offer them hospitality and protection. The need for protection becomes apparent that night when "all the men from every part of the city of Sodom— both young and old—surrounded the house," demanding that the visitors come out so they can have sex with them (19:4–5). Needless to say, this episode illustrates the depth and breadth of the sinfulness of the city. And after escorting Lot and his family out of the city, God destroys the city and kills its inhabitants. But what exactly is the sin of Sodom here?

To many, the answer is obvious, and they point to the sexual nature of the sin. But we should not jump too quickly to that answer. Most later biblical reflections on the sin of Sodom and Gomorrah either do not mention the specific sin (Isa. 1:9, 10; 13:19; Jer. 23:14; 49:18; 50:40; Amos 4:11; Zeph. 2:9), or if they do, they do not typically name homosexual practice (Ezek. 16:49–50; Matt. 10:9–15; Luke 10:8–12). Also, in the ancient Near East, when men had sex with other men, it was sometimes an assertion of power over another, as seems to be the case in Sodom. The penetrator

---

32. For a helpful analysis of Gen. 19 and Judg. 9, as well as the David and Jonathan relationship, see Himbaza, Schenker, and Edart, *Question of Homosexuality*, 5–44.

asserted his superiority over the penetrated in an act of dominance. We should not consider the city of Sodom to be filled with men who have same-sex attraction. Rather, these men want to humiliate their foreign visitors.

At the same time, it is not quite true to say that later biblical texts never point to the sexual nature of the sin at Sodom. In his denunciation of false teachers, Jude cites a number of analogies from the Old Testament, including "Sodom and Gomorrah and the surrounding towns" that "gave themselves up to sexual immorality and perversion" (v. 7). But even here we should be careful not to use the example of Sodom and Gomorrah as illustrative of the sin of homosexual behavior. After all, we are not talking about consensual sexual relations but attempted rape, and gang rape at that. In a word, the story of Sodom and Gomorrah really has no bearing on the discussion at hand.

After reading Genesis 19, Judges 19 sounds fairly familiar. Indeed, it is likely that the author intends to draw an analogy between Gibeah, which will be King Saul's hometown, and Sodom. A Levite's concubine has left him and returned to her father's house in Bethlehem. After four months, he goes to get her to return to their home in the hill country of Ephraim. The father appears reluctant to let his daughter go and does everything he can to delay their departure. Eventually, though, the Levite insists on leaving, but it is so late in the day that they have to spend the night en route. The Levite refuses to stay in Jebus, a non-Israelite city, so they push on to Gibeah.

When they enter Gibeah, they are not greeted with hospitality; instead, an out-of-towner (an Ephraimite) who is living there anxiously tells them not to stay out in public but to come home with him. When evening comes, we find out why he is anxious, as the men of the town come and demand to have sex with the Levite. The host tells them that this would be an outrageous breach of hospitality, and he offers his daughter and the concubine.

They push the concubine out into the street, where she is raped. She ultimately dies, and her death becomes the occasion for a civil war.

There are no "good guys" in this story. The book of Judges presents it in order to highlight the moral depravity, spiritual confusion, and political fragmentation of this period. We, though, are interested in this story because it has often been pressed into service to bolster the idea that the Bible is against homosexual acts. But, as with the Sodom story, Judges 19 has nothing directly to say about the subject. The focus again is on lack of hospitality; the sex is not that of same-sex-attracted men but that of men who want to assert power over the visitor.

Excursus

David and Jonathan (2 Samuel 1:26)

While Genesis 19 and Judges 19 do not in and of themselves support a nonaffirming viewpoint, the story of David and Jonathan has been wrongly used to suggest a more positive position on committed homosexual relationships.

There is no question that Saul's son Jonathan has a loving relationship with the young David. And when his friend Jonathan dies in battle, David emotionally proclaims, "I grieve for you, Jonathan my brother; you were very dear to me. Your love for me was wonderful, more wonderful than that of women" (2 Sam. 1:26).

Many people read David's statement against the background of the close relationship between these two men and believe, or at least wonder whether, they were engaged in a sexual relationship. But, as Susan Ackerman and others have pointed out, such deep affection is characteristic of young warriors who bond together in crisis situations. While it may be appropriate to speak of the relationship as having overtones of the homoerotic, it is not likely at all that the biblical text presents David and Jonathan as sexually involved.[33]

Romans 1

THE TRADITIONAL INTERPRETATION

Jesus himself does not speak about homosexuality (see below for comments on this), but we do find three passages in Paul's writings that address the issue. And all three, according to traditional interpretations, reaffirm the message that he observed in the Old Testament that homosexual behavior violates God's will concerning human sexuality (as does a host of other activities, including adultery and premarital sexual intercourse). Debate surrounds the interpretation of each, so it is necessary to look carefully at all three of these passages.

In the book of Romans, Paul wants to talk about "the power of God that brings salvation to everyone who believes" (1:16), but he starts by talking about humanity's sin (1:18–3:20). As Douglas Moo points out, Paul realizes that it is "only by fully understanding the 'bad news'" that we can "appreciate the 'good news.'"[34]

Thus, in Romans 1 Paul turns his attention to the "wrath of God" that comes against "all godlessness and wickedness of people" (1:18). He argues that this wrath is justified because God has made himself known to all people, but they have suppressed this knowledge. They know God but do not glorify (praise) him. They substitute the worship of idols for that of the true God. In a word, they worship the creation rather than the Creator.

33. Ackerman, *When Heroes Love*. As the subtitle (*The Ambiguity of Eros in the Stories of David and Gilgamesh*) indicates, Ackerman similarly analyzes the homoerotic language used in the Gilgamesh Epic to describe the relationship between Gilgamesh and Enkidu.
34. Moo, *Romans*, 59.

Paul then identifies the consequences, the first of which is that "God gave them over in the sinful desires of their hearts to sexual impurity for the degrading of their bodies with one another" (1:24). Before going on, we need to notice that this verse does not specify homosexual desire or behavior. In other words, every one of God's human creatures, every one of us, is implicated in this statement. Anyone who thinks they escape Paul's condemnatory words here is quite wrong and acting like the Pharisee who says, "God, I thank you that I am not like other people—robbers, evildoers, adulterers—or even like this tax collector" (Luke 18:11).

It is true that after acknowledging the pervasive nature of human sexual sin, Paul does name homosexual acts as an example: "God gave them over to shameful lusts. Even their women exchanged natural sexual relations for unnatural ones. In the same way the men also abandoned natural relations with women and were inflamed with lust for one another. Men committed shameful acts with other men, and received in themselves the due penalty for their error" (1:26–27). For centuries the idea of "natural (sexual) relations" has been understood against the background of Genesis 2, in which God instituted marriage as the proper vehicle for sexual intercourse and marriage is described as between one man and one woman. Thus, the definition of "natural (sexual) relations" is defined by the creation ideal of Genesis 2:24 ("That is why a man leaves his father and mother and is united to his wife, and they become one flesh").

All sexual sins, heterosexual and homosexual, are violations of this creation purpose. Furthermore, perhaps to make sure that people do not feel themselves acquitted, Paul adds a long list of sins that again implicate every human being (1:28–32). I am emphasizing this in order to avoid the error that many make of placing homosexual sin in some kind of special category. But it is also wrong to suggest that Paul does not consider homosexual desires and actions sinful.

Rereadings of Romans 1

The traditional understanding of Romans 1 has been challenged on a number of fronts in recent years. Some argue that this passage is not relevant to the discussion by suggesting that Paul is not citing homosexual behavior in general (particularly committed mutual relationships) but rather a particular Roman form known as pederasty. Older men would take boys as lovers, and when the boys grew older, they, in turn, would take younger male lovers. But if this were so, why are lesbian relationships also cited here? In addition, if the practice of pederasty were meant, why not use the Greek word for pederasty (*paiderastia*)?

Others suggest that we should understand the language of "natural" and "unnatural" to refer to individual human nature. That is, if a person is heterosexual, then it is according to that person's natural desires to be with a person of the opposite sex; but if a person's natural inclination is to be with a person of the same sex, then that type of relationship is natural. Thus, a person sins if they go against their natural propensities—for example, a gay man sleeping with a woman or a heterosexual woman sleeping with a woman. But to connect it to the individual seems a very modern understanding of *natural*. As we pointed out above, and as is widely held, we should understand Paul's use of *natural* against the background of Genesis 2:24, and this view is supported by the fact that Paul shares the general Jewish view on homosexuality,[35] which is based on the Old Testament. Paul echoes what we learn in the Old Testament about homosexuality.

---

35. Moo (*Romans*, 66) cites *Sibylline Oracles* 3.594–600 as representative of contemporary Jewish attitudes toward Greek cultural opinions: "Surpassing, indeed all humans, they [Jewish men] are mindful of holy wedlock and do not engage in evil intercourse with male children, as do Phoenicians, Egyptians, Romans, spacious Greece and many other nations, Persians, Galatians, and all Asia, transgressing the holy law of the immortal God."

1 Corinthians 6:9 and 1 Timothy 1:10

THE TRADITIONAL INTERPRETATION

In 1 Corinthians 6 Paul chastises those who bring lawsuits against their fellow Christians, arguing that it is better to be cheated than to bring such disputes out into public view. After all, he argues, "you yourselves cheat and do wrong, and you do this to your brothers and sisters" (6:8). He then expands the category of wrongdoing that leads to the loss of the kingdom of God: "Do not be deceived: Neither the sexually immoral nor idolaters nor adulterers nor men who have sex with men nor thieves nor the greedy nor drunkards nor slanderers nor swindlers will inherit the kingdom of God" (6:9–10).

Let's first be clear that Paul gets all of us with this list. Everyone has violated God's intention for our sexuality, and we are all sexually immoral. We have all treated someone or something as more important than God and therefore are idolaters. And many have had too much to drink, cheated someone out of something small or large, and been greedy.

But included in this list is "men who have sex with men," which is a translation of two Greek words, one that identifies the passive member of a pair (*malakoi*) and the other the active member (*arsenokoitai*; more on these two terms below). The only reason we are highlighting "men who have sex with men" is that, while I know plenty of greedy people in the church, none of them is owning it and defending it as the way God made them and therefore OK. When confronted with greed, they may deny it, but no one in the church is saying "Greed is good, so leave me alone."

The case of 1 Timothy is similar. In the opening to his letter to Timothy, Paul[36] directs his disciple to oppose false teachers who claim to be teachers of the law but "do not know what they are

---

36. While I remain unconvinced by the arguments that someone other than Paul wrote this letter, my point here is not affected if it turns out to be the case that the letter is pseudonymous.

talking about or what they so confidently affirm" (1:7). He goes on to affirm the goodness of the law particularly as it convicts evildoers of their sin. He says the law is made "for lawbreakers and rebels, the ungodly and sinful, the unholy and irreligious, for those who kill their fathers or mothers, for murderers, for the sexually immoral, for those practicing homosexuality, for slave traders and liars and perjurers—and for whatever else is contrary to sound doctrine that conforms to the gospel concerning the glory of the blessed God, which he entrusted to me" (1:9–11).

As in 1 Corinthians, Paul leaves no one off the hook. We can all find ourselves described in this list. Paul does not give us the idea that it is worse in the eyes of God to lie than it is to kill our parents in terms of our standing before God. But the question we are dealing with in this chapter and in our contemporary churches is whether homosexual behavior (*arsenokoitais*, one of the words that Paul uses in 1 Cor. 6, is also used here) is OK in a way that we would recognize that the other descriptions in this list are not. In these passages, the church has traditionally understood *arsenokoitai/arsenokoitais* and *malakoi* to specifically refer to homosexual practice, an interpretation that can be seen reflected in most major Bible translations, and has held that such practice is sinful. Thus, 1 Corinthians 6:9 and 1 Timothy 1:10 agree with Romans 1 and with the testimony of the Old Testament in censuring same-sex behavior.

Rereadings of 1 Corinthians 6:9 and 1 Timothy 1:10

Some object to the translation of the Greek *arsenokoitai*, which occurs in both passages, as "homosexual," since that English word was created in the nineteenth century and thus is considered an anachronism of sorts. This involves the confusion of concept and word. That the word *homosexual* is not found in English until the nineteenth century has nothing to do with Greek words that refer to the behavior. Indeed, besides *arsenokoitai*, Paul in 1 Corinthians

6:9 uses a second word, *malakoi*, thus mentioning both the active and passive partners in a homosexual act.

Some confuse the issue by suggesting that it is unclear exactly what these terms mean.[37] That might be the case if *malakoi* were used alone, but "an analysis of *arsenkoitēs* reveals no ambiguity. This term literally means 'sleeping (*koitē*: lit. 'bed, couch,' *keisthai*: 'to be asleep') with a man (*arsen*: 'male').' [It is] formed by the association of two words present in [the Greek text of] Lv. 18:22 and 20:13)."[38]

After surveying the biblical material, the eminent New Testament scholar Robert H. Gundry, my former colleague, correctly observes that "(1) the Bible never puts homosex[39] in a favorable light; (2) homosex always appears in association with evil; and (3) everywhere an explicit judgment is rendered we have a condemnation or a prohibition."[40] I find the attempt at reinterpreting the relevant texts or trying to render them irrelevant to the present situation unpersuasive. To repeat, the vast, vast majority of interpreters, scholars, and pastors around the world still maintain the traditional understanding of these texts and their import, which has been held with virtually no significant objections in the history of the church until the past generation. The bar is high to change that understanding, and, in spite of the fact that many in the West, under the influence of strong cultural factors, would like to be able to affirm same-sex relationships, I submit that the effort has failed.

Summary

There are three passages that speak about homosexual practice in the New Testament, and they all agree with the Mosaic law of

37. Gushee, *Changing Our Mind*, 74–80.

38. Himbaza, Schenker, and Edart, *Question of Homosexuality*, 77. See also Grenz, *Welcoming but Not Affirming*, 56–59; R. B. Hays, *Moral Vision*, 391–92; R. B. Hays, *1 Corinthians*, 97.

39. Gundry uses *homosex* as "shorthand for engaging in homosexual intercourse."

40. Gundry, "On Homosex and Homosexual Marriage." Thanks to the author for allowing me to have the manuscript.

the Old Testament. Attempts to reread the passages as if the terms are ambiguous are, in my opinion, unsuccessful. We have nothing to suggest that there is any difference between the Old and the New Testaments on this subject. This lack of movement will be critically important as we consider the teaching of the canon as a whole and its mandate to the church today.

Responding to Objections

We have just looked at the biblical texts that support the traditional Christian view on sexuality and interacted with recent attempts to challenge that interpretation. Now we move to other, more general arguments used to move opinion toward an affirming attitude.

"Jesus Said Nothing about Homosexuality"

If same-sex acts were sinful, wouldn't Jesus have made a point of it? Jesus truly is the apex of divine revelation, and he doesn't seem bothered by the issue, so why should we?

Such questions make a faulty assumption and also forget something important about Jesus as he is presented in the Gospels (the only place where we today learn about him and his teachings during his earthly ministry). In the first place, these questions assume that Jesus addresses or needs to address every issue, and these questions forget that Jesus fully affirms the Old Testament as the Word of God. We made this point in the section about divine violence as well. Unless the New Testament gives us indication that Jesus's coming somehow fulfills an Old Testament law so that we no longer observe it or that the sociological situation has changed in a way that the law no longer has relevance, we should assume that the principle is still valid (particularly when there are New Testament passages that explicitly reaffirm it).

To put it another way, Paul's words are as authoritative as those of Jesus, since they are the divinely inspired interpretation of the redemptive acts and teaching of Jesus. That Jesus said nothing about homosexuality tells us nothing about his attitudes toward homosexuality except that it implies his agreement with the Old Testament, but Paul's teaching based on the Old Testament law does inform us of the attitudes of this divinely commissioned apostle. And, actually, Jesus is not really silent about this matter. When Jesus tells the disciples that "what comes out of a person is what defiles them," he lists, among other things, "sexual immorality" as well as "adultery" (Mark 7:20–23), which we have every reason to think would include homosexual acts for this first-century Scripture-affirming Jewish man.

"Homosexual Relationships Don't Hurt Anyone"

Those who, like me, are old enough to remember the 1960s and '70s marvel at the rapid shift in attitudes toward homosexuality and same-sex marriage that has taken place over the past decade or so. There are many reasons for this shift in attitudes, including the sinful actions of the church and individual Christians as they ostracized people in the LGBTQ community. But for those of us who can remember forty to fifty years ago, the more positive attitude toward homosexuality also coincides with a shift of attitude and strategy by the gay community itself.

The predominant strategy in the 1960s and '70s was to attack marriage as a bourgeois institution. Of course, this move was a part of a broader cultural trend connected with the sexual revolution that wanted to free sexual expression from the institution of marriage and encouraged (and still encourages) all kinds of pre- and extramarital sexual activity.

At some point, that strategy changed, so that rather than attacking marriage, the gay community started lobbying for the right to marry.[41] This move was brilliant as a way to make homosexuality

41. The influential political commentator and author Andrew Sullivan is often credited as an early advocate for this change of strategy.

an accepted part of Western culture. There is much to respect about this movement, as it promotes virtues like fidelity in relationships. Indeed, as I will say below, I believe the church wastes capital and energy contesting the legalization of same-sex marriage, and same-sex marriage has not, as far as I can see, led to the crumbling of Western culture (unless one thinks that same-sex marriage itself is a sign of that crumbling culture, as many do).

But it is not really true to say that what happens in the bedroom is a private act and is no one's business but our own. That is a very Western idea connected with our idea of individuality. But individuals affect families, families affect communities, and so on. We are social animals, and what we say, advocate for, and do affects the mental and physical life of everyone in our communities. Sex and marriage are public, social acts, not private acts, even if the sexual acts are done behind closed doors.

There are, of course, those who want to make long lists of social harms of homosexual behavior in an attempt to justify the biblical teaching. Some of these claims are bogus and easily refuted; others may have merit but certainly can be contested. I am not going to repeat them here. My point here is a bit more radical. For those of us who take the Bible as God's Word revealing to us who God is and what his will is for how we live our lives, the only question is what God tells us on this matter. We don't have the luxury of saying, "Well, God tells us not to do x, but you know, I think we know better about x, so I am going to do x."

At this point I am reminded of Genesis 3. That Genesis 3 is a figurative depiction of an actual event (see chap. 1) does not undermine the point that humans rebelled against a divine prohibition that they came to think was misguided. After all, what good reason could be given for not eating the fruit of the tree of the knowledge of good and evil? God does not give reasons, such as "because it will poison you" (it won't). The sin itself is the assertion of moral autonomy.

My point here is not about whether there are good reasons to refrain from same-sex relations for individual and societal flourishing. My point is that for those of us who believe our ethic derives from Scripture, we don't need to name or be convinced of such reasons if the biblical text clearly prohibits it. Paul Copan's comment about divine violence in the book of Joshua is equally relevant here: "An omniscient God will have reasons for commanding or prohibiting—reasons that we ourselves may not or even cannot know. So God's motivational state will be different from our own, which is why we need commands even if we don't know all the reasons behind them."[42] But of course not everyone, and not every Christian, is so convinced. Thus, the ultimate rebuff is simply to reject Scripture as a guide to life.

"Who Cares about the Bible Anyway?"

Let me begin by reminding readers that this book addresses the Christian community and not the broader culture. Those outside the church are not going to accept the Bible as divine revelation. Indeed, as I will discuss later, it is a waste of time and wrongminded to try to make non-Christians act like Christians, which is a horrific mistake the church has made in the past.

But there are Christians who ultimately throw up their hands when they realize that the Bible holds the view that it does on the issue of homosexual practice; they then conclude that the Bible isn't the Word of God, except maybe in some kind of general sense. This book is not the place to make the argument for accepting the Bible as God's divine self-revelation through human authors, but I will say that not accepting the Bible as such puts us in a rather tenuous place. If we as Christians reject the Bible as God's divine revelation, then in a crucial sense we are, as one of my seminary professors put it, placing ourselves as the ultimate authority over

---

42. Copan and Flannagan, *Genocide*, 170.

the canon, which is God's standard of faith and practice.[43] We become the judge of what is right and what is wrong rather than being under God.

Yes, the Scriptures need to be interpreted, and there is room for debate over interpretation. That is the process we have been engaged in here. I welcome counterarguments to my biblical interpretations (as I have argued against certain interpretations with which I disagree). But to conclude that the Bible says x on a subject but is wrong is an approach that I think Christians should dismiss.

"Shouldn't We Follow the Spirit's Leading?"

Well, yes. But the deeper question is, Can the Spirit lead us into new understanding of the issue of same-sex relationships beyond that articulated in the Bible? Just last night I had a spirited yet irenic conversation with a friend of mine who is an evangelical theologian, and he adopted this line of thought. He reminded me about the story of Peter and Cornelius (Acts 10–11).

Peter was utterly convinced of the separation of Jews and gentiles, and so he would not eat food identified as unclean in the Old Testament, a law whose purpose was to keep Jews from fraternizing with gentiles. But three times a voice from heaven commands him in a vision to eat what he considers unclean food. At the same time, messengers from the gentile Cornelius come and invite Peter to Cornelius's house. An angel from God had told Cornelius to invite Peter. When Peter arrives, he comes to realize that "God does not show favoritism but accepts from every nation the one who fears him and does what is right" (Acts 10:34–35). The Holy Spirit then comes on "all who heard the message" (10:44), and Cornelius is baptized. In the next chapter, Peter explains to the leaders in Jerusalem what has happened, and they conclude, "So then, even to Gentiles God has granted repentance that leads to life" (11:18).

---

43. See "The Nature of the Word of God" in chap. 1.

My friend went on to ask, "Could the Spirit today be moving us to see that same-sex committed unions are not incompatible with the will of God, even though the Bible itself teaches us otherwise?" He appealed to the compelling stories of faith coming from those who are gay and Christian as evidence that the Spirit is so moving.

I told him that I found the stories he referred to as moving and had no reason to doubt that they are testimonies of true faith. But I did not find the analogy that he was drawing compelling. For one thing, beginning with the promise to Abraham that God would bless not only him and his descendants but through him all the nations of the world (Gen. 12:3), it was obvious that God was there not just for Israel but for all people. This was not a totally new idea that the Spirit presented to Peter. In the Old Testament it is true that gentiles like Ruth had to in essence become Israelite in order to be part of the covenant community, but the whole Old Testament yearned for the day when the wall of separation between Jew and gentile would come down (Eph. 2:14–18).

Even more importantly, if we were to adopt such an approach toward the Spirit and homosexuality, how would we be able to tell the difference between what the Spirit is purportedly teaching us and our own wishes and desires? I find interesting the parable of the rich man and Lazarus (Luke 16:19–31). At the end of this parable, the rich man wants to go and warn his brothers to repent to avoid his fate. Father Abraham responds, "They have Moses and the Prophets; let them listen to them" (16:29). After all, he says, "if they do not listen to Moses and the Prophets, they will not be convinced even if someone rises from the dead" (16:31). The parallel is not exact, but to me it is a warning not to accept a presumed "movement of the Spirit" that contradicts the Scriptures. Again, knowing myself, what I might perceive as the Spirit speaking to me may just be a form of wish fulfillment. Scripture is there to help us navigate what might be of the Spirit and what might not be.

"What Is the Relationship between the Bible and Experience?"

I take up this question about the Bible and experience because many who adopt an affirming position realize that it is hard to bring Scripture in support of their position. Certainly, as we have seen, when the Bible does reference homosexual acts, it does so only negatively.

So scholars like Dan Via will say, "I take the Bible to be the highest authority for Christians in theological and ethical matters, although I also recognize the legitimacy of tradition, reason, and experience. . . . The authoritative norm is the one you finally listen to in a situation of competing norms."[44] Indeed, Via states that "the biblical texts that deal specifically with homosexual practice condemn it unconditionally," but he believes that various factors, including the "experience of gay Christians," overrule the uncontested biblical teaching.[45] Thus, it appears that he will listen to "experience" over the text in what he calls "competing norms."

Let me begin by saying that I too believe God can and does speak to us through "tradition, reason, and experience," but the Bible has a special place among them. Reason and experience can be deeply affected by sin, and in consequence so can tradition (though tradition here would support a traditional view). The Bible, when properly interpreted, trumps reason and experience. Certainly, as has been abundantly clear throughout this book, our interpretations can be wrong; indeed, it is right to bring experience and reason to the Bible to question our interpretations, including those concerning same-sex relationships. We certainly did that with the question of creation and evolution. However, to come to the conclusion that Via comes to (and many others with him), that the Bible is just one competing norm and that our experience trumps what we know the Bible teaches, is deeply theologically

44. Via and Gagnon, *Homosexuality and the Bible*, 2.
45. Via and Gagnon, *Homosexuality and the Bible*, 93–95.

problematic, since in that way we can just ignore the Bible on any number of issues.

"Doesn't Love Trump the Text?"

The answer to this question is no. Why? Because love and the text are not in conflict. God is love, and the Bible is God's Word. Our problem is that we, as modern Westerners, believe that love should allow us all as individuals to find our own personal happiness in the here and now. But personal happiness is not the greatest good in the Bible. The greatest good is to know God and follow his commandments. It's not just those who are same-sex attracted who feel frustrated and often don't understand why God puts us through various experiences or prohibits us from certain actions that would lead to our emotional happiness (or at least that we think would lead there).

Now What?

As I said at the beginning of this chapter, the question of what the Bible says about homosexual practice is straightforward. The understanding that the Bible prohibits homosexual practice has been the view of the church through the ages until recently and is still the main position held globally, with exceptions primarily in the Western world. The hard question is, Now what? Given what we now know about same-sex attraction, how can the church demonstrate love to all people?

The Theology and Politics of Same-Sex Marriage in Society

In this section I speak mainly of the American church and society, because as an American citizen I am most familiar with the situation in my own country. I travel and teach widely, however, so I know that there are similarities with other places, particularly in the West (including Australia); this is less the case in Asia and South America, and much less so in Africa. As I mentioned above, the non-West, both society and church, has a much more traditional attitude toward the topic of homosexuality. Some in the West make the presumptuous accusation of backwardness toward Asia and particularly Africa.[46] However, the different attitude in the West can equally—and, in my opinion, more likely—be the result of the influence of modern cultural ideas, particularly on the church.

Anyone who lives in or knows the American situation marvels at the rapid change in attitudes that has taken place over the past thirty years. But the change has to do with more than attitude. There has been a change in law, most notably now a national legal acceptance of same-sex marriage. In the light of the biblical position on homosexuality, what should the church do? And in the light of these legal realities, what should individual Christians do?

In the process leading up to the legalization of same-sex marriage, many Christians and many churches decided to protest and to garner votes to prevent the present situation legislatively.[47] Of course, in such times the media seems to pick up on the most egregious and hateful types of protests. Think again of Westboro Baptist Church, which pickets at the funerals of fallen soldiers who gave their lives for their country (which this particular church says is at war because of homosexual sins). We might also think of people carrying obscene banners and posters as they march. The church and individual Christians should have uniformly and more loudly condemned such tactics (and in the future they must), which smear the name of Christ. That said, in a Western democ-

46. Jenkins, *Next Christendom*, 198–202.
47. In 2008 in California, Proposition 8, which proposed that "only marriage between a man and a woman is valid or recognized in California" be added to the state's constitution, gained widespread support from the church and passed, only to be declared unconstitutional in 2010.

racy like the United States, Christians are certainly well within their rights to argue their case and cast their vote in a way that is consonant with their conscience. Indeed, out of care for our fellow humans' flourishing, we should work to persuade others of biblical values.

But I believe some Christians, and I am not here referring to the radical fringe, unnecessarily and at times inappropriately express frustration and exasperation (in private and sometimes in public) at the present situation now that we have been through the main legal battle on same-sex marriage in our society. I think this attitude is at least partly the result of muddling the relationship between the state and the church. Should we really care that much about the policy of the state? I suggest not.

While he was not speaking about same-sex marriage, I have found the words of Martin Lloyd-Jones, the great Welsh preacher of the previous generation, extremely helpful. Where he speaks of the attitude of the "New Testament," I think it is fair to think of the Bible as a whole:

> The New Testament is never interested in conduct and behavior in itself. I can go further and say that the New Testament does not make an appeal for good behavior to anyone but to Christian people. The New Testament is not interested, as such, in the morality of the world. It tells us quite plainly that you can expect nothing from the world but sin, and that in its fallen condition it is incapable of anything else. In Titus 3:3 Paul tells us that we were all once like that: "For we ourselves were sometimes foolish, disobedient, deceived, serving divers lusts and pleasures, living in malice and envy, hateful, and hating one another. . . ." Thus there is nothing, according to the New Testament that is so fatuous and so utterly futile, as to turn to such people and appeal to them to live the Christian life. . . . The truth is that it only has one message for people like that—the message of repentance.[48]

48. Lloyd-Jones, *Faith on Trial*, 63.

Lloyd-Jones gives us a healthy reminder that God is interested not in lives of external conformity to his will but in hearts that lead to thankful obedience.[49]

Every Christian has to think through these issues and act according to their conscience, but as I argued above, I personally think it is wrong-minded for denominations and churches to try to change the law of the land. I also think it is wrong-minded in most cases for Christians to refuse services to gay couples that they would offer to non-Christian heterosexual couples.[50]

The Theology and Politics of Same-Sex Marriage in the Church

The church is not the society at large. While Christians should not expect the broader society to reflect biblical values, they should care deeply about the beliefs and practices of the church. The church must find its guidance in all matters of faith and practice from the Bible, which represents God's disclosure of his nature and his will for his people. We know the Triune God through Scripture in a way that our experience and our reason (also avenues to knowledge of the divine) will not contradict. Our exploration of Scripture on the topic of sexuality concluded that the Bible as a whole treats homosexual behavior, along with pre- and extramarital intercourse, as a violation of God's intention in human sexuality.

Before proceeding, however, I need to address a particularly American misconception: the myth that America is a Christian

---

49. The book of Daniel, particularly chaps. 1–2, is a helpful study for how God's followers live a life of faith in a toxic culture. See Longman, *Daniel*, esp. 62–69.

50. An example is the well-publicized case of the baker who refused to supply a cake for a same-sex marriage. Of course, the baker has to act according to his conscience, but he is providing a service to the general public. The cake is not his celebration of the event; it is the couple's celebration. In October 2017, the Supreme Court decided in favor of the baker, but in a way that leaves open the question of whether religious beliefs trump antidiscrimination laws.

nation. It is probably this error that leads many Christians to worry that America is not acting like the church.

The whole idea of a Christian nation is a non sequitur. Nations are not intended by God to be religious entities, with the exception of ancient Israel. What made Israel a religious nation? God's choice of them that was rooted in the call to Abraham. This call did not give ancient Israel favored status but rather singled them out for special service that would lead to the blessing of "many nations" (Gen. 12:3). Indeed, this "election" often entailed suffering.[51]

Even if our nation was founded by Christians (some of the founders were Christians, but many weren't) on purely Christian principles (but it wasn't; think of the influence on our founding fathers of the philosophy of John Locke and other sources), that would not make America a Christian nation. Even if the vast majority and indeed every single citizen were practicing Christians, that would not make America (or any nation) a Christian country. Only God's choice would make that happen, and according to the New Testament, God is not in the business of doing that these days. Rather, his people are drawn from many nations.

Returning now to the question of the church and homosexuality, we ask the question, What is the church to do in the light of the biblical perspective on homosexual desire and practice? In my opinion, there are certain things that are clear and other matters that Christians need to explore.

First, the church must recognize that, at least in most cases, same-sex desire is not a choice. Many in the previous generation believed, as do some today, that same-sex desire is a choice and that a person can choose to become heterosexual. This understanding led to the idea that a person must become heterosexual in order to join a church. Such a position is as cruel as it is ignorant. I base this on the testimony of many gay men and women who say that if it were a choice, they would certainly not choose to be

51. Kaminsky, *Yet I Loved Jacob*.

gay, particularly in the past when gays were ostracized and worse by society and the church. Accordingly, the church must warmly welcome people who have same-sex attraction but have chosen a celibate life because of their conviction that the Bible teaches that homosexual activity is a violation of God's will.[52] The church should not only welcome them but also encourage them to be honest about their desires and struggles.

And that leads to the next point. Not only should the church welcome those who have same-sex attraction and follow God by living a life of celibacy; the church also should take care to warmly embrace these brothers and sisters by entering into deep and meaningful relationships with them.

Let's be honest. The church typically has a very poor track record of welcoming single people into fellowship both inside and outside the church. Ed Shaw, a British minister who has chosen a celibate life, describes the typical church situation:

> Moms, dads and their 2.4 children tend to settle in quickly, but you can arrive as a single parent, a divorcee, a widow or widower, a single man or woman for whatever reason, and find that people don't know what to do with you—unless you are in your twenties and can join the singles group (and get married quick). The impression that we unintentionally give is that the church is made up of biological families, and that unless you are part of one of these conveniently shaped building blocks, you won't ever fit in.[53]

We all need to be mindful of loving our single friends not just by including them in church functions but by spending time with them outside of church. It's odd that couples and families have a hard time integrating singles into their lives, because it is far from a burden to hang out with single people—going to movies, having dinner, and so forth. But, of course, true friendship involves

52. See the testimonies of Shaw, *Same-Sex Attraction*; Allberry, *Is God Anti-Gay?*; and Hill, *Washed and Waiting*.
53. Shaw, *Same-Sex Attraction*, 44.

more than activities; it also means sharing hopes and aspirations, struggles and failures. Couples and families have the opportunity to invite singles into their lives, building deep relationships with them through mutual support.

Christians who are attracted to the same sex are in one sense in the same situation as all Christians, struggling with unwanted desires and sometimes failing, as well as wanting someone to share joys and successes with. But there is a difference that we all need to acknowledge, and that is that heterosexuals, married ones who struggle with sexual sin as well as single ones who yearn for an intimate relationship, all have the potential of marriage or the improvement of a struggling marriage. Heterosexual Christians should be especially mindful of loving same-sex-attracted brothers and sisters, who from a biblical standpoint don't have that same possibility open to them.

In addition, Christians who are same-sex attracted and have shown aptitude at ministry should be encouraged to seek ordination. Every minister who ever lived has struggled with sexual sin. If you are in a church with a minister who claims otherwise, run for the door. Of course, I am not talking here about people—homosexual or heterosexual—who act on those desires as if they are not violations of God's will. That is a different story.

The matters above seem clear to me. But there are a number of issues about which the church needs to do more thinking. Although some churches have thought about these issues, from where I sit, there remain a lot of specific situations that raise questions that I don't think have been adequately discussed. While I may betray my leanings on these issues, I am not going to give definitive answers, or even discuss the issues fully. This is partly because I have not resolved these issues in my mind and partly because in talking about the "church" I am incorporating a lot of different traditions that have different views on, say, the status of ordination or what it means to be a member or even what church discipline looks like. In the final analysis, how one responds to these situations ultimately depends on the specifics of the situations. My hope is that my questions and proposals will give church leadership something to think about.

First, how should Christian leaders communicate the biblical perspective on homosexuality to the church, both at large and locally? What is nonnegotiable is that the biblical perspective must be spoken in love, not in anger or in defensiveness. The truth spoken in anger is not the truth.

In the Sermon on the Mount Jesus taught that when we speak to others, we should do so with a humility that rules out anger:

> Do not judge, or you too will be judged. For in the same way you judge others, you will be judged, and with the measure you use, it will be measured to you.
>
> Why do you look at the speck of sawdust in your brother's eye and pay no attention to the plank in your own eye? How can you say to your brother, "Let me take the speck out of your eye," when all the time there is a plank in your own eye? You hypocrite, first take the plank out of your own eye, and then you will see clearly to remove the speck from your brother's eye. (Matt. 7:1–5)

Though it is frequently done, it is wrong and overly literalistic to quote this verse as if it prohibits any kind of judgment of others. If it did, it would contradict a host of other passages that not only permit but encourage Christians to help one another discover and deal with sin in their lives (Luke 17:3; Gal. 6:1; 1 Tim. 5:20). Paul gets upset with the Corinthian church for neglecting to discipline a man who was sleeping with his stepmother (1 Cor. 5). What Jesus condemns here is a proud judgment that points the finger at others without owning up to one's own sin. Thus, some attempts to address the issue of homosexuality are ineffective and even backfire.

In the summer of 2017, a group of evangelical leaders published a statement on gender and sexuality with an emphasis on homosexuality commonly referred to as the Nashville Statement.[54] I find little to quarrel with in terms of content. I think it well reflects the biblical teaching on the subject. As true as it is, however, the form of the statement strikes me as unwise, if not simply inappropriate. The sixteen affirmations and denials come across, as one critic said, as "passive aggressive" rather than sensitive and loving.[55] The gay community and their supporters simply responded with their own aggressive statement.[56]

My perception is that these two statements only served to energize their bases and showed no real awareness of the thinking of the others by way of thoughtful critique. Even some, including me, who are sympathetic to the message of the Nashville Statement and also respect the signers (at least most of them) have distanced themselves from the statement. That said, as I am sure I will discover when this book is published, just articulating the traditional Christian viewpoint on this topic will be taken as a form of aggression. There are those who take any disagreement as a form of abuse. Still, pronouncements alone only aggravate the situation and risk violating Jesus's teaching in Matthew 7.

Every church and Christian institution needs to think of the best way to present the biblical teaching. And this is not an easy matter. When I was speaking on another topic (creation/evolution) at a large evangelical church in Pittsburgh, one of the pastors told me that they decided that homosexuality was a "pastoral" but not a "preaching" topic. They knew that they had many same-sex-attracted attenders and members who would be driven from the church if they felt "preached at" on this topic.

I am not sure exactly what I feel about this approach. I can see the wisdom in it, at least for some churches, but something in me

---

54. See http://cbmw.org/nashville-statement.

55. P. Enns, "Lansdale Statement (See What I Did There? Get It?)," *Pete Enns* (blog), accessed June 26, 2018, http://peteenns.com/lansdale-nashville-statement.

56. The Denver Statement, http://www.patheos.com/blogs/nadiabolzweber /2017/08/the-denver-statement/.

hesitates to consider any biblical topic "off limits" for proclamation. But not all proclamation has to be through a sermon. Perhaps a more sensitive way to handle the topic is in a teaching/discussion session where people can ask questions and make comments. More, of course, can be said about how best to communicate the biblical perspective on homosexual practice, but I hope there is enough here to stimulate thinking.

Second, how should the church respond to an openly gay couple who visit the church? And then, how should the church respond to a same-sex couple who are Christians and want to become members? The first question is simple to answer. We should greet every person who comes to the church with love and warmth. The church isn't for perfect people. If it were, it would be empty. Unfortunately, at least according to the testimony of some same-sex-attracted people, that is not how they experienced the church, causing them to leave one church in search of another that welcomes gay members or simply to leave the faith altogether. Churches that are unwelcoming to visitors of any kind simply are not living up to their call to respect all human beings as created in God's image and loved by Jesus.[57]

While the question of how to greet visitors is easy (or should be), the second question is more complex, and I am not going to provide a concrete and specific answer here. Rather than there being a general principle, much will depend on what a particular church regards as a criterion for membership and on the situation of the people who desire membership.

Of course, it is clear that same-sex-attracted individuals who have decided to obey what they consider to be the Bible's teaching on the issue and thus practice celibacy should be warmly welcomed into membership like any other Christian individuals who struggle with anger or greed or lust or alcohol or drugs (and the list goes

57. For an excellent guide on how to love same-sex-attracted people in church, see the thoughtful and practical advice given by Allberry in *Is God Anti-Gay?*

on and on). The issue comes to a head, however, for those who deny that there is anything wrong with same-sex behavior. They reject the idea that their sexual desires and actions are anything like anger, greed, lust, or alcoholism. God made them that way, they reason, and so their feelings are good and holy and not a result of the brokenness of sin.

For many churches, this attitude becomes an insurmountable obstacle to membership. After all, membership involves discipline. If a member demonstrates a resistance to the guidance of the church's teaching on what the leadership considers a clear teaching of Scripture, then such people are subject to discipline and, if they are unrepentant, removal from membership. An example would be someone who has an anger issue, creating chaos around their family or community. No decent church should leave such a situation unaddressed (though many unfortunately do). If confronted, an angry person may deny or minimize the problem, but it is unlikely that they would say, "My anger is natural to me. There is nothing wrong with anger."

The situation of homosexual individuals and church membership is further complicated by the fact that the church is inconsistent here. One common objection to the idea that openly gay and affirming people and same-sex couples can't be full members is that many churches allow people who have been divorced on nonbiblical grounds (and perhaps remarried) to join the church or maintain their membership. Jesus is pretty clear in saying that the only reason for a divorce that allows remarriage is "adultery" (Matt. 19:1–12; see specifically v. 9). Paul likewise says to Christian married couples: "To the married I give this command (not I, but the Lord): A wife must not separate from her husband. But if she does, she must remain unmarried or else be reconciled to her husband. And a husband must not divorce his wife" (1 Cor. 7:10–11). He even goes on to say that a woman should stay married to her nonbelieving husband unless he leaves her (7:12–16).

Let's just say not many churches, even "Bible-believing" ones, pay much attention to this biblical teaching when it comes to membership. True, two wrongs don't make a right, and I am not advocating a change in membership requirement for those who have suffered the pain of divorce. And I should point out that many churches that are not consistent on this issue when it comes to divorce and membership do promote healthy marriages and a high view of the importance of marriage.

The first step I believe we should take is to acknowledge that it is possible to be a Christian and to be gay and not be celibate, even though as an advocate of the traditionalist ethic I believe such people are sinning if they are sexually active. After all, especially in this cultural environment, people may (wrongly) believe that they are not sinning, especially if they listen to some of the flawed attempts to reinterpret the key texts we looked at above.

Now I know that this will anger just about everyone. On the one hand, those who are unapologetically gay and Christian won't be happy to think that I and others like me think they are sinning. On the other hand, many traditionalists will believe that I am not taking seriously texts like 1 Corinthians 6:9 that "men who have sex with men" will not inherit the kingdom of God. But I think it is a rare person who doesn't find himself or herself implicated in the list of vices that Paul gives us here. I acknowledge, for instance, my greediness and pray that the Spirit will help me with it, but I suspect that greed will follow me to the grave.

What makes a person a Christian is neither being morally perfect nor even being aware of the full scope of God's desires for how we live but a vital relationship with God. Even though I am unwilling to say that homosexual acts are good or morally neutral, I am also unwilling to deny that noncelibate gays have a relationship with God through Christ (any more than I am willing to deny that people who have divorced on unbiblical grounds and remarried, those who are living together without being married, alcoholics, or people addicted to painkillers are Christians, and the list could go on). If a noncelibate gay person has a relationship with Christ, then the church should recognize that they are, like every Christian, a broken sinner in need of Christ's grace. But they have their praxis wrong in a serious way.

That said, we have to reckon with the idea that church membership may be more restrictive than even salvation. If a church rightly affirms the biblical sexual ethic and believes that same-sex acts even in the context of what society recognizes as marriage are sinful, then the church would have to apply its discipline immediately to the same-sex couples who are unwilling to submit to that standard or the consequent discipline.

Conclusion

I suspect that this chapter will be the most controversial one in this book. For many, the reminder that the Bible prohibits same-sex relations will be upsetting; for others, the appeal for a more welcoming attitude toward same-sex-attracted people will be taken as compromising.

I believe that the Bible is clear on the issue of homosexuality and that attempts to reread the Bible to make it more amenable to same-sex relationships are desperate attempts to make the Bible say what it clearly does not. That is why advocates have turned more to the testimony of same-sex people to make their case. As Ed Shaw notes, "It's people, not theology, that seem to be powering the rejection of the traditional Christian ethic."[58] But this will do little to convince those of us who hold that the Bible is canon to change our opinion. Rebekah Eklund, a leader in the Evangelical Covenant Church, has been quoted as saying, "The two sides in this debate are almost having two different conversations. The conservative side wants to talk about the Bible. The other side

58. Shaw, *Same-Sex Attraction*, 18–19.

is sharing stories. You can tell stories all day long, and they're wonderful and they're valuable, but for people who think the Bible says no to this issue, it's not going to say anything."[59]

This is an issue that can split churches, split generations within the church (Christians who are under thirty tend to be much more affirming), and cause the church to experience ostracism and even eventually persecution from society. The possibility of persecution should not really be a concern. The church tends to flourish under persecution, and if the past few decades have witnessed anything, it is that the church has been embarrassed by Christians who have political power. What is important, beyond holding firmly to the biblical view on sexuality, is that this sensitive and controversial issue be discussed with love and wisdom.

DISCUSSION QUESTIONS

1. What is meant by the "traditional understanding of the biblical ethic on sexuality"? What is the biblical argument in its favor?

2. What is the significance of the fact that the church has held this view virtually unanimously since its founding and still today widely across the global church?

3. Did you find any of the reasons given for changing that traditional biblical ethic convincing? Why or why not?

4. Are you acquainted with same-sex-attracted Christians who are either friends or relatives? How have they chosen to live? Do you agree or disagree? Are you same-sex-attracted and a believer? How have you decided to live?

5. If a close relative or friend told you that he or she was gay, how could you react in a way that would show the love of Christ?

59. Quoted by Jeff Chu in his collection of stories about gays in the evangelical church (*Does Jesus Really Love Me?*, 195).

6. How do you think your church would react to the presence of openly same-sex-attracted people in the congregation? Do you agree or disagree? Why or why not?

7. If you are from the United States or another country where same-sex marriage is allowed, what has been your reaction to the acceptance of same-sex marriage? On what grounds?

8. What do you think Jesus would say about same-sex marriage? How do you think Jesus would love same-sex-attracted individuals and even married couples?

9. Should same-sex-attracted people be allowed to join your church? Be ordained to the ministry? Under what conditions, if any?

10. Where do you experience sexual brokenness in your life?

Final Word

We have completed our examination of what I consider to be the four most controversial issues of the Old Testament: evolution, history, violence, and sexuality. I believe many will agree with my choices here. In the process, we have also said a few words about other topics that people find vexing (including slavery, polygamy, and patriarchy in chap. 4). I selected the four main topics because of recent attempts from within the evangelical or conservative Christian movement to reconsider our views on them.

In terms of evolution (chap. 1), I have sided with those who want to push back against an imposition of a wooden reading that would lead us to think that it was the intention of the biblical author to provide us with a straightforward description of the *how* of creation. But I also wanted to push back against those evangelical Christians who affirm evolution but deny that humans created in the image of God were ever morally innocent, that there was a historical fall, or that there is original sin. I find myself critical of young earth creationists, the intelligent design community, and even old earth creationists who reject evolution. On the other side, I am also critical of evolutionary creationists like Peter Enns and John Schneider whose views deny a historical fall and a concept of original sin. I rather argued that the biblical text is not in conflict with evolutionary theory. The Bible is interested in the who and why of creation, while science is interested in how creation happened.

When it comes to questions of history (chap. 2), my discussion partners were those in the evangelical movement who have come to think that certain redemptive events like the exodus and conquest did not happen (including Kenton Sparks, Peter Enns, Megan Bishop Moore, and Brad Kelle). These scholars defend the theological value of these stories, but I argued that unless they happened, and there are good reasons to think that they did, they have no such significance.

Our third controversy was the issue of divine violence (chap. 3). Does God harm people, even kill them? A number of works have been written to deny that God actually did hurt anyone, even though the Bible pictures him as doing precisely that (Eric Seibert, Peter Enns, and Greg Boyd). Others give interpretations that minimize the harm (Paul Copan, Matthew Flannagan, David Lamb, and Preston Sprinkle). I also took the occasion to address a new book by John and Harvey Walton. I did not find any of these people's discussions fully satisfying. I reasserted the basic view that I have held on the topic since the early 1980s as providing the best understanding of the biblical material and how we are to relate to it today: the Bible presents one coherent account from Genesis to Revelation of God's fight against and final defeat of evil.

Finally, in chapter 4 I tackled the emotionally charged issue of same-sex relations and the Bible. Though the traditional biblical ethic has been held virtually unanimously throughout church history and is by far the predominant view of the church today, I asked whether there is anything to recent attempts to say that same-sex relations are compatible with the Bible and therefore should be normalized by the church. My response was negative, but that just leads to the even more difficult issue of how we love our same-sex-attracted brothers and sisters. No doubt there is much more to say about this issue.

Though I disagree with my many discussion partners and those who agree with them, I certainly respect them and have learned much from them—if not on these topics, then certainly on others. I am not vain enough to claim that I have the final word on these vexed issues. My hope here is to contribute to the discussion of these hard issues and encourage open, faithful dialogue about the message of Scripture. I look forward to the future responses to this book and its ideas that I expect to receive. All of us need to remain open to other perspectives.

My final comment will be a reminder. We are dealing with controversial issues about which there is considerable disagreement. But this not the important focus of the Bible. What is certain in the Bible is that God created us, but we rebelled against him. He did not give up on us but pursues a restored relationship with us. That pursuit led ultimately to the cross, the death and resurrection of Jesus. To be reconciled with God, we must be in a relationship with Jesus. He will come again in the future to bring us to himself. For this we can all praise God.

Bibliography

Ackerman, S. *When Heroes Love: The Ambiguity of Eros in the Stories of David and Gilgamesh.* New York: Columbia University Press, 2005.

Alexander, D. R. "Creation, Providence, and Evolution." In Torrance and McCall, *Knowing Creation*, 259–83.

Allberry, S. *Is God Anti-Gay? And Other Questions about Homosexuality, the Bible and Same-Sex Attraction.* London: The Good Book Society, 2013.

Allender, D., and T. Longman III. *Bold Love: The Courageous Practice of Life's Ultimate Influence.* Colorado Springs: NavPress, 1992.

———. *God Loves Sex: An Honest Conversation about Sexual Desire and Holiness.* Grand Rapids: Baker Books, 2014.

———. *Intimate Allies.* Colorado Springs: NavPress, 1999.

———. *The Intimate Mystery of Marriage.* Downers Grove, IL: InterVarsity, 2005.

Ansberry, C. B. "The Exodus: Fact, Fiction or Both?" In C. M. Hays and C. B. Ansberry, *Evangelical Faith*, 55–73.

Augustine. *The Literal Meaning of Genesis: Volume 1, Books 1–6.* Ancient Christian Writers 41. New York: Paulist Press, 1982.

Bandy, A. S. "Vengeance, Wrath, and Warfare as Images of Divine Justice in John's Apocalypse." In Thomas, Evans, and Copan, *Holy War in the Bible*, 108–29.

Barker, W. S., and W. R. Godfrey. *Theonomy: A Reformed Critique.* Grand Rapids: Zondervan, 1990.

Beale, G. K. "The Cognitive Peripheral Vision of Biblical Authors." *Westminster Theological Journal* 76 (2014): 263–93.

Beckwith, R. T. *The Old Testament Canon of the New Testament Church.* London: SPCK, 1987.

Bell, Rob. *Love Wins: A Book about Heaven, Hell, and the Fate of Every Person Who Ever Lived.* San Francisco: HarperOne, 2011.

Berman, J. "The Kadesh Inscriptions of Ramesses II and the Exodus Sea Account (Exodus 13:17–15:19)." In Hoffmeier, Millard, and Rendsburg, *"Did I Not Bring Israel Out of Egypt?,"* 93–112.

Bimson, J. J. *Redating the Exodus and Conquest.* Sheffield: University of Sheffield Press, 1978.

Bird, P. "The Bible in Christian Ethical Deliberation concerning Homosexuality: Old Testament Contributions." In *Homosexuality, Science, and the "Plain Sense" of Scripture,* edited by David L. Balch. Grand Rapids: Eerdmans, 2000.

Boyd, G. A. *Crucifixion of the Warrior God: Interpreting the Old Testament's Violent Portraits of God in the Light of the Cross.* 2 vols. Minneapolis: Fortress, 2017.

Bright, J. *The History of Israel.* 4th ed. Louisville: Westminster John Knox, 2000. First edition published in 1969.

Brueggemann, W. *Genesis.* Interpretation. Louisville: Westminster John Knox, 1982.

Butterfield, R. *Openness Unhindered: Further Thoughts of an Unlikely Convert on Sexual Identity and Union with Christ.* Pittsburgh: Crown & Covenant, 2015.

Calvin, John. *Commentaries on the First Book of Moses Called Genesis.* Vol. 1. Translated by John King. 1847. Available online, Grand Rapids: Christian Classics Ethereal Library, 2005. https://www.ccel.org/ccel/calvin/calcom01.

———. *A Commentary on the Psalms of David.* Vol. 1. Oxford: D. A. Talboys, 1840.

———. *Institutes of the Christian Religion.* 2 vols. Translated by Ford Lewis Battles. Library of Christian Classics. Philadelphia: Westminster, 1960.

Carlson, R. F., and T. Longman III. *Science, Creation and the Bible.* Downers Grove, IL: IVP Academic, 2010.

Chapman, S. "Martial Memory, Peaceable Vision: Divine War in the Old Testament." In Thomas, Evans, and Copan, *Holy War in the Bible*, 46–67.

Charles, J. D., ed. *Reading Genesis 1–2: An Evangelical Conversation.* Peabody, MA: Hendrickson, 2013.

Childs, B. S. *Biblical Theology of the Old and New Testaments: Theological Reflection on the Christian Bible.* Minneapolis: Fortress, 1993.

Chu, J. *Does Jesus Really Love Me? A Gay Christian's Pilgrimage in Search of God in America.* New York: Harper, 2013.

Cline, E. H. *From Eden to Exile: Unraveling Mysteries of the Bible.* Washington, DC: National Geographic Society, 2007.

Collins, C. J. *Genesis 1–4: A Linguistic, Literary, and Theological Commentary.* Phillipsburg, NJ: Presbyterian and Reformed, 2006.

———. "Reading Genesis 1–2 with the Grain: Analogical Days." In *Reading Genesis 1–2: An Evangelical Conversation*, ed. J. Daryl Charles, 73–92. Peabody, MA: Hendrickson, 2013.

———. *Science and Faith: Friends or Foes?* Wheaton: Crossway, 2003.

Collins, J. J. *The Bible after Babel: Historical Criticism in a Postmodern Age.* Grand Rapids: Eerdmans, 2005.

Copan, P. *Is God a Moral Monster? Making Sense of the Old Testament God.* Grand Rapids: Baker Books, 2011.

Copan, P., and W. L. Craig. *Creation out of Nothing: A Biblical, Philosophical, and Scientific Exploration.* Grand Rapids: Baker Books, 2004.

Copan, P., and M. Flannagan. *Did God Really Command Genocide? Coming to Terms with the Justice of God.* Grand Rapids: Baker Books, 2014.

Copan, P., T. Longman III, C. L. Reese, and M. G. Strauss. *Dictionary of Christianity and Science: The Definitive Reference for the Intersection of Christian Faith and Contemporary Science.* Grand Rapids: Zondervan, 2017.

Cowles, C. S. "The Case for Radical Discontinuity." In Cowles et al., *Show Them No Mercy*, 11–44.

Cowles, C. S., E. H. Merrill, D. L. Gard, and T. Longman III. *Show Them No Mercy: God and the Canaanite Genocide.* Grand Rapids: Zondervan, 2003.

Cullmann, O. *Christ and Time: The Primitive Christian Conception of Time and History.* Philadelphia: Westminster, 1964.

Cunningham, C. *Darwin's Pious Idea: Why the Ultra-Darwinists and Creationists Both Get It Wrong.* Grand Rapids: Eerdmans, 2010.

Davies, P. R. *In Search of "Ancient Israel."* Sheffield: JSOT Press, 1992.

Dawkins, R. *The God Delusion.* Boston: Houghton Mifflin, 2006.

———. *The Selfish Gene.* 30th anniversary ed. Oxford: Oxford University Press, 2006.

Dembski, W. "Science and Theology (Dialogue View)." In Copan et al., *Dictionary of Christianity and Science,* 610–14.

Dever, W. G. *What Did the Biblical Writers Know and When Did They Know It? What Archaeology Can Tell Us about the Reality of Ancient Israel.* Grand Rapids: Eerdmans, 2001.

Dunn, J. D. G. *Romans 1–8.* Word Biblical Commentary. Waco: Word, 1988.

Earl, D. S. "Joshua and the Crusades." In Thomas, Evans, and Copan, *Holy War in the Bible,* 19–43.

Eller, V. *War and Peace from Genesis to Revelation.* Scottdale, PA: Herald, 1981.

Enns, P. *The Bible Tells Me So: Why Defending Scripture Has Made Us Unable to Read It.* San Francisco: HarperOne, 2014.

———. *The Evolution of Adam: What the Bible Does and Doesn't Say about Human Origins.* Grand Rapids: Brazos, 2012.

———. *Inspiration and Incarnation: Evangelicals and the Problem of the Old Testament.* 2nd ed. Grand Rapids: Baker Academic, 2015.

———. *The Sin of Certainty: Why God Desires Our Trust More Than Our "Correct" Beliefs.* San Francisco: HarperOne, 2015.

Exum, C. *The Song of Songs.* Old Testament Library. Louisville: Westminster John Knox, 2005.

Falk, D. R. "Francis Collins." In Copan et al., *Dictionary of Christianity and Science,* 100–101.

Finkelstein, I., and N. A. Silberman, *The Bible Unearthed: Archaeology's New Vision of Ancient Israel and the Origin of Its Sacred Texts.* New York: Free Press, 2001.

Fleisher, M. C. *The Old Testament Case for Nonviolence.* Oklahoma City: Epic Octavius the Triumphant, 2018.

Friedman, R. E. *The Bible with Sources Revealed.* San Francisco: HarperOne, 2005.

————. *The Exodus: How It Happened and Why It Matters.* San Francisco: HarperOne, 2017.

Fuentes, A. *The Creative Spark: How Imagination Made Humans Exceptional.* New York: Dutton, 2017.

Gane, R. E. *Old Testament Law for Christians: Original Context and Enduring Application.* Grand Rapids: Baker Academic, 2017.

Garr, W. R. "'Image' and 'Likeness' in the Inscription from Tell Fakhariyeh." *Israel Exploration Journal* 50 (2000): 227–34.

————. *In His Own Image and Likeness: Humanity, Divinity, and Monotheism.* Leiden: Brill, 2003.

Giberson, K. W., and F. S. Collins. *The Language of Science and Faith.* Downers Grove, IL: InterVarsity, 2011.

Gombis, T. "The Rhetoric of Divine Warfare in Ephesians." In Thomas, Evans, and Copan, *Holy War in the Bible*, 87–107.

Grabbe, L. L., ed. *Can a "History of Israel" Be Written?* Sheffield: Sheffield Academic, 1997.

Grenz, S. *Welcoming but Not Affirming: An Evangelical Response to Homosexuality.* Louisville: Westminster John Knox, 1998.

Grisanti, M. A. "תעב." In *New International Dictionary of Old Testament Theology and Exegesis*, edited by W. A. VanGemeren, 4:314–18. Grand Rapids: Zondervan, 1997.

Grudem, W. "Biblical and Theological Introduction: The Incompatibility of Theistic Evolution with the Biblical Account of Creation and with Important Christian Doctrines." In Moreland et al., *Theistic Evolution*, 61–77.

Gundry, R. H. "On Homosex and Homosexual Marriage." In *Extracurriculars: Teaching Christianly outside Class*, 171–81. Eugene, OR: Wipf & Stock, 2014.

Gunn, D. M. *The Fate of King Saul.* Journal for the Study of the Old Testament Supplement Series 14. Sheffield: JSOT Press, 1978.

Gushee, D. P. *Changing Our Mind.* 3rd ed. Canton, MI: Read the Spirit Books, 2017.

Gwaltney, W. C. "The Biblical Book of Lamentations in the Context of Near Eastern Literature." In *Scripture in Context II: More Essays on the Comparative Method*, edited by W. W. Hallo, J. C. Moyer, L. G. Perdue, 191–211. Winona Lake, IN: Eisenbrauns, 1983.

Hamilton, V. P. *The Book of Genesis: Chapters 1–17*. New International Commentary on the Old Testament. Grand Rapids: Eerdmans, 1990.

Hawking, S., and L. Mlodinow. *The Grand Design*. New York: Bantam Books, 2012.

Hawkins, R. K. *How Israel Became a People*. Nashville: Abingdon, 2013.

Hays, C. M., and C. B. Ansberry, eds. *Evangelical Faith and the Challenge of Historical Criticism*. Grand Rapids: Baker Academic, 2013.

Hays, C. M., and S. L. Herring. "Adam and the Fall." In C. M. Hays and C. B. Ansberry, *Evangelical Faith*, 24–54.

Hays, R. B. *1 Corinthians*. Interpretation. Louisville: John Knox, 1997.

———. *The Moral Vision of the New Testament: A Contemporary Introduction to New Testament Ethics*. San Francisco: HarperSanFrancisco, 1996.

———. *Reading Backwards: Figural Christology and the Fourfold Gospel Witness*. Waco: Baylor University Press, 2016.

Heinzerling, R. "On the Interpretation of the Census Lists by C. J. Humphreys and G. E. Mendenhall." *Vetus Testamentum* 50 (2000): 250–52.

Hess, R. "The Jericho and Ai of the Book of Joshua." In *Critical Issues in Early Israelite History*, edited by R. S. Hess, G. A. Klingbeil, and P. J. Ray Jr., 33–46. Bulletin for Biblical Research Supplement 3. Winona Lake, IN: Eisenbrauns, 2008.

———. "Onomastics of the Exodus Generation in the Book of Exodus," in Hoffmeier, Millard, and Rendsburg, *"Did I Not Bring Israel Out of Egypt?,"* 37–48.

Hill, W. *Washed and Waiting: Reflections on Christian Faithfulness and Homosexuality*. Grand Rapids: Zondervan, 2010.

Himbaza, I., A. Schenker, and J.-B. Edart. *The Bible and the Question of Homosexuality*. Washington, DC: Catholic University of America Press, 2011.

Hoffmeier, J. K. "Egyptian Religious Influences on the Early Hebrews." In Hoffmeier, Millard, and Rendsburg, *"Did I Not Bring Israel Out of Egypt?,"* 3–35.

————. *Israel in Egypt: The Evidence for the Authenticity of the Exodus Tradition.* New York: Oxford University Press, 1997.

————. "What Is the Biblical Date for the Exodus? A Response to Bryant Wood." *Journal of the Evangelical Theological Society* 50 (2007): 223–24.

Hoffmeier, J. K., A. R. Millard, and G. A. Rendsburg, eds. *"Did I Not Bring Israel Out of Egypt?,"* Biblical, Archaeological, and Egyptological Perspectives on the Exodus Narratives. Bulletin for Biblical Research Supplement 13. Winona Lake, IN: Eisenbrauns, 2016.

Hollenback, G. M. "Who Is Doing What to Whom Revised: Another Look at Leviticus 18:22 and 20:13." *Journal of Biblical Literature* 136, no. 3 (Fall 2017): 529–37.

Hubbard, R. L., Jr. *Joshua.* The NIV Application Commentary. Grand Rapids: Zondervan, 2009.

Humphreys, C. J. "The Number of People in the Exodus from Egypt: Decoding Mathematically the Very Large Numbers in Numbers 1 and 26." *Vetus Testamentum* 48 (1998): 196–213.

————. "The Numbers in the Exodus from Egypt: A Further Appraisal." *Vetus Testamentum* 50 (2000): 322–28.

Hylen, S. "Metaphor Matters: Violence and Ethics in Revelation." *Catholic Biblical Quarterly* 73, no. 4 (October 2011): 777–96.

Jack, J. *The Date of the Exodus in the Light of External Evidence.* Edinburgh: T&T Clark, 1925.

Jacobsen, T. "The Battle between Marduk and Tiamat." *Journal of the American Oriental Society* 88 (1968): 104–8.

Jenkins, P. *The Next Christendom: The Coming of Global Christianity.* Oxford: Oxford University Press, 2002.

Jones, G. L. "Sacred Violence: The Dark Side of God." *Journal of Beliefs and Values* 20 (1999): 184–99.

Kaiser, W. *Malachi: God's Unchanging Love.* Grand Rapids: Baker, 1984.

Kaminsky, J. *Yet I Loved Jacob: Reclaiming the Biblical Concept of Election.* Nashville: Abingdon, 2007.

Kitchen, K. A. "Egyptians and Hebrews, from Ra'amses to Jericho." In *The Origin of Early Israel—Current Debate: Biblical, Historical and Archaeological Perspectives*, edited by S. Ahituv and E. D. Oren, 65–131. Beer-sheva: Ben-Gurion University of the Negev Press, 1998.

————. *On the Reliability of the Old Testament.* Grand Rapids: Eerdmans, 2003.

Kline, M. G. "Because It Had Not Rained." *Westminster Theological Journal* 20 (1957/58): 146–57. Reprinted in Kline, *Essential Writings*, 9–19.

————. *Essential Writings of Meredith G. Kline.* Peabody, MA: Hendrickson, 2017.

————. "The Intrusion and the Decalogue," *Westminster Theological Journal* 16 (1953): 1–22.

Koester, C. R. *Revelation and the End of All Things.* Grand Rapids: Eerdmans, 2001.

Kynes, W. *An Obituary for "Wisdom Literature": The Birth, Death, and Intertextual Reintegration of a Biblical Corpus.* New York: Oxford University Press, forthcoming.

Lamb, D. T. *God Behaving Badly: Is the God of the Old Testament Angry, Sexist and Racist?* Downers Grove, IL: InterVarsity, 2011.

LeFebvre, M. "Calendars and Creation: Israel's Festival Calendars and the Genesis 1:1–2:3 Creation Week." Unpublished manuscript. To be published as *The Liturgy of Creation: Understanding Calendars in Old Testament Context.* Downers Grove, IL: IVP Academic, forthcoming.

Lemche, N. P. *The Israelites in History and Tradition.* Louisville: Westminster John Knox, 1998.

Lind, M. C. *Yahweh Is a Warrior.* Scottdale, PA: Herald, 1980.

Lindsey, H. *The Late Great Planet Earth.* Grand Rapids: Zondervan, 1970.

Lloyd-Jones, D. M. *Faith on Trial: Studies in Psalm 73.* London: InterVarsity Fellowship, 1965.

Lockyer, H. "In Wonder of the Psalms." *Christianity Today* 28 (March 2, 1984): 72–78.

Longman, T., III, ed. *The Baker Illustrated Bible Dictionary.* Grand Rapids: Baker Books, 2013.

————. *Daniel.* The NIV Application Commentary. Grand Rapids: Zondervan, 1999.

————. "The Divine Warrior: The New Testament Use of an Old Testament Motif." *Westminster Theological Journal* 44 (1982): 290–307.

————. *The Fear of the Lord Is Wisdom: A Theological Introduction to Wisdom in Israel.* Grand Rapids: Baker Academic, 2017.

———. "Firmament." In Copan et al., *Dictionary of Christianity and Science*, 284.

———. "Genealogy." In Copan et al., *Dictionary of Christianity and Science*, 301–2.

———. *Genesis*. The Story of God Bible Commentary. Grand Rapids: Zondervan, 2016.

———. "God's Law and Mosaic Punishments Today." In Barker and Godfrey, *Theonomy*, 41–58.

———. "History and Old Testament Interpretation." In *Hearing the Old Testament: Listening for God's Address*, edited by C. G. Bartholomew and D. J. H. Beldman, 96–121. Grand Rapids: Eerdmans, 2012.

———. *How to Read Exodus*. Downers Grove, IL: InterVarsity, 2009.

———. *How to Read Genesis*. Downers Grove, IL: InterVarsity, 2005.

———. *Immanuel in Our Place*. Phillipsburg, NJ: Presbyterian and Reformed, 2001.

———. *Introducing the Old Testament: A Short Guide to Its History and Message*. Grand Rapids: Zondervan, 2012.

———. *Jeremiah, Lamentations*. Understanding the Bible Commentary. Grand Rapids: Baker Books, 2008.

———. *Job*. Baker Commentary on the Old Testament Wisdom and Psalms. Grand Rapids: Baker Academic, 2012.

———. "Nahum." In *The Minor Prophets: An Exegetical and Expository Commentary*, edited by T. E. McComiskey, 2:765–829. Grand Rapids: Baker, 1993.

———. "An Old Testament Professor Celebrates Creation." In *How I Changed My Mind about Evolution: Evangelicals Reflect on Faith and Science*, edited by K. Applegate and J. B. Stump, 48–53. Downers Grove, IL: IVP Academic, 2016.

———. *Proverbs*. Baker Commentary on the Old Testament Wisdom and Psalms. Grand Rapids: Baker Academic, 2006.

———. "Psalm 98: Divine Warrior Hymn." *Journal of the Evangelical Theological Society* 27 (1984): 267–74.

———. *Psalms*. Tyndale Old Testament Commentaries. Downers Grove, IL: InterVarsity, 2014.

———. *Reading the Bible with Heart and Mind*. Colorado Springs: NavPress, 1997.

―――. *Song of Songs*. New International Commentary on the Old Testament. Grand Rapids: Eerdmans, 2001.

―――. "'What Was Said in All the Scriptures concerning Himself' (Luke 24:27): Reading the Old Testament as a Christian." In *Evangelical Scholarship Retrospects and Prospects: Essays in Honor of Stanley N. Gundry*, edited by D. R. Buursma, K. Covrett, and V. D. Verbrugge, 119–36. Grand Rapids: Zondervan, 2017.

Longman, T., III, and R. B. Dillard. *An Introduction to the Old Testament*. 2nd ed. Grand Rapids: Zondervan, 2006.

Longman, T., III, and D. G. Reid. *God Is a Warrior*. Grand Rapids: Zondervan, 1995.

Longman, T., III, and John Walton. *The Lost World of the Flood*. Downers Grove, IL: IVP Academic, 2018.

Magruder, K. "Galilei, Galileo." In Copan et al., *Dictionary of Christianity and Science*, 298–300.

Matthews, K. A. *Genesis 11:27–50:26*. New American Commentary. Nashville: Broadman & Holman, 2005.

McDowell, C. L. *The "Image of God" in Eden: The Creation of Mankind in Genesis 2:5–3:24 in the Light of the* mīs pî pīt pî *and* wpt-r *Rituals of Ancient Mesopotamia and Egypt*. Siphrut. Winona Lake, IN: Eisenbrauns, 2016.

McDowell, J., and S. McDowell. *Evidence That Demands a Verdict: Life-Changing Truth for a Skeptical World*. Nashville: Thomas Nelson, 2017.

Meek, T. J. *Hebrew Origins*. New York: Harper and Brothers, 1936.

Merrill, E. "The Case for Moderate Discontinuity." In Cowles et al., *Show Them No Mercy*, 61–94.

Meyer, S. C. "Neo-Darwinism and the Origin of Biological Form and Information." In Moreland et al., *Theistic Evolution*, 105–38.

―――. "Scientific and Philosophical Introduction: Defining Theistic Evolution." In Moreland et al., *Theistic Evolution*, 33–60.

Milgrom, J. "On Decoding Very Large Numbers." *Vetus Testamentum* 49 (1999): 131–32.

Millard, A. R. "Amorites and Israelites: Invisible Invaders—Modern Expectations and Ancient Reality." In *The Future of Biblical Archaeology: Reassessing Methodologies and Assumptions*, edited by J. K.

Hoffmeier and A. R. Millard, 148–60. Grand Rapids: Eerdmans, 2004.

———. *The Eponyms of the Assyrian Empire, 910–612 BC.* State Archives of Assyria Studies 2. Helsinki: Neo-Assyrian Text Corpus Project, 1994.

Miller, R. D., II. *The Dragon, the Mountain, and the Nations: An Old Testament Myth, Its Origins, and Its Afterlives.* Winona Lake, IN: Eisenbrauns, 2017.

Moo, D. J. *Romans.* The NIV Application Commentary. Grand Rapids: Zondervan, 2000.

Moore, M. B., and B. Kelle. *Biblical History and Israel's Past: The Changing Study of the Bible and History.* Grand Rapids: Eerdmans, 2011.

Moreland, J. P., S. Meyer, C. Shaw, A. K. Gauger, and W. Grudem, eds. *Theistic Evolution: A Scientific, Philosophical, and Theological Critique.* Wheaton, IL: Crossway, 2017.

Noonan, B. J. "Egyptian Loanwords as Evidence for the Authenticity of the Exodus and Wilderness Traditions." In Hoffmeier, Millard, and Rendsburg, *"Did I Not Bring Israel Out of Egypt?,"* 49–68.

Olyan, S. M. "'And with a Male You Shall Not Lie the Lying Down of a Woman': On the Meaning and Significance of Leviticus 18:22 and 20:13." *Journal of the History of Sexuality* 5 (1994): 179–206.

Pritchard, J. B., ed. *Ancient Near Eastern Texts Relating to the Old Testament.* 3rd ed. Princeton: Princeton University Press, 1969.

Provan, I. *Ecclesiastes and Song of Songs.* The NIV Application Commentary. Grand Rapids: Zondervan, 2000.

———. *Lamentations.* New Century Bible Commentary. Grand Rapids: Zondervan, 1991.

Provan, I., V. P. Long, and T. Longman III. *A Biblical History of Israel.* 2nd ed. Louisville: Westminster John Knox, 2015.

Ramsey, G. W. *The Quest for the Historical Israel.* Eugene, OR: Wipf & Stock, 1999.

Ridderbos, H. N. *Redemptive History and the New Testament Scriptures.* Phillipsburg, NJ: Presbyterian and Reformed, 1963.

Schneider, J. "The Fall of 'Augustinian Adam': Original Fragility and Supralapsarian Purpose." *Zygon* 47 (2012): 949–69.

Schwab, G. *The Song of Song's Cautionary Message concerning Human Love.* New York: Peter Lang, 2002.

Seibert, E. A. *Disturbing Divine Behavior: Troubling Old Testament Images of God.* Minneapolis: Fortress, 2009.

Shaw, E. *Same-Sex Attraction and the Church: The Surprising Plausibility of the Celibate Life.* Downers Grove, IL: InterVarsity, 2015.

Smedes, L. *Sex for Christians: The Limits and Liabilities of Sexual Living.* Grand Rapids: Eerdmans, 1994.

Smith, J. K. A. "What Stands on the Fall? A Philosophical Exploration." In *Evolution and the Fall*, edited by W. T. Cavanaugh and J. K. A. Smith, 48–64. Grand Rapids: Eerdmans, 2017.

Sparks, K. L. *God's Word in Human Words: An Evangelical Appropriation of Critical Biblical Scholarship.* Grand Rapids: Baker Academic, 2008.

Sprinkle, P. *Fight: A Christian Case for Nonviolence.* Colorado Springs: David C. Cook, 2013.

Strawn, B. A. *The Old Testament Is Dying: A Diagnosis and Recommended Treatment.* Grand Rapids: Baker Academic, 2017.

Strickland, G. *Structuralism or Criticism? Thoughts on How We Read.* Cambridge: Cambridge University Press, 1981.

Stump, J. "Science and Theology (Reconciliation View)." In Copan et al., *Dictionary of Christianity and Science*, 614–17.

Tennyson, A. "In Memoriam A.H.H." In *The Complete Works of Alfred Tennyson*, 108–35. New York: R. Worthington, 1879.

Thiele, E. *The Mysterious Numbers of the Hebrew Kings.* Rev. ed. Grand Rapids: Zondervan, 1983.

Thomas, H. A. "A Neglected Witness to 'Holy War' in the Writings." In Thomas, Evans, and Copan, *Holy War in the Bible*, 68–83.

Thomas, H. A., J. Evans, and P. Copan, eds. *Holy War in the Bible: Christian Morality and an Old Testament Problem.* Downers Grove, IL: IVP Academic, 2013.

Thompson, T. L. *The Mythic Past: Biblical Archaeology and the Myth of Israel.* New York: Basic Books, 1999.

Torrance, A. B., and T. H. McCall, eds. *Knowing Creation.* Vol. 1 of *Perspectives from Theology, Philosophy, and Science.* Grand Rapids: Zondervan, 2018.

Torrey, C. C. "The Prophecy of Malachi." *Journal of Biblical Literature* 17 (1898): 1–15.

Trible, P. *God and the Rhetoric of Sexuality*. Philadelphia: Fortress, 1978.

Van Seters, J. *Prologue to History: The Yahwist as Historian in Genesis*. Louisville: Westminster John Knox, 1992.

Venema, D. "Genesis and the Genome: Genomics Evidence for Human-Ape Common Ancestry and Ancestral Hominid Population Sizes." *Perspectives on Science and Christian Faith* 62 (2010): 166–78.

Venema, D. R., and S. McKnight. *Adam and the Genome: Reading Scripture after Genetic Science*. Grand Rapids: Brazos, 2017.

Via, D. O., and Robert A. J. Gagnon. *Homosexuality and the Bible: Two Views*. Minneapolis: Fortress, 2003.

Vines, M. *God and the Gay Christian: The Biblical Case in Support of Same-Sex Relationships*. New York: Convergent Books, 2014.

Volf, M. *Exclusion and Embrace: A Theological Exploration of Identity, Otherness, and Reconciliation*. Nashville: Abingdon, 1996.

———. *Free of Charge: Giving and Forgiving in a Culture Stripped of Grace*. Grand Rapids: Zondervan, 2006.

von Rad, G. "The Origin and Concept of the Day of Yahweh." *Journal of Semitic Studies* 4 (1959): 97–108.

Walsh, J. T. "Leviticus 18:22 and 20:13: Who Is Doing What to Whom?" *Journal of Biblical Literature* 120 (2001): 201–9.

Walton, J. H. "Genesis." In *Zondervan Illustrated Bible Background Commentary*, edited by J. H. Walton, 1:2–159. Grand Rapids: Zondervan, 2009.

———. *Genesis 1 as Ancient Cosmology*. Winona Lake, IN: Eisenbrauns, 2011.

———. "Human Origins and the Bible." *Zygon* 47 (2012): 875–89.

———. "Serpent." In *Dictionary of the Old Testament: Pentateuch*, edited by T. D. Alexander and D. W. Baker, 736–39. Downers Grove, IL: InterVarsity, 2003.

Walton, J. H., and T. Longman III. *How to Read Job*. Downers Grove, IL: IVP Academic, 2016.

Walton, J. H., and J. Harvey Walton. *The Lost World of the Israelite Conquest: Covenant, Retribution, and the Fate of the Canaanites*. Downers Grove, IL: IVP Academic, 2017.

Warfield, B. B. "On the Antiquity and the Unity of the Human Race." *Princeton Theological Review* 9 (1911): 1–25.

Weaver, J. D. "Narrative Christus Victor: The Answer to Anselmian Atonement Violence." In *Atonement and Violence: A Theological Conversation*, edited by J. Sanders, 1–32. Nashville: Abingdon, 2006.

Webb, W. J. *Slaves, Women and Homosexuals: Exploring the Hermeneutics of Cultural Analysis*. Downers Grove, IL: InterVarsity, 2001.

Wenham, G. J. *Genesis 1–15*. Word Biblical Commentary 1. Waco: Word, 1987.

Whitelam, K. W. *The Invention of Ancient Israel: The Silencing of Palestinian History*. New York: Routledge, 1996.

Williams, R. J. "'A People Come Out of Egypt': An Egyptologist Looks at the Old Testament," in *Congress Volume: Edinburgh 1974*, Supplements to Vetus Testamentum 28, 231–52. Leiden: Brill, 1975.

Willits, J. "Bent Sexuality." In Wilson, *Mere Sexuality*, 143–63.

Wilson, T. *Mere Sexuality: Rediscovering the Christian Vision of Sexuality*. Grand Rapids: Zondervan, 2017.

Wood, B. G. "The Rise and Fall of the 13th Century Exodus-Conquest Theory." *Journal of the Evangelical Theological Society* 48 (2005): 475–89.

Wright, N. T. *The Day the Revolution Began: Reconsidering the Meaning of Jesus's Crucifixion*. San Francisco: HarperOne, 2016.

———. *Surprised by Scripture: Engaging the Contemporary Issues*. San Francisco: HarperOne, 2015.

Younger, K. L. *Ancient Conquest Accounts: A Study in Near Eastern and Biblical History Writing*. Sheffield: JSOT Press, 1990.

———. "Recent Developments in Understanding the Origins of the Arameans." In Hoffmeier, Millard, and Rendsburg, *"Did I Not Bring Israel Out of Egypt?,"* 199–222.

Zachman, R. C. "Why Should Free Scientific Inquiry Matter to Faith? The Case of John Calvin." In Torrance and McCall, *Knowing Creation*, 69–86.

Author Index

285

Scripture Index

289

Subject Index

Tremper Longman III (PhD, Yale University) is Distinguished Scholar and Professor Emeritus of Biblical Studies at Westmont College in Santa Barbara, California. Before coming to Westmont, he taught at Westminster Theological Seminary in Philadelphia for eighteen years. He has authored or coauthored more than thirty books, including *An Introduction to the Old Testament*, *How to Read Proverbs*, and commentaries on Genesis, Job, Proverbs, Ecclesiastes, Song of Songs, Jeremiah and Lamentations, and Daniel.

An **Essential** Dictionary for *Study* and *Teaching*

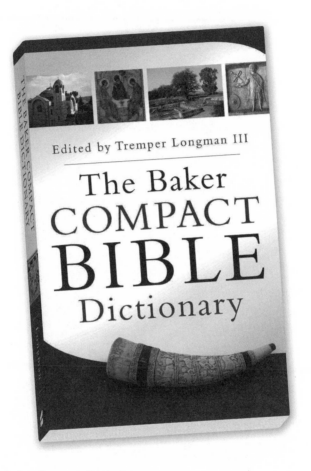

The Baker Compact Bible Dictionary provides access to the essential information and key Scripture references needed to read the Bible with increased understanding. Its A-to-Z entries succinctly define biblical terms, events, people, and places.

CLEAR, CONCISE, AND *ACCURATE* DEFINITIONS OF MORE THAN **500 BIBLICAL TERMS** AND **TOPICS**

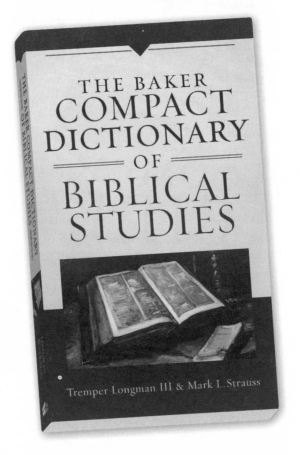

"An ideal source for students of Scripture."

—THOMAS R. SCHREINER,
Southern Baptist Theological Seminary

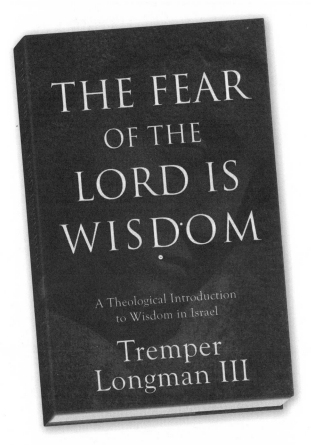

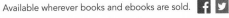

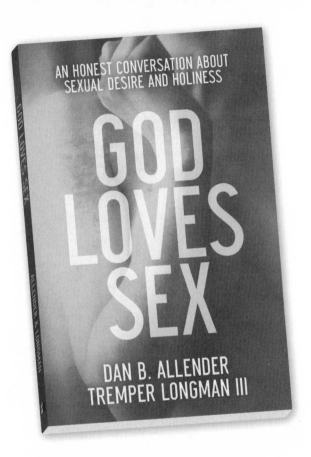